ALFARABI AND THE FOUNDATION OF ISLAMIC POLITICAL PHILOSOPHY

Alfarabi
and the Foundation of
Islamic Political Philosophy

MUHSIN S. MAHDI

With a Foreword by
Charles E. Butterworth

THE UNIVERSITY OF CHICAGO PRESS
Chicago & London

The University of Chicago Press, Chicago 60637
The University of Chicago Press, Ltd., London
© 2001 by The University of Chicago
All rights reserved. Published 2001
Paperback edition 2010
Printed in the United States of America

19 18 17 16 15 14 13 12 11 10   2 3 4 5 6

ISBN-13: 978-0-226-50186-4 (cloth)
ISBN-13: 978-0-226-50187-1 (paper)
ISBN-10: 0-226-50186-8 (cloth)
ISBN-10: 0-226-50187-6 (paper)

Library of Congress Cataloging-in-Publication Data

Mahdi, Muhsin.
Alfarabi and the foundation of Islamic political philosophy / Muhsin S. Mahdi.
p. cm.
Includes bibliographic references and index.
ISBN-13: 978-0-226-50186-4 (cloth : alk. paper)
ISBN-10: 0-226-50186-8 (cloth : alk. paper)
1. Fārābī. 2. Philosophy, Islamic. 3. Political science—Philosophy. I. Title.
B753.F34 M33 2001
181'.6—dc21

00-012720

For L. S.

If we had to repay the debt of gratitude

incurred by his kindness to us,

not even the whole of time

would suffice.

CONTENTS

PART TWO
The Virtuous City

FOREWORD

$\mathscr{M}$uhsin Mahdi presents here a full and totally new account of Alfarabi's teaching with respect to religion and politics. He does so with a depth of understanding and philosophic insight based on decades of scholarly investigation and textual recovery as well as on his rediscovery of the scope and focus of medieval political philosophy in the Islamic tradition. He does so, moreover, primarily with a view to showing how an accomplished philosopher addresses religious and political questions generally and those that arise within the medieval Islamic context more particularly. Thus he places the reader directly before these and related questions without dwelling on traditional procedures in such an undertaking, that is, without providing an elaborate account of what the book is about or how it proceeds and without saying much about where it fits in the contemporary scholarly literature on Alfarabi. Defensible as is the author's decision to pass over such matters in order to focus, from the outset, on the more important task of demonstrating how Alfarabi founded Islamic political philosophy, it may not be amiss to offer here a brief account of both subjects.

๛

In the introduction, Mahdi focuses on the major stumbling block that faces all those who seek to understand Alfarabi, the apparent Neoplatonic character of his works. He speaks briefly about Alfarabi's life and the intellectual context in which he flourished, his goal being to indicate that in formulating his political philosophy Alfarabi leaned more to the movement that preceded Neoplatonism—Middle Platonism. This school of Platonic interpretation flourished from about 25 B.C.E. until about A.D. 250, that is, from the time of Antiochus of Ascalon until about the time of Plotinus. Though the *Didaskalikos* of Alcinous is the extant text that best represents the tenets of this movement, Mahdi makes no at-

tempt here to identify putative sources upon which Alfarabi may have
drawn. His emphasis is on how Alfarabi's use of this line of Platonic
interpretation, rather than the Neoplatonic one connected with theological issues, allowed him to focus on Plato's political concerns and attempt
simultaneously to render Aristotle more acceptable to his readers. In addition, Mahdi notes why in pursuing such a course Alfarabi nonetheless
utilized the basic themes and language of Neoplatonism to suggest a
harmonization of sorts between philosophy and religion, even though
he ultimately subordinates the latter to the former. The significance of
Middle Platonism for Alfarabi is Mahdi's discovery, as is his recognition
that the two works usually taken as representative of Alfarabi's full political teaching—the *Principles of the Opinions of the Inhabitants of the Virtuous City* and the *Political Regime*—actually play another role that can
be fully appreciated only in the light of the new project Alfarabi sets forth
in the *Enumeration of the Sciences,* chapter 5, and especially in the *Book
of Religion.*

Acknowledging the merit of Ibrahim Madkour's early work on Alfarabi, incomplete as it necessarily was, Mahdi identifies Leo Strauss as the
scholar who first discerned the importance of Alfarabi's trilogy, the *Philosophy of Plato and Aristotle,* and then explored Alfarabi's use of Plato in
his review essay of the *Philosophy of Plato.* For Mahdi, Strauss's insights
made it possible to think anew about the *Enumeration of the Sciences,*
chapter 5. And Mahdi's own discovery of the all-important *Book of Religion* allowed him to see in what sense the *Virtuous City* and *Political Regime* needed to be understood primarily as models or patterns for Alfarabi's new presentation of political science and especially of the relationship between politics and religion that he brings to light in the *Book of
Religion.* The discovery of Alfarabi's new political teaching is central to
the argument of the entire book and forms the core of Mahdi's unique
contribution to the understanding of Alfarabi as well as to scholarship
on this all-important philosopher. It is for this reason that he devotes the
bulk of the introduction to an explanation of why one must learn to read
the *Virtuous City* and the *Political Regime* in a new manner and come
to understand, in addition, why it is perfectly appropriate for Alfarabi
to preface what appears first and foremost as a political teaching with a
cosmological teaching.

Consequently, with one exception, Mahdi says nothing about scholarship on Alfarabi since Leo Strauss's article on Alfarabi published in
1945. The exception is his indirect reference to Richard Walzer's erroneous interpretation of the *Virtuous City*—as set forth in his edition and

translation of the work, along with a commentary, published four decades later. Mahdi's silence is understandable, for in those intervening
years nothing of significance with respect to Alfarabi's political philosophy appeared. D. M. Dunlop's introduction to his edition and translation of Alfarabi's *Aphorisms of the Statesman* (1961) merely repeats the
standard notions about Alfarabi's Neoplatonism, and Ann K. S. Lamb-
ton's appendix about Alfarabi's political philosophy in her *State and Government in Medieval Islam, an Introduction to the Study of Islamic Political Theory: The Jurists* (1983) relies extensively on Mahdi's own writings.

Since then, two books on Alfarabi's political teaching have been published, both by students of Muhsin Mahdi. The year 1990 marked the
appearance of Miriam Galston's *Politics and Excellence: The Political Philosophy of Alfarabi.* Five years later, the volume *Metaphysics as Rhetoric:
Alfarabi's Summary of Plato's "Laws"* by Joshua Parens was issued. Both
volumes represent an attempt to explain Alfarabi's full political teaching.
Galston addresses that subject thematically, looking at the way different
subjects are treated in Alfarabi's various writings—including the logical
writings—and contrasting her own understanding of his teaching with
those set forth by the different interpreters of Alfarabi since Madkour.
Her book is important both for the careful manner in which she follows out particular themes in these different texts by Alfarabi and for her
gentle but firm use of these analyses to correct the earlier interpretations.
Parens, on the other hand, addresses Alfarabi's political teaching by ex-
amining different aspects of the little known *Summary of Plato's "Laws."*
The undertaking obliges him to consider Plato's *Laws, Republic,* and
other relevant dialogues as well as several of Alfarabi's writings—most
notably the *Political Regime, Virtuous City, Enumeration of the Sciences,*
and *Book of Religion*—in addition to the vast array of scholarship sur-
rounding Alfarabi generally as well as his *Summary* and Plato's *Laws* in
particular.

Once the reader grasps the way Mahdi speaks about the secondary
literature in the introduction—namely, to identify those writings that led
him to his own understanding of Alfarabi's teaching and to suggest ever
so discreetly how that differs from the dominant opinion about that
teaching in recent times—his silence about these books by his own students is perfectly understandable. Moreover, given that these books necessarily draw upon his research and reflect his influence, his reticence to
speak about them appears even commendable. So, too, does his reluc-
tance to quarrel with, even to attempt to correct, those whose interpretations he finds faulty. Mahdi's arguments and interpretations are grounded

in thorough scholarship and based on painstaking research into the primary sources, on the careful investigation and presentation of manuscripts that he discovered, on the consideration of doctrines and schools
of thought relevant to Alfarabi's undertaking but not heretofore examined in this context, and on his own thoughtful appreciation of the secondary literature. But these arguments and interpretations are presented
here as reasoned conclusions, as philosophic judgments based on ratioci-
nation rather than on scholarly dialectic.

Again, because others who have written on Alfarabi's broader philosophical teaching in recent times—Dominique Mallet, Thérèse-Anne
Druart, and Shukri Abed, to name but a few—have also studied with
Mahdi, he refrains from citing their writings. The desire that the book
become no more an encomium than a polemic seems to keep him from
citing or discussing the works of those with whom he agrees as well as
disagrees, except in the one case already noted. In a related respect as
well, Mahdi follows a unique approach in this book: noted as he is for
painstaking and thorough scholarship, he eschews here the traditional
scholarly convention of citing secondary literature that is more or less
relevant to a particular topic. He does so, I think, in order to oblige the
reader to consider with him the texts of Alfarabi passed in review and
to think primarily about their philosophical implications. His book is,
therefore, without parallel in the history of scholarship on Alfarabi.

§

Mahdi's goal is to encourage the interested reader to reflect about how
Alfarabi shows the way to his full political teaching. The questions raised
in the introduction—especially those concerning the relationship between religion and philosophy, on the one hand, and politics and religion, on the other—are addressed in the essays constituting the book
itself in such a manner as to show how Alfarabi resolves them while keeping the philosophic enterprise of the ever masterful second teacher fully
before the reader's eyes. The chapters are divided into three parts.

The goal of the first part is to provide a general sense of the philosophical debate, an orientation as it were to the respective spheres of
philosophy, political thought, theology, and jurisprudence within Islam
simply and within medieval Islam at the time of Alfarabi more particularly. Here, a clear distinction between political philosophy and political
theology as well as between political philosophy and mysticism is evoked.
In addition, attention is drawn to the way Alfarabi differs from his immediate predecessor al-Kindī and near contemporary al-Rāzī by focusing on

Plato as one who sought primarily to explain how human beings might live together well in political community. Alfarabi's Plato is not the Plato of the *Timaeus*, intent upon understanding the heavens, but the Plato of the *Republic* and especially of the *Laws*, intent upon understanding what needs to be said about the heavens and the gods to the citizens of the city so that they may live in a well-ordered and fully responsible manner.

Part 2 focuses on the city and, above all, on the virtuous city. Here, philosophy is distinguished from science and from religion. In addition, the role of the founder as founder—whether founder inspired by revelation or founder prompted by reason—is examined, and the considerations Alfarabi deemed basic to founding qua founding are made explicit. The exposition centers on a careful exegesis of Alfarabi's *Enumeration of the Sciences* and *Book of Religion* as works that set forth the fundamental principles for his political science or political philosophy. It is followed by a novel, perhaps even completely unprecedented, attempt to demonstrate that the other books usually taken to be indicative of Alfarabi's political philosophy are nothing of the sort. To this end, the *Selected Aphorisms*, the *Political Regime* (whose full title is *Political Regime, Nicknamed "Principles of the Beings"*), and especially the *Virtuous City* are subjected to close analysis and comparative readings as a means of unraveling Alfarabi's attempt to present a number of different examples of the ways in which his principles of political science or political philosophy might be applied. The argument is surely novel, and it runs counter to the assumptions currently held as sacrosanct by scholarship on Alfarabi, most notably that branch of it stemming from Richard Walzer and his disciples. It will stand or fall on its merits.

Chapter 4, that having to do with Alfarabi's *Enumeration of the Sciences*, may strike some readers as difficult to fathom and certainly as exceedingly prolix. To appreciate the merit of this chapter, it is necessary to discern the remarkably thorough interpretation of the work it provides. Indeed, this chapter represents the first attempt anyone has made to analyze the work as a whole. In a literal and a figurative sense, Mahdi considers the parts of the treatise carefully and from several different perspectives in order to show how the work fits together as a whole and to suggest the way in which it serves as an introduction to Alfarabi's larger political teaching. No one who follows his interpretation of the *Enumeration of the Sciences* through to the end, difficult as such an undertaking is, will ever again fall prey to the temptation to consider that work as a mere summary or popular encyclopedic account of the sciences. With great exegetical skill, Mahdi shows here how the key to the understanding of Alfarabi's broader philosophical teaching rests in a firm grasp of its minutest details.

In the third part, particular attention is paid to the work that first prompted thoughtful students of Alfarabi to entertain the notion that his teaching might be primarily political, namely, the trilogy known as the *Philosophy of Plato and Aristotle*. This work opens with a treatise entitled *Attainment of Happiness*, in which Alfarabi explores the relationship between the theoretical and practical sciences, especially the way in which the pursuit of theoretical science repeatedly comes to an impasse that can be overcome only after looking anew at practical science. That treatise is followed by the *Philosophy of Plato*, and it, in turn, by the *Philosophy of Aristotle*. The focus here is above all on the last treatise, this in order to explain the novel use Alfarabi made of Plato in his writings and to indicate the unusual role he assigned to Aristotle. The interpretation also draws on Alfarabi's little known *Book of Letters* (one of the treatises Mahdi discovered at the beginning of his research into Alfarabi) and on Aristotle's *Metaphysics*, book Lambda, as well as on a fragment from one Aristoteles/Aristocles entitled *On Philosophy*. In this part, the reader is also urged to consider the importance of Alfarabi's opinion about the cycles through which human life tends to pass and how this becomes manifest in his political teaching.

The chapters in this part, as in the book as a whole, are so written that the inattentive reader will wonder what Mahdi is trying to accomplish. Why, for example, does he spend so much time on the *Attainment of Happiness* in chapter 8 and on the *Philosophy of Plato* and *Philosophy of Aristotle* in chapter 9? Similarly, why does the book end with an account of the different cyclical views of history? To repeat that Mahdi does so in order to indicate how Alfarabi suggests what the relationship between theoretical and practical science might be, how the two need to be pursued independently and yet in conjunction, and that the two are interrelated, but not interdependent, is the beginning of an answer. More to the point, Mahdi dwells so on such issues in order to explain their nuances and point to their ramifications without reducing them to a simple formula. Aware that these are better understood as problems than as issues that have been resolved, he strives to provide the reader with all the tools for appreciating Alfarabi's approach to, and use of, them. This is also why he insists on the novel use Alfarabi makes of Plato in his writings and alerts the reader to the importance Alfarabi attaches to cyclical theories of human development.

In sum, Muhsin Mahdi presents here a philosophical reading and in-

terpretation of one of the most important philosophers in the medieval
Arabic and Islamic tradition. Grounded in decades of pathbreaking research and informed by a deep understanding of the history of philosophy, especially of philosophy as it relates to political life, this account of
Alfarabi as founder of political philosophy in Islam clearly provides the
fullest and most masterful explanation of what the second teacher sought
to do in these writings that intrigue even as they elude or baffle all but
the most persistent and thoughtful reader.

Charles E. Butterworth

INTRODUCTION

𝒜lfarabi (Abū Naṣr al-Fārābī, ca. 870–950) was held in high esteem in medieval times by major philosophers such as Avicenna in eastern Islam and Averroes in western Islam. Although his fame was partially eclipsed by his two great successors, he remained the greatest *political* philosopher of the period. This judgment was confirmed during the second half of the twentieth century with the publication of the rest of his surviving political-philosophic works, including such fundamental treatises as the *Philosophy of Plato, Plato's "Laws,"* and the *Philosophy of Aristotle.*

Having instituted a new epoch in human history and a new religious-political order, the revealed religions challenged the tradition of Greek philosophy to investigate and make intelligible a religious-political order based on prophecy, revelation, and the divine law. Alfarabi can be said to have been the first major philosopher to take up this challenge.

Little is known for certain of Alfarabi's life apart from his having died in A.D. 950 at an advanced age near Damascus. It can be assumed that he was born in the district of Fārāb in Central Asia and that he lived and studied in Central Asia before coming to Baghdad to continue his studies. After that, he traveled to Byzantium—apparently for more-advanced studies in some of the Arabic-teaching institutions across the border—before returning to Baghdad, where he taught until conditions in the 'Abbāsid capital forced him to leave for Syria and subsequently Egypt. Later, he returned to Syria, where he died. Among his teachers in Central Asia and in Baghdad were Christian clerics who traced the origin of their philosophic studies to the school of Alexandria, the pagan Platonic school of philosophy that had been Christianized during the later Roman period and its remnants transplanted in Antioch, Ḥarrān, Baghdad, and Central Asia. To judge by their functions and surviving theological writings, these teachers were Nestorian Christians who had inherited the

1

Christian Neoplatonic tradition handed down by the last representatives of the Alexandrian school.

Through his Nestorian Christian teachers and his reading of the works of the great Neoplatonic teachers and commentators of the Athenian and Alexandrian schools, Alfarabi was well versed in the Neoplatonic philosophic tradition and the Christian Neoplatonic theological tradition. Were he to have followed these two traditions and developed a Neoplatonic Islamic theology, no one would have been surprised. What does evoke wonder is his rejection of the main tenets of both the pagan and the Christian Neoplatonic traditions and his return to the pre-Neoplatonic philosophic tradition, namely, the tradition he found in the works of Plato and Aristotle themselves and in the works of earlier, pre-Neoplatonic, especially Middle Platonic, commentators. Alfarabi's appreciation of the significance and possible use of the different periods and levels of Platonic political philosophy is a topic that has yet to be investigated and understood. Its surface features are the recovery of Platonic political philosophy and the use of certain elements drawn from the post-Platonic philosophic tradition—principally Aristotelian and Middle Platonic—in his political writings. Part 3 of this volume, "On the Philosophy of Plato and Aristotle," touches on certain features of this aspect of Alfarabi's thought, leaving a fuller account for a companion volume on Alfarabi and the Platonic philosophic tradition.

In addition to showing the relevance of the philosophy of Plato and Aristotle and their successors for the study of the revealed religions, Alfarabi presents political science or political philosophy as the philosophic discipline within whose purview such a study falls. Thus, one aspect of the importance of Alfarabi in the history of philosophy is that he was the first philosopher to develop a philosophy of religion based on the Platonic-Aristotelian philosophic tradition in general and Platonic political philosophy in particular, presented in a context analogous to that provided by Plato's *Republic, Timaeus,* and *Laws,* while making use of the Greek philosophic tradition that preceded the doctrinal innovations introduced by Neoplatonism.

Alfarabi was fully aware of the works of the major Neoplatonic philosophers and of the incorporation of Neoplatonic doctrines into Christian theology, the dominant philosophic theology of his Christian teachers and students in Baghdad. He read and made use of the works of the distinguished Neoplatonic teachers of philosophy in Alexandria and Athens during Roman times that were translated into Arabic during the ninth and the first part of the tenth century. He understood the value of the Neoplatonic philosophic tradition for bringing together, or harmonizing, philosophy and religious orthodoxy and for constructing a Platonism for the people. It is therefore understandable that historians of philosophy who had not studied his works with sufficient care should have thought that he must have followed the Neoplatonic tradition that had dominated the Platonic school in Alexandria and Athens. Yet the complete absence from his authentic writings of the central Neoplatonic philosophic doctrines—of the One, Intellect, and Soul—should have been sufficient to suggest to students of Islamic philosophy who read him that they were in the presence of a philosopher who made use of certain elements drawn from the Neoplatonic philosophic tradition but whose Neoplatonism must remain suspect.

҈

Alfarabi initiated in Islamic philosophy the tradition of returning to the works of those he calls the two primary sources of philosophic investigation, Plato and Aristotle, without, however, ignoring later developments and their possible contributions to the human and natural sciences. His successors in all three revealed religious communities confirmed his high position as the greatest philosophic authority since Aristotle, calling him the "second teacher" after Aristotle.

It will be apparent to the reader of the following chapters that Alfarabi revived Platonic political philosophy and established it as the discipline with which to approach the study of the establishment of the revealed religions and the societies founded by them. He brought to the fore the theme of the relationship between philosophy and politics in a context where the overriding question was the relationship between philosophy and religion. And he raised the question of the relationship between religion and politics, between the philosophy of religion and political philosophy.

How his approach was then used or modified by his successors in their discussion of the revealed religions is a chapter in the history of philosophy that has yet to be written. It is already clear, however, that without Alfarabi and his writings in the field of the philosophy of religion, much of the history of Islamic philosophy, and medieval philosophy more generally, remains unintelligible.

Alfarabi's works in the field of political philosophy and religion range from the most popular to the most properly philosophic. Until World War II, his most popular works—the *Harmonization*, the *Virtuous City*, and the *Political Regime*—provided readers with almost all of what was thought to be his political philosophy. Even relatively popular works that may have explained what treatises like the *Virtuous City* and the *Political Regime* are all about, such as chapter 5 of the *Enumeration of the Sciences* and the *Book of Religion,* were either not published or not taken into account in interpreting the *Virtuous City* and the *Political Regime.* The more difficult, yet fundamental, works that give the reader some sense of how Alfarabi read and interpreted the writings of Plato and Aristotle, such as the *Philosophy of Plato* and the *Philosophy of Aristotle,* were but names in medieval bibliographies.

Under these conditions, it was difficult for students who read such works as the *Virtuous City* and the *Political Regime* to raise and answer significant questions regarding their respective presuppositions. Do the same sets of presuppositions explain the doctrines present in both works? Is one "more scientific" than the other? Why do they begin differently? Why do questions concerning the active intellect, the imagination, prophecy, and the universal state tend to be present or to occupy a more important place in one and not in the other?

Some of these questions could have been answered by means of a close comparison of the two works, yet much that is left unsaid remained beyond the ken of readers in the absence of the programmatic works and the more fundamental works. One tended to wonder about the outdated cosmology, biology, and psychology in the *Virtuous City* and in the *Political Regime.* Of course, any child knows that major aspects of the cosmology and biology presented in these two works became outdated with the introduction of the telescope and microscope, not to speak of more recent tools. But have all the questions become outdated? What about the relationship between politics, religion, and cosmology? What do they have to do with one another? What is the relationship between man, society, the natural environment, and the physical universe? What about the vision of the unity of science?

Crude as they may look, the *Virtuous City* and the *Political Regime* provide the reader with the opportunity to consider such questions. These two comprehensive political works begin a discourse on the universe and its principles, placing man and society in this broader context; yet both the cosmology and the politics presented in them differ in the two works and differ significantly from our view of cosmology and politics. The outdated character of the parts on cosmology is to some extent remedied by the contemporary relevance of the question. And in science, it is the question or the framework that is important.

To take but one example, chapter 5 of the *Enumeration of the Sciences,* whose main subject matter is political science, concludes with short accounts of what look like Islamic jurisprudence *(fiqh)* and Islamic theology *(kalām)*, even though a closer look indicates that Alfarabi is thinking of jurisprudence and theology as disciplines that may be present in any regime. Apart from the juxtaposition of political science, on the one hand, and jurisprudence and theology, on the other, there is no explanation of what the accounts of jurisprudence and theology are doing as appendages to a chapter on political science. This is a question Alfarabi addresses explicitly only in the *Book of Religion*, where it becomes clear that opinions about God and the world are not the preserve of the sciences enumerated prior to chapter 5 in the *Enumeration of the Sciences;* they are for the most part legislated, defined, and defended by human beings who are not scientific inquirers, who do not necessarily know logic, mathematics, physics and metaphysics, or political science. Here are arts that compete with the true sciences, both theoretical and practical. Moreover, the political significance of the rhetorical, dialectical, sophistical, or poetical methods, practical experience, imitation of earlier lawgivers and rulers, and so forth used by them needs to be understood and appreciated.

෴

The first comprehensive study of Alfarabi's place in Islamic philosophy was published before World War II by Ibrahim Madkour (1934). This was the first full-fledged study of Alfarabi in modern times, representing what scholarship was able to achieve on the basis of Alfarabi's published works and such manuscripts of unpublished works as were known at the time to exist in European libraries. At about the same time Leo Strauss (1936), having examined Falaquera's *Reschith Chokhmah*, was able to identify the structure of Alfarabi's most important philosophical work, the trilogy entitled *Philosophy of Plato and Aristotle* and consisting of the *Attainment of Happiness,* the *Philosophy of Plato,* and the *Philosophy of Aristotle.* But the more important steps were the publication of the *Philosophy of Plato* (1943) and the review essay on this crucial work by Strauss (1945).

Of the works studied here, the *Enumeration of the Sciences* has been well known since medieval times. Indeed, it was frequently quoted and summarized in Arabic, Hebrew, and Latin. But it was thought to be a mere "encyclopedic" account of the sciences. The importance of chapter 5, "On Political Science, the Science of Jurisprudence, and the Science of Theology," was nonetheless recognized, and it tended to be quoted,

in part because the relatively extended account of political science that
followed the Platonic tradition could hardly be found elsewhere, political
science having almost disappeared from view as a philosophic discipline.
Yet it was not clear what jurisprudence and theology, appended to political science, had to do with the latter discipline or with philosophy in
general. The relationship between political philosophy, jurisprudence,
and theology becomes intelligible only in the account of political science
in Alfarabi's *Book of Religion,* a work not available to students of Alfarabi's political philosophy until after its publication in 1968; and, until
its publication, one could only have guessed at how Alfarabi conceived
of the connection between political science, on the one hand, and jurisprudence and theology, on the other. Above all, however, it was the *Book
of Religion* that stated and explained explicitly and unequivocally Alfarabi's view of the relationship between the city *(madīna)* and religion
(milla) as subject matters of political science or political philosophy.

Alfarabi's *Virtuous City* has also been frequently read and cited since
medieval times, in addition to being frequently printed and translated in
modern times. Its companion work, the *Political Regime,* which seems
to have been better known and appreciated in western Islam in medieval
times, was translated by Dieterici at the end of the nineteenth century
and printed in Hyderabad early in the twentieth century. Little attention
was paid to it, however, on the assumption that it was just another version of the *Virtuous City.* As for the *Virtuous City* itself, the common
opinion persisted that it was a sort of encyclopedia representing yet another summary of the philosophic sciences, another version of the *Enumeration of the Sciences* apart from the omission of such disciplines as
logic and mathematics—a view repeated in the introduction and commentary accompanying the latest edition of the work (1985).

One of the first tasks of the analysis and interpretation of Alfarabi's
political philosophy was to establish the relationship between chapter 5
of the *Enumeration of the Sciences* and the *Book of Religion,* both of which
present accounts of political science or political philosophy, and then to
clarify the relationship between these general accounts of political science and the *Virtuous City* as well as the *Political Regime,* two construc-
tions produced by the kind of political science described by Alfarabi. In
other words, the *Virtuous City* and the *Political Regime* can now be seen
as examples, patterns, or models constructed by Alfarabi according to
some of the rules described in his account of political science. Such models are meant to be imitated by future founders and lawgivers and to
be used by students of philosophy to understand their own political-

theological predicament. These two works do not, therefore, embody either Alfarabi's theoretical philosophy or his practical philosophy but are only examples of the kind of regimes that can be constructed by political philosophy.

One of the main questions posed by the *Virtuous City* and the *Political Regime* is the status of the first part of each work—the part beginning with the enumeration of divine attributes and concluding with the generation of man and the initial description of his faculties—and its relation to the second part, that is, the political part proper. This question is not fully resolved in the *Enumeration of the Sciences*, where the last section of chapter 4 (which enumerates some of the topics covered by the third and last part of divine science, or metaphysics) and the beginning of chapter 5 (where Alfarabi begins his account of political science) are merely juxtaposed without the relationship between metaphysics and political science being explained. In addition, one notices that the section on political science (excluding jurisprudence and theology) is initially practical in orientation. Only when Alfarabi presents the component parts of the virtuous royal craft (in 105.15ff.), do we find a reference to the theoretical sciences or theoretical philosophy (106.1 and 16).

Descriptions of God and the world are central in the account of theology, including the need to refute false opinions—presumably opinions that do not accord with the account of nature and the divinity in the preceding chapters of the *Enumeration of the Sciences*, especially chapter 4, and, in particular, its last part. In the accounts of jurisprudence and theology, it is assumed that opinions about God and the world are legislated in every religion and that, after the passing away of the prophet-lawgiver, jurisprudence and theology exist in every religion in order to continue the effort of deducing new views and defending old ones. The sections on jurisprudence and theology follow directly upon the last explanation in political science of ignorant leaderships and their not needing philosophy, either theoretical or practical. It is assumed, further, that opinions about God and the world are components of the virtuous as well as of the nonvirtuous royal art, of every lawgiver and his religion, of every religion.

Therefore, Alfarabi's treatment of these subjects in his works on political philosophy and religion is not an innovation. It points to the similarity between the virtuous royal craft or art and the art of the lawgiver, between the virtuous city as envisaged by Plato and the religious community based on revelation. This points to the need to understand the Platonic philosophic account of the virtuous royal art, an account more

accessible now with the coming of the revealed religions. It hardly needs
to be emphasized that Platonic politics and the revealed religions, different as they may be, bear certain resemblances that can encourage the
student of both philosophy and religion to learn what Platonic politics
can teach about revealed religions. Of course, the presence of opinions
about God and the universe in a community is not sufficient to identify it
with the virtuous city constructed by Plato or to identify every prophet-
lawgiver with the Platonic philosopher-king. There are true and false
prophets, and the arts of theology and jurisprudence exist in good and
bad religious communities. Alfarabi hints at all this in chapter 5 of the
Enumeration of the Sciences by the neutral account of jurisprudence and
theology as practiced in different religions and by the comical fashion in
which certain theological activities are described.

In other words, one cannot take at face value the word of jurists and
theologians with regard to what they say about the character of the opinions and actions prescribed in their own religions. They are defenders of
their own religion, not scientists with neutral perspectives. Unlike Alfarabi's political science, jurisprudence and theology are not scientific but
practical arts based on the opinions and actions prescribed by the founder
of each religious community. Still, the emphasis placed on opinions by
jurists and theologians requires that political science, too, pay equal attention to opinions and actions. Thus, an Aristotelian political science
that is largely action-oriented will have to be abandoned altogether or
else incorporated within a Platonic political science that pays equal, if
not greater, attention to opinions. In addition, more attention needs to
be paid to the royal virtuous art and the virtuous city. This is one reason
why in chapter 5 of the *Enumeration of the Sciences* Alfarabi moves from
a summary description of a practical political science—placed after the
description of the theoretical sciences in chapter 4 and hence concentrat-
ing on the practical aspect of political science—to a more Platonic political science.

The *Virtuous City* and the *Political Regime* are works that are clearly
identified in their titles as forming part of practical philosophy—that is,
as political works. Yet they contain matters that properly belong to the
theoretical sciences, to physics and metaphysics. I cannot sufficiently
emphasize the political character of these works in their entirety, including the so-called metaphysical and physical parts, or sufficiently emphasize the political character of those parts that appear as purely theoretical.
For we learn from chapter 5 of the *Enumeration of the Sciences* and from

the *Book of Religion* that opinions about God and the world, as well as opinions about human activities, can be presented in ways other than purely theoretical and scientific. It is crucial to determine whether and to what extent the *Virtuous City* and the *Political Regime* are scientific, especially since they do not claim to be such, do not follow the order of investigation that the sciences are supposed to follow, and are assertoric rather than investigative or demonstrative. This ought to be an evident and generally acceptable ground for not taking everything presented by Alfarabi, especially if it is political in character and does not even pretend to be scientific, as a scientific account simply. The point is well worth keeping in mind, given the simplistic manner in which the views expressed in the *Virtuous City* and the *Political Regime* are frequently taken to represent Alfarabi's philosophic or scientific views.

The opinions expressed in these two works not only originate in a political context (in that they are legislated) but are politically relevant, important, and even crucial. For they point to the ends (or the view of happiness) for which the actions are performed, a fundamental subject matter of political science. They display the varying views of, or opinions about, happiness, again one of the main subject matters of political science (see *Enumeration of the Sciences,* 102.6 and 8ff.). And they indicate the basis of the distinction between the goods, beautiful things, virtues, and useful things, and their opposites (102.14ff.), as well as the basis of the distinctions among regimes and types of rulerships (103.1ff.).

❧

To resume. The *Virtuous City* and the *Political Regime* are parallel works, yet not identical in every respect. Broadly speaking, both are divided into what looks like a cosmological part (a political cosmology or a political theology) and a political part. They contain elements derived from the philosophy of Plato and Aristotle, but the overall framework is Platonic and not Aristotelian.

The *Enumeration of the Sciences* and the *Book of Religion* enumerate the functions of political science, which in part correspond to the subject matter of the *Virtuous City* and the *Political Regime.* Therefore, the division of the subject matter of these two works into cosmological and political is not precise. The political is assimilated to the cosmological, and the cosmological is assimilated to the political. If we disregard the political, we will have no way of explaining why man and society occupy such a dominant position in these two works in contrast, for example, to Proclus's *Elements of Theology;* for man is not the highest being (God is) or the highest body (the celestial bodies are). And we will have no way of defining the science that these works treat.

According to the account of the *Book of Religion,* everything in these two works is part of the subject matter of political science. On the other hand, it is not clear at first why a political work should begin in this manner and proceed in this way. There are various lines of inquiry that need to be followed up in these two books: (1) One is man's place within the whole (the principles and bodies with which the *Political Regime* begins) and the relation of his soul, form, and matter to the rest of the principles and bodies in the world. (2) Political science is asked in the *Book of Religion* to inquire into the cosmos, the body, and the city in order to bring out certain aspects or particular characteristics that are *in them;* these activities of political science are enumerated in detail in the *Book of Religion.* One needs to look again at the *Political Regime* and the *Virtuous City* in order to find out how political science performs some of the tasks ascribed to it in chapter 5 of the *Enumeration of the Sciences* and in the *Book of Religion* and how it applies some of the general rules described there in these two particular cases. (3) Since political science signifies the science that has to do with the city, special attention should be paid to those parts of the *Political Regime* and the *Virtuous City* that deal with the city in order to find out how the city is patterned after the cosmos or the human body. Conversely, one needs to find out how the cosmos and the human body are presented in these two works, that is, whether they aim at giving or emphasizing those characteristics that are politically relevant and can be imitated. That is, Alfarabi may not be interested in the investigation of nature as such but wishes to use the most likely account of the cosmos, that of Aristotle as modified by Ptolemy, which he further modifies by politicizing the account of the cosmos as an introduction to his account of the city. The question here is whether, and to what extent, the cosmos and the human body are already interpreted politically or certain conclusions of scientific inquiries are modified to make them more adequate opinions for the citizens and to present them as patterns for the construction of the city. In this respect, it is perhaps not quite fair to speak of "political cosmology" or "myth," that is, of a cosmos or a human body presented with no attention to the scientific accounts of the cosmos or of the human body. For it is precisely the *relationship* between science and the city that is at issue, a dilemma Alfarabi discusses more fully when explaining the roots of the opinions of ignorant and erring cities (or religions) at the end of the *Virtuous City* and of the *Political Regime*. The implication is that just as corrupt ancient opinions explain the view of these cities, noncorrupt modern opinions should be at the root of the views of the virtuous city. But "noncorrupt" means that scientific knowledge should not be corrupted in the process of modifying it and presenting it politically. Differently stated, the integrity of scientific knowledge should be maintained even when it is used to help form the opinions of the citizens.

PART ONE

Orientation: Philosophy, Jurisprudence, and Theology

The Political Orientation of Islamic Philosophy

First, I beg leave to speak of our Church Establishment, which is the first of our prejudices, not a prejudice destitute of reason, but involving in it profound and extensive wisdom. I speak of it first. It is first and last and midst in our minds. For, taking ground on that religious system of which we are now in possession, we continue to act on the early received and uniformly continued sense of mankind. That sense not only, like a wise architect, has built up the August fabric of states, but, like a provident proprietor, to preserve the structure from profanation and ruin, as a sacred temple, purged from all the impurities of fraud and violence and injustice and tyranny has solemnly and forever consecrated the commonwealth and all that officiate in it. This consecration is made that all who administer in the government of men, in which they stand in the person of God Himself, should have high and worthy notions of their function and destination, that their hope should be full of immortality, that they should not look to the paltry pelf of the moment nor to the temporary and transient praise of the vulgar, but to the solid, permanent existence in the permanent part of their nature, and to a permanent fame and glory in the example they have as a rich inheritance to the world.

*I*n this statement from *Reflections on the Revolution of France* (446–47), Burke sums up a fundamental premise on which Western political theology and political philosophy before the sixteenth century was based and against which Western political philosophers since the sixteenth century have rebelled. (While one can certainly find ancient Epicureans and modern Western religious philosophers who do not fit this general picture, they neither seriously challenged the dominance of the above view in earlier times nor hampered the subsequent successful rebellion against it.) This chapter will examine the same issue as it arose in Islamic philosophy.

It is a common opinion that the human activity called philosophy is neither necessary nor useful, and the prevalence of this belief compels philosophy to justify itself. The justification often involves asking, first, about what is necessary and useful for man, and eventually about the nature of man himself. One way to approach the question "What is man?" is to look at man's place in the world and speculate about the things that might distinguish men from other beings that one sees or imagines. The question comes down to this: Is man's reason or intelligence something different from the rest of the world of nature and from those other parts of man's being that he shares with the higher animals? Or is man's reason simply a more complex mental mechanism than those of other animals, merely an extension of, or an improvement on, animal faculties—one that serves to satisfy the same needs, desires, and passions that animals experience, but in a more efficient and perfect fashion? This question is inseparable from the question of what constitutes politics. Both ancients and moderns understood man to be a "political animal," an animal who differs from the others in living and acting and pursuing his goals in a political community. What man is all about and what politics is all about are questions that approach the same point from two different directions.

Islamic philosophy shared the ancient view that man is a special kind of being; that his ability to reason—his power to know himself and the whole—is the activity that marks him as different from other animals; and that reasoning is therefore the ultimate purpose of his existence. It regarded this difference between man and other living beings as a radical one—as radical as, if not more radical than, the difference between inanimate and animate beings, the soulless and the souled.

This is a philosophic view. However, the philosopher does not live among, confront, argue with, or justify his position to inanimate beings or other animals, but to other men; and other men are, like him, already members or citizens of a political community. Yet they are, by and large, immune to philosophy and the way of life it entails. Instead they stand by their common conviction that the fundamental opinions accepted by and pursued in the political community are normative and are not to be questioned; to question them may in fact be considered a form of treason that justifies banishment or death. This presents the philosopher with the following dilemma. If—and he is convinced that it is so—man's reason for existence and his distinction from other animals is his exercise of intelligence and his ability to know, if such knowledge is predicated on questioning convictions and opinions and investigating everything, and if a political community denies the need for such an investigation and makes it impossible, then that political community has already decided in favor of the view that the proper aim of political life and of man himself is to gain greater efficiency in attaining ends that are not specifically human but are more elaborate versions of ends pursued by certain other animals— pleasure, wealth, honor, and so forth. It is at this point that the classic conflict between philosophy and the political community begins.

Philosophy and the Divine Law

If there is a single attitude that has characterized the entire Muslim community throughout the centuries, it is gratitude for revelation and the divine law; commitment to the exemplary deeds and sayings of the Prophet, the vehicle of that revelation; adherence to the way of life of the Prophet and his companions as the correct way, which the community must preserve and imitate and to which it must return; and the conviction that deviation from the way of these pious ancestors is wrong and constitutes a rebellion that leads to strange byways, to forsaking God's command, to estrangement, and to exile to a world of infidelity, from which the Muslim community must return and again find its home. No amount of interpretation, legal devices, reliance on the consensus of the community and its common interest, or justification based on necessity and the change of times can undermine the fundamental belief that genuine progress requires a return. There is no rainbow on the horizon, no golden age at the end of man's time whether resulting from the perfection of human sciences and arts or from man's controlling or conquering nature. Progress consists in resisting estrangement and false paths and in returning to one's origins by completing the circle—in their end is their beginning. The Muslim community is therefore never satisfied with its present. It looks to the future, but only insofar as it is called upon to bring about the revolution that will suppress its own rebellion and, beyond all this, as it must think of the final end and of the final accounting. Beyond the return to the right way of pious ancestors is the final return of all men to their Maker, to the other world, the world beyond this world. A state of forgetfulness or indifference to the final end can only be seen as the ultimate rebellion and infidelity and as exile by a community that began with an overwhelming sense of the imminence of that end.

The demands of Islamic philosophy and the demands of the Islamic divine law as commonly understood did not agree in every respect. For the modern Western student of Islam the agreements loom large. For Muslim philosophers and theologians the disagreements demanded attention and in some cases an adequate resolution.

To begin with, man is the central concern of both philosophy and divine law: philosophy is a human activity, and the divine law is addressed to man and not to animals, stars, or angels. In addition, both call on man to reach for something higher than himself, to become divine, to relate himself to what is above and beyond himself. Man is confronted with a demand, a duty, to open himself to the whole or the highest principle of the whole. Further, neither philosophy nor the divine law is meant to be at man's service; rather, man is meant to be at the service of both. They are not meant to meet his needs or improve his condition as they existed before he became aware of philosophy or of the divine law, for those needs and that condition are seen by philosophy and the divine law as miserable and unworthy of his capacities as a human being. Man's humanity is now constituted or reconstituted by a higher calling. Philosophy calls upon man to know the visible universe and its principles through his highest faculty, his reason or intelligence; the divine law calls upon him to obey faithfully the commands of God. In both cases, however, he is primarily performing a duty rather than demanding his rights. The highest rights are not the rights of man but the rights of the universe and its highest principle, the right of God to be known and obeyed. Therefore, both the city constructed by the philosophers and the city established by the divine law demand a comprehensive view of the universe and its highest principle and require man to understand his place in that comprehensive order of things.

The emphasis on man's duty is also the overarching principle of political and social life as seen by both the philosophers and the divine law. Political and social life are constituted by the duty to act in a virtuous way. To perform virtuous activity does not mean to pursue one's desires and passions and pleasures but to meet the demands of goodness as established by human intelligence or by the divine law. Virtuous activity is not at the service of pleasure; it is a by-product of activity according to virtue. Therefore, both the city constructed by the philosophers and the city established by the divine law are cities devoted to virtue—they are virtuous cities. Virtue is at their center; it is the principle of their regimes and of their organization, in contrast to the tyrannical city, whose end is not the common good of the ruler and the ruled but the private good only of the ruler. The virtuous city is ruled by the wise; the tyrannical city is ruled by the ignorant who pursue their lower passions, desires, and pleasures.

The chief virtue in both the city constructed by the philosophers and the city established by the divine law is justice; and justice means obedience to the law, which in both cases is a comprehensive law, covering what we now call civil and penal law, public and private law, moral and religious law, or the law relating to both deeds and beliefs. Muslim philosophers and Muslim theologians have argued at length for the superiority of such comprehensive laws over laws that restrict themselves to deeds alone or to such deeds as are considered socially or politically relevant. These arguments will not be reviewed here. Instead, we will look into how a comprehensive law tends to tempt certain members of the Muslim community into trying to transcend the common legal demands of virtue and justice and even to impose on them the duty to go beyond these demands, how the additional activity tends to be an asocial or private activity, and how the philosopher in his view of what this activity ought to be tends to part ways with certain other followers of the divine law.

To understand how this parting of the ways develops, it is necessary to begin with the common legal demands of the divine law regarding belief, worship, and the conduct of social transactions. The divine law comes equipped with certain underpinnings meant to ensure obedience by encouraging the formation of certain states of character, mind, and feeling commonly placed under the headings of piety and humility, fear and hope—the fear of God and of divine punishment and retribution, and the hope for future rewards and divine mercy. In contrast to the common legal demands of the divine law, piety and humility admit degrees of more or less. Similarly, while the divine law demands that man inquire into the universe and come to know its highest principles, especially the highest principle, God Himself, this, too, obviously admits of degrees. And while in both cases the minimal demands may be incumbent on all, the maximal possible demands can be imposed only on the chosen few.

Now it so happens that the states of character, mind, and feeling best suited to carry out these two kinds of demands are quite different from, if not antithetical to, each other; to meet the two kinds of demands more than minimally requires additional virtues that are different in kind, and therefore two different kinds of training or education. A life lived in constant fear and trembling is not conducive to acquiring knowledge, to inquiry and understanding and contemplation. These require rather that man be serene, take pleasure in looking about him and in wondering at what he sees, and be fearless in facing whatever presents itself to him in his inquiry, in considering various views, in admitting the truth of what he discovers to be demonstrably true, and in confessing his ignorance or doubt when he does not find certainty.

Neither inquiry nor piety, it is true, require knowledge of the highest principles or the so-called essence of God, nor do they presuppose wisdom about the whole. The unknown can either be feared or it can be inquired into—both are equally possible attitudes to take, and either can just as well go hand in hand with initial ignorance. But men do not usually confine themselves to confessing their ignorance; they argue with each other and seek a ground to stand on that is firmer than ignorance, one that can support certain positive views about the universe, its structure, and its highest principles.

Islamic Jurisprudence and Theology

Let us begin at a time when the juridical study of the divine law, theology, mysticism, and philosophy had reached a degree of maturity and follow the path that a concerned Muslim would have taken to learn these disciplines and to try to cut his own trail through them. Toward the end of the twelfth century, al-Ghazālī surveyed these various paths to knowledge in his famous *Al-Munqidh min al-Ḍalāl* (Deliverer from Error), but since he was seeking the ultimate ground of knowledge, he did not concern himself with the juridical study of the divine law, in which he was already an expert practitioner. His reason was rather simple: according to him, this study deals primarily with practical and worldly matters. Starting from the explicit statements in the Quran and the sayings and deeds of the Prophet-Lawgiver and of his immediate followers, and using such logical procedures as analogy, this discipline attempts to arrive at correct determinations of cases for which there are no explicit precedents. The jurist's perspective is confined within the horizon established by the Lawgiver and the divine law. As a jurist, he does not inquire into the divine law in the sense of asking questions about its grounds: Why a divine law at all? Why this divine law rather than another? Why a regime based on this divine law rather than another? Why this way of organizing a human community rather than another?

Of course, the majority of the faithful and many of their leaders may think, perhaps properly, that the attempt to go beyond ascertaining what the divine law demands and faithfully obeying those demands is either a waste of time or a form of rebellion. This equation of the just with the legal is the hallmark of good citizenship, but it does not satisfy those members of the religious community who believe that the divine law calls upon them to search for the secrets of God's creation. And they need to learn the secrets of the divine law itself, especially when the community becomes splintered in its opinions regarding such questions as God's attributes, the character of the revelation, and man's responsibilities, or when it is faced with outsiders who deny the truth of the divine law and argue for the superiority of other divine or human laws.

Theology is the discipline of defending the divine law—of establishing the truth of a particular revelation, the genuineness of the mission of the Lawgiver, and the correctness of the beliefs and deeds his law demands. To do this, however, theology needs to go beyond the explicit statements of the divine law to develop a rational, relatively coherent view of what the ultimate source of the divine law, God, is and what kind of demands he is likely to make or not to make, what prophecy is and how to distinguish genuine prophets from false prophets, and what man is and what demands he can legitimately meet. Otherwise it will not be possible to argue for the validity of a particular divine law, the justice of its demands, or the virtue or goodness of those who faithfully fulfill these demands. All this presupposes that these matters are knowable to man, not merely on the basis of the divine law but independently of it. It also assumes that the way to this knowledge is a particular type of theological discourse or inquiry.

But are these matters knowable independently of the divine law? This seems to be the question that divided Muslim theologians into so-called rationalists and traditionalists. It was a difficult question to deal with, primarily because the intention of Islamic theology was to defend the divine law, while it could not perform that function without going beyond the divine law and elaborating what it meant, what its intentions were, and what made it possible—that is, without first obtaining a more comprehensive view of the structure of the universe and its guiding principles, of God's essence and attributes, and of the structure of the human self and will. The different schools of Islamic theology explored the various possible comprehensive views, but, if we are to believe al-Ghazālī, their point of departure, which remained the divine law, and their primary intention, which remained the defense of that law, prevented them from pushing such inquiries as far as they needed to go if they were to satisfy his thirst for knowing the truth of things or overcome his uncertainty in the face of so many conflicting positions. Moreover, Islamic theology, already held suspect by many students of the Islamic law who felt that it was impious to conduct inquiries of this sort into the divine law to begin with, now had to face philosophers and mystics who asserted that they had found better and more fruitful ways to conduct these inquiries.

Like the juridical study of the law, Islamic theology was initially very much concerned with politics. In fact, the question of the leadership of the Islamic community was one of the primary questions, if not the primary question, that led to the rise of Islamic theology. By al-Ghazālī's time, however, politics in the wider sense had receded into the background in both the juridical study of the law and theology. The legal qualifications of rulers continued to be discussed, but the rulers themselves had long since ceased to act as worthy successors of the Prophet. They had become secular kings who had to meet certain minimal legal requirements and whose legal function was now limited to appointing the judges who administered the divine law; they no longer engaged in elaborating, interpreting, or even applying the divine law. These functions were now assumed by the jurists and the theologians, who had succeeded in establishing themselves as the custodians of the divine law and separating the legislative and juridical from the administrative sphere. The divine law was to be protected and preserved by the jurists and the theologians, and the Muslim community became coextensive with the operation of this law rather than with the rule of any particular dynasty. But this also meant that the sphere of the divine law tended to become limited to personal law and the law of transactions, leaving the rulers and their bureaucracies in control of constitutional and administrative law and aspects of criminal justice. Correspondingly, theology became increasingly preoccupied with questions of ethics rather than politics in the broad sense, except when it incorporated some of the accounts of the political regimes expounded by the philosophers.

Politics became the preserve of its practitioners: kings, viziers, and bureaucrats. Islamic jurisprudence and theology saw to it that worldly kings did not attempt to claim any divine rights or the right of dynastic succession on the basis of the divine law, or to function as intermediaries between their Muslim subjects and the Prophet or God, and in so doing they succeeded in thoroughly demythologizing the status of the rulers and definitively uprooting the ancient Near Eastern views on the divinity of kings. Furthermore, jurists and theologians discussed whether the Muslim community was under a legal obligation to remove, by force if necessary, an unjust ruler, but they held such diverse views on this question that it was hardly possible to speak of a consensus among them. More important, they also remained largely oblivious to the broad questions of political life. Therefore, they were equipped neither to understand nor to discuss the overall character of the political orders or regimes under which Muslims lived, their diversity as Islam spread over a large part of the civilized world, or the changes that took place in them as one ruler succeeded another, as power extended or contracted, and as the community underwent social and economic changes that were bound over time to transform the character of the community, its ideas, and its practices.

Nature and Convention

Concerning philosophy, al-Ghazālī said that its practitioners held three opinions not shared by the rest of the Muslim community: that the world has always existed and was not made out of nothing, that God knows universals rather than particulars, and that rewards and punishments in the world to come pertain to souls or spirits rather than bodies. These questions had already been treated by Alfarabi in the *Harmonization* and were to be taken up again by Averroes in the *Decisive Treatise,* both of whom attempted to show that, in the form presented by al-Ghazālī, the charges were false: the philosophers' positions on these issues were varied, complex, and not as dogmatic as al-Ghazālī made them out to be. But Alfarabi and Averroes showed also that the dogmatic way in which a revealed religion tends to assert its views on the creation of the world, God's knowledge of particulars, and bodily resurrection presents philosophic inquiry with grave and, in some cases, insurmountable difficulties. Al-Ghazālī, who treated the views of the philosophers as a collection of doctrines or dogmas, does nothing to help us appreciate these difficulties. To ferret them out, we must begin by recognizing the importance that philosophy attaches to the discovery of nature and the distinction between nature and convention.

Let us start with a cursory look at the history of the expressions *ṭabīʿa* (nature) and *sunna* (convention) in Arabic. In prephilosophic usage, the abstract form *ṭabīʿa* is not common, and the other forms of the expression (such as *ṭabaʿa, ṭabʿ,* which mean "stamping," "making an impression" or an imprint, and hence temper or character as something stamped or imprinted in men's souls in consequence, e.g., of food and drink) are hardly distinguishable from *sunna,* "tradition," "custom," or "way"; in fact, *ṭabʿ* can in some cases be understood as subordinate to *sunna,* which can have a more comprehensive and permanent connotation than *tabʿ* especially when *sunna* is used to refer to the form or conduct of life, the "way of the ancients," or the "way of God." The philosophic discovery of nature required the modification of the meaning attached to the expression *tabʿ* and the use of the more abstract forms *tabīʿa* (nature) and *tabīʿī* (natural) to mean, not an impression or an imprint, but an expression   nature expresses itself, and natural beings are those beings that express or expose themselves as they *are* to our eyes and reveal *what* they are to our mind's eye.

Al-Ghazālī knew, of course, that the philosophers had such a view of nature, and he could not condemn it because, as he said at the end of his *Incoherence of the Philosophers,* there were Muslim theologians who held a similar view. He had to admit that this understanding of nature was a possible and legitimate Muslim interpretation of the world. But there was another possible and legitimate interpretation, and that was the one developed by the theologians whom al-Ghazālī followed, namely that the world has no nature but only a convention, habit, or custom. Atomism and the denial of inner causality was a rational effort to elaborate systematically the notion that nothing in the world has a nature of its own: it merely has a convention external to it. Everything has a *sunna,* which means that everything is prescribed, or sanctioned, from outside itself and by something else.

In short, these theologians understood God's creation by analogy to man-made things, and God himself by analogy to human makers or artisans. The philosophers, on the other hand, began with the distinction between man-made things and non-man-made things that have their principles in themselves. To them, the visible world is a natural world whose parts have a natural order and whose highest principle is a supreme intelligence: the creator, knower, and sustainer of this order. Man, too, is a natural being. His nature is revealed in the realization of his innate capacities. It is expressed through his desires, passions, and power to reason, his ability to labor in order to satisfy his needs, and his aptitude for developing the arts and the social, moral, and political orders that fulfill his needs and enable him to achieve the perfection the human species is meant to achieve by nature. Man's nature is the source of his happiness. Everything that man does has to be understood in terms of his nature, his place in the natural whole, and the ends of his nature as a being within this natural whole which is the visible world.

It is not difficult to understand why those having such a perception of nature in general and of human nature in particular would see grave difficulties in the conventional perception that the highest principle of the world is an omnipotent being that is in no way restricted by its knowledge of the world or by the nature of creation, a God conceived ·by analogy to a manager who concerns himself with all particular incidents and accidents and who promises material rewards and threatens material punishment. One way to meet these difficulties is to regard this conventional view as necessary for the education of the overwhelming majority of the faithful, who are not able, or do not have the opportunity, to pursue these matters and yet need well-defined and easily understood opinions to strengthen their attachment to the divine law. To this end, philosophers and mystics tended to agree that the divine law contained a surface meaning suitable for everyone and a higher meaning suitable only for the chosen few. In this way, they could try to transcend the common juridical and theological view of the divine law without denying its validity or utility. Here, however, ends the resemblance between philosophy and mysticism.

Philosophy and Mysticism

For mystics like al-Ghazālī (see Shehadi 1964; Sherif 1975), God is unknowable, inaccessible, and wholly unpredictable because He is absolutely free. Even the relative stability and predictability according to which the believer acts in response to the divine law is not a sure passport to heaven or to the vision of God in the hereafter. One needs to be patient and hopeful of God's kindness and mercy, go beyond the strict demands of the divine law, and practice the additional mystical virtues that culminate in trust and love, the only virtues with which man can counter an utterly unpredictable relation between himself and his Lord.

For the philosophers, however, this type of mystical attitude assumed a kind of divine wisdom that they did not claim to possess. Instead, their understanding of nature and order in the visible world and their understanding of human nature and its place within the natural whole led them to a fresh appreciation of convention. Beginning with the notions that human nature, unlike the rest of the natural world, is not eternally perfect; that it does not spontaneously achieve perfection but contains certain capacities for perfection that need to be developed; and that the development of these capacities takes the form of activities and habits that require society and political life, the philosophers then turned to inquire into the nature of these activities and habits through which man achieves his happiness in this world and the world to come.

They asked about the nature of the human body and about man's natural needs, desires, and passions, which either force or lead him to associate with others and to abide by the minimal rules required to make even the simplest and most necessary forms of social life possible. They inquired into the way in which human society develops into the elaborate political communities that enable men to satisfy further their desire for pleasure and play, wealth, honor, or freedom, or some combination of these. They investigated the various forms that political communities or regimes take and the particular part of the human soul that dominates each variety, the type of ruler who leads it, the kind of convention and law that promotes and preserves it, and the causes of the revolutions or changes that take place in it and transform it into a different regime. They investigated the different units that make up society and the political regime—families, tribes, villages, cities, nations, and empires—and inquired into the role of such natural and quasi-natural factors as race, common character, language, geography, and the natural environment in the formation and determination of the special character of political regimes.

They paid particular attention to the relation between human laws and divine laws, and to the variety of human laws and the variety of divine laws. They emphasized the view that the variety of human and divine laws does not necessarily invalidate any one of them but simply reflects the differences among men and can accord with, or take account of, the different stages of development in which human communities find themselves and the different conditions and conventions under which they live. This led them to consider the art of the lawgiver, both the universal lawgiver who legislates for the entire human race and particular lawgivers who legislate for individual nations or cities.

In all these investigations, the philosophers did not lose sight of their original point of departure. They understood convention to be, not something that is wholly arbitrary or is accepted merely because it is "our way" or the "ancestral way," but something that completes and perfects nature; it is a second nature, as it were, indispensable if man is to achieve the ends intended for him by nature. That there is a certain measure of arbitrariness in convention, law, and political life can be accepted without undermining the possibility of inquiring into convention and even developing a science of conventional things. Such a science can be anchored in the science of human nature, its needs, and its ends. It will be, not a science of nature, but a science of man, this unique being who can reshape himself with a view to certain ends. These ends are not all of the same rank: some are easier to achieve than others, and some—perhaps even the highest—remain for the most part unattainable. Such, for instance, is the political regime devoted to knowledge—the regime in which philosophers come to be kings or kings come to be philosophers and in which, in the case of the ruling part, man's highest end is identical with the highest end of the political regime. But, for the most part, man's political life and its ends are not identical with man's highest end, and he will have to pursue his highest end alone or in the company of a few friends and disciples. Only gods and beasts can dispense altogether with arbitrariness and with agreement on common actions and opinions that are theoretically uncertain or problematical.

The Divine Law and Philosophy

One can perhaps say that Islamic philosophy agreed with Islamic jurisprudence, theology, and mysticism on the practical orientation of the divine law, on its character as law, and on its superiority to mere human laws—that is, on the superiority of a law that requires its followers both to perform certain actions and avoid others and to profess certain opinions and reject others. But Islamic philosophy refused to accept the notion that the divine law forbids—indeed, it argued that it demands—free inquiry, and it proceeded to conduct this inquiry according to the best available method, the method of trusting what can be seen rather than what has been said, nature rather than ancestral opinion. Philosophy was thus understood by analogy to the human arts whose practice is demanded by the divine law, but a divine law that left man free to perfect these arts according to his natural light. Averroes reminds his reader in the *Decisive Treatise* that, on occasion, the divine law demands the ritual slaughter of an animal, but that it is man's responsibility to determine the best instrument for that purpose.

To express this notion another way, one can say that Islamic philosophy accepted the practical relevance of legal opinions but perceived a certain disjunction—at the highest level, among the guardians of the law, so to speak—between the requirement of practice and the requirement of theory. Practice requires decisions: they must be based on solid conviction, must have a certain finality, and are incompatible with hesitation or lack of resolution. Theory requires open-mindedness, confession of ignorance, suspension of premature judgment, openness to new evidence, and willingness to reconsider. This, one could say, is how Islamic philosophy found or understood human nature—there is a permanent disjunction or duality, or even conflict, between the requirements of practical life and the requirements of theoretical life at the highest level.

Since theoretical life cannot be conducted in isolation from practical life but depends upon it, the philosopher recognized this duality in his own life, performed the actions and accepted the belief demanded by the divine law, and at the same time attempted to preserve the integrity of inquiry and of theoretical life. Such a harmonization between the demands of practical life and the demands of theoretical life is not without its problems; but then such problems cannot be avoided without sacrificing one or the other side, either abandoning one's desire to know, or abandoning one's attachment to one's own community and its divine law, or subordinating the one to the other, or doing what, according to the "Condemnation of 219 Propositions," the Latin Averroists are said to have done—saying that X is true according to philosophy even though Y is true according to theology.

This last solution implies a belief that philosophy has been converted to wisdom or that it is no longer the love of wisdom and the search for it because the search has already been completed and truth found. Should that be the case, then what was called above the duality in man's nature becomes a so-called theory of the double truth, which is somewhat hard to live by. It is perhaps easier to say, "I believe and inquire," than to say, "I believe one thing and know the truth to be otherwise." Islamic philosophy resisted the claims that philosophy had been converted to wisdom, whether by the theologians, the mystics, or certain schools within its own fold. The political orientation of Islamic philosophy was in no sense dependent on settling the ultimate philosophic questions; it was, on the contrary, an integral part of philosophic inquiry into those questions.

Philosophy and Political Thought

*T*he dialogue called *Laws* or *On Leg-islation*, where Plato sets forth the best possible political order, begins with a question regarding the origin of laws: the Athenian Stranger asks his two companions whether they attribute their laws to "a god or some human being" (Plato, *Laws*, 624a1). When Alfarabi recognized that Plato's *Laws* asked questions pertinent to divine laws—that it was, as Avicenna maintained afterward, the standard work on prophecy and the divine law—philosophy turned to politics, and political philosophy proper emerged in the Islamic community. Though the question whether "a god or some human being" was the giver of their laws was answered definitively and emphatically by the followers of the revealed religions, many questions still needed discussion and clarification: the relation between God, the man who serves as the intermediary, and the religious community; the extent to which divine laws regulate man's private and communal life; the reach of the religious community beyond national and geographic borders; and the relation between what is revealed and what is attainable by the unassisted human mind.

Questions such as these were also of concern to the theologians and jurists of the revealed religions and formed what is known as their political thought, which was not a continuation of pagan political thought or classical political philosophy. The victory of the revealed religions over the religions of pagan antiquity transformed what had been the prepolitical basis of political life as well as the prephilosophic basis of philosophy. Men's perception of the world about them and their views about pleasure and pain, the useful and the harmful, good and bad, virtue and vice, happiness and misery, and this world and the next—all underwent radical change. No one who did not recognize the new conditions could henceforth lead or rule them; no one could explore practical or theoretical matters with them, impart knowledge to them, or engage them in a dia-

logue on the nature of things—including political things—except by
starting from their new perception of the world and of themselves.

The reintroduction of political philosophy into these religious communities was, therefore, a task that demanded more than the recovery of
the classical tradition, itself no mean task in the new circumstances. For
reasons that have not yet been fully investigated or understood, political
philosophy did not begin its career in the new environment until the
tenth century of the Christian era, when Alfarabi succeeded in reviving
the political philosophy of Plato and Aristotle and thus liberating Socratic philosophy from Christian theology and initiating what became
the main tradition of philosophic thought in the Islamic community. It
was not until the twelfth century that political philosophy penetrated
Judaism through Maimonides, and not until the thirteenth that it penetrated Latin Christianity through the Averroists, Albert the Great, and
Thomas Aquinas.

To speak about philosophy and political thought in the times of the
revealed religions—"in our time," as philosophers used to say in those
times—can mean speaking about a special branch of philosophy such as
the one treated by Aristotle in the *Politics*. It can mean speaking about all
of philosophy and all of religion; about the way philosophy approaches
religion, develops a philosophy of religion, and deals in this context with
theology and jurisprudence as practiced in the revealed religions; or
about the way philosophy proposes new ways of conducting theological
and legal investigations in a particular revealed religion. Or it can mean
speaking about how a religious tradition approaches philosophy, transforms it and subordinates it to theology, and makes its peace with it; or
about how a divine law proscribes or sets limits to philosophic inquiry.
These questions have for long been dominated by the attractive thesis
proposed by Étienne Gilson, who submerged the relation between philosophy and revelation in Latin Christianity in what he called a "Christian philosophy" (Gilson 1955, 5, where the reader can find the argument against Adolph Harnack on this issue)—a thesis imitated by some
students of Islam and Judaism who speak of a comparable "Islamic philosophy" and "Jewish philosophy" and by some students of comparative
philosophy who speak of a more general "religious philosophy." "Christian philosophy" in this latter sense is absurd and deserves Heidegger's
(1961, 6) remark that it is no more credible than a round square.

What needs to be investigated is how political philosophy reoriented
itself to face the new environment of the revealed religions, what difficulties it had to surmount, what opportunities it took advantage of, and,

above all, what problems it found worthy of reflection and inquiry. To do so, one need not necessarily abandon the use of "Islamic," "Jewish," or "Christian" in tagging the philosophy practiced in the communities adhering to these revealed religions; one need only abstain from prejudging the nature of the relation between philosophy and the religious sciences.

The Challenge of the Revealed Religions

Arabic and Islamic political philosophy, like Arabic and Islamic philosophy in general, appears as a synthesis of Aristotelianism, Platonism, and Neoplatonism. These three traditions were not strangers to one another. Aristotle may have modified Plato's thought in fundamental ways, but Plato was often his point of departure. Contemporary students of Arabic and Islamic philosophy should be careful not to be misled by the fashion that dominated the history of Greek philosophy for some time, one that saw Plato and Aristotle as opposed to one another and considered earlier attempts in Hellenistic and medieval times to look for common themes in their thought or possible agreements between them to be historical misunderstandings rather than legitimate interpretations. Similarly, Plotinus and the other Neoplatonists were careful students of the writings of the two great masters. The Platonists (the Academics), the Aristotelians (the Peripatetics), and the Neoplatonists had much in common and interacted constantly. In a sense, they formed a single tradition of "divine" philosophers and distinguished themselves from the "naturalists" among the pre-Socratics and from the Epicureans and the Stoics. They were aware that they disagreed about important issues, including the nature of the supreme principle, and concerned themselves with understanding the grounds of their agreements and disagreements.

Although it is not reasonable to suggest that Arab and Muslim philosophers were totally ignorant of those differences and disagreements, one must recognize that their writings present the modern reader with a difficult problem. Many of them appear more interested in stressing the unity of the philosophic tradition than with explaining its diversity; they tend to hide rather than publicize differences of opinion about difficult and unresolved issues in philosophy. Not being modern historians of philosophy, they were concerned primarily with the issues themselves rather than with their genesis. And they seem to have thought it more important that the potential philosopher not be discouraged by disagreements among philosophers and fall prey to the doctrines of the skeptics and the preaching of those who claimed that disagreements among philosophers prove that philosophy is a fruitless enterprise. There was, finally, the impact of the revealed religions, which presented philosophy—all philosophy—with a massive and unprecedented challenge.

The consequences of this challenge for political philosophy were far-reaching. The revealed religions are based on the premise that the supreme principle of the world, the maker, originator, creator of the universe and all the beings in it, has revealed to man, indirectly through angels and prophets or directly by His Incarnation, the highest and most comprehensive knowledge man can ever hope to obtain about God Himself, his own soul, the purpose of life on earth, how he ought to conduct himself here, and his final end or the rewards and punishments that await him in the world to come. Compared to this revealed knowledge, what man has tried and keeps trying to achieve by his own efforts is at best incomplete or confused, at worst erroneous. Seen from this perspective, the highest wisdom of paganism will appear as dark ignorance or unfulfilled yearning.

To begin with Aristotle's political philosophy, the view that practical life is self-sufficient and closed upon itself and that man can live a good, virtuous, and noble life without necessarily possessing correct opinions about God, obeying His commands, or caring for salvation in the world to come would now seem the height of foolishness and pride. As for Plato's view that theoretical wisdom is not available to man, that he is condemned to a life of quest and search, and that practical and political life should be seen in the light of this quest and placed in its service—all this was no doubt a true account of man's condition before the coming of revelation. What Plato would have had to add, but could not have even guessed, is that wisdom is not available to man as long as he relies on his own devices: God in His mercy can terminate the state of bewilderment and ignorance; and man may obtain the object of his wish, though not through philosophy. And now that the object of man's wish has been obtained, his life on earth must be based on revealed knowledge, his practical and political life placed at the service of his salvation, and everything subordinated, not to philosophy, but to the quest of what he has now been assured is true virtue and wisdom and perfection.

The Neoplatonists' view, finally, that the principle of the world is beyond being and theoretical knowledge, and that the way to imitate Him is ultimately through practical devotion and spiritual activity (an *ergon* rather than a *logos*), may be a truer account than the accounts of both Aristotle and Plato. Yet, here again, man's unaided effort only intuited the ultimate Mystery from its veiled appearance or emanation in the natural world. Now, however, the ultimate Mystery has chosen to reveal itself to man and teach him how to conduct his life, alone or in association with others, in order to achieve life everlasting in the presence of this ultimate Mystery. The natural and limited wisdom achieved by Neoplatonists about the ultimate Mystery, the structure of the universe, and the human soul, through which the ultimate Mystery reveals itself, and what man must do to achieve his salvation—all this must be set aside; man must now believe in God's own revelation of Himself and obey His commands.

In the case of each revealed religion, there followed centuries of sustained effort on the part of philosophers to understand the implications of the revelation and come to terms with them and equally sustained efforts on the part of theologians and jurists to define how and to what extent religion can make use of philosophy. Different attempts were made to set limits to each party's claims or harmonize them by redefining the one, the other, or both. All this came to form part of the Western tradition, making it difficult to imagine that philosophy and the revealed religions were not always on intimate terms. Yet Arabic and Islamic philosophy, like medieval philosophy in general, remains almost unintelligible unless one recovers the difference in the origin and perspective of philosophy and of the revealed religions, the initial incompatibility of their claims, and the realization in each camp that the other camp presents a serious challenge and an alternative way of life. Only the seriousness of the conflict can explain the interest in accommodation during the late Hellenistic and early medieval period.

Implications for Philosophy

Initially, the claims of the revealed religions were directed, not against a particular philosophic school, but against philosophy as such, against the "idea" of philosophy and the premise that philosophy is the best way of life and the path to the most comprehensive knowledge available to man. Gradually, it became clear to philosophers, just as it was clear to the theologians and jurists of the revealed religions, that division in the rank of the philosophers was detrimental to the cause of philosophy—theologians and jurists exploited it at every opportunity—and that it might be prudent to make up their differences and present a common front wherever possible. This did not mean that they were now ready to hold incompatible views or that Peripatetics were ready to embrace Epicureanism. There was sufficient community of interest and doctrinal affinity between Academics, Peripatetics, and Neoplatonists to make room for the formation of a common front. It did not take them long to realize that almost all of Aristotle, or the essential Aristotle, was unacceptable to the revealed religions, that certain Platonic doctrines were readily accepted by theologians, and that Neoplatonism was welcomed with open arms in certain theological circles. When the indisputable success of the revealed religions finally convinced Hellenistic philosophers that coexistence, accommodation, and a more harmonious relation with the revealed religions was the only prudent and practical alternative to the fruitless defense of decaying pagan religions, the most urgent question was how to protect and preserve Aristotle. This was achieved by hiding him from public view.

The common front marched to embrace the revealed religions with Plotinus (the other-worldly Greek sage who enchanted everyone with his divine speech) in front, followed by the divine Plato, with Aristotle kept in the background, hardly to be seen, and not to be read by students unless prepared for reading him first by Plotinus and then by Plato. It is well known that at some undetermined date a clever fellow decided that Aristotle deserved to become known as the author of certain extracts from Plotinus's *Enneads* and Proclus's *Elements of Theology* put together under the title the *Theology of Aristotle*. Some like-minded students of philosophy (smiling smugly, no doubt, under their beards) thought this a capital idea and attributed to him other Neoplatonic writings also. After that, whenever one of their coreligionists repeated the accusation that Aristotle believed in the eternity of the world or did not believe in survival after death, they could say to him: "This is not quite fair. Look at what he writes here. Could this be said by someone who believes in the eternity of the world or denies survival after death?" (Consider Alfarabi's treatment of these questions in the *Harmonization*.) Another way to protect and preserve Aristotle was not to teach most of his works in public sessions but to read them in private sessions only; still another, to cover his writings with commentaries, interlaced with Platonic and Neoplatonic doctrines.

Finally, there is the curious case of Aristotle's *Politics*. This book seems to disappear from view in the late Hellenistic period and throughout the medieval period, until the second half of the thirteenth century. It must have always been there, since the Latins encountered no difficulty in finding manuscripts of it when they went to look for them. Yet during the revival of interest in Aristotle's works in Hellenistic and early medieval times, when they were translated into Latin, Syriac, and Arabic, hardly anything was said about this book. No one knows whether or how much of the book was translated into Syriac or Arabic; and if anyone wrote a commentary on it in Greek, Syriac, or Arabic, we know nothing of it.

Philosophers in the Islamic community knew of the book and the subject matter it treated but did not expound its doctrine in detail. If they had no access to it, one would expect them to miss it and to mention this fact, which—with one notable exception—is not the case. The only philosopher who needed to say something about this question was Averroes, who planned to comment on all of Aristotle's writings. He did not say that the book was not translated into Arabic or that his predecessors had no access to it—only that *he* could not get hold of it and therefore would comment on Plato's *Republic* instead. He gave no indication that this substitution presented certain problems or that Plato's *Republic* might not agree with the spirit or letter of Aristotle's *Politics*—things he, as the most knowledgeable student of Aristotle's works, must have known. He read and commented on the *Nicomachean Ethics,* where he could find (in bk. 6) Aristotle's main discussion of practical and political science, and on the *Rhetoric,* where he could find Aristotle's classification of the regimes. He was in a position to form a clear idea of Aristotle's view of political science. Yet he proceeds as though it went without saying that if after finishing Aristotle's *Ethics* one could not come across his *Politics,* Plato's *Republic* would do just fine.

One could, I suppose, insist that the disappearance of the *Politics* was just an accident and that men like Averroes could not tell the difference between Aristotle and Plato in any case. But such statements are not quite convincing: they do not take into account the question of the compatibility between Aristotle's *Politics* and the revealed religions or the implications of introducing this book into the discussion of political philosophy at a time and within a context in which Plato, or a combination of Plato and Plotinus, could do much more to clarify political life as it then existed and avoid the kind of frontal attack on religion about an issue (the self-sufficiency of practical wisdom) that was no longer vital for the fate of philosophy. Aristotle's view of the self-sufficiency of political life could be studied and understood in a less exposed context, in the *Ethics* and the *Rhetoric,* for instance.

The counterpart of "hiding" Aristotle's political science is the recovery and exposition of Platonic politics. Plato's *Republic* and *Laws* became the basic textbooks of Arabic and Judeo-Arabic political philosophy, a state of affairs that has no parallel in Latin Christianity, where Aristotle's *Politics* was translated in the thirteenth century and Aristotle's *Politics,* rather than Plato's *Republic* and *Laws,* became the basic textbook of political philosophy. Again, a purely historical account of the survival of texts and of the influence of earlier traditions is neither sufficient nor helpful in clarifying the character or intention of political philosophy as developed in the Islamic community and, later, in the Jewish community and in Latin Christianity, respectively.

To begin with, one might have expected the situation in the Islamic community and in Latin Christianity to be the reverse. After all, Islam is thought to be more of a political, this-worldly religion; certainly it pays more attention to things that appear to be exclusively this-worldly. Therefore, Aristotle's *Politics* should have appealed to philosophers in the Islamic community as the more "realistic" account of political life, in which worldly things retain their relative independence and dignity. Plato's writings, on the other hand, should have been especially appealing to Christian theologians. His transpolitical, "idealistic," "other-worldly" views and his best city somewhere "in heaven" had in fact appealed to the church fathers (e.g., to Augustine) in the Hellenistic period. Furthermore, the Plato transmitted to philosophers in the Islamic community, as Alfarabi points out in the *Harmonization,* was a "Hellenistic," ascetic, divine, and other-worldly Plato whose way of life was contrasted to that of a this-worldly Aristotle. This was the received account, which they had to modify and correct. The traditional Plato transmitted to them was a nonpolitical Plato, a Plato for whom philosophy was an exercise in and preparation for death. Plato was still known as the author of the *Republic* and the *Laws* and the *Statesman,* but the immediate political context of these works had been lost sight of.

This background does not explain the Plato recovered and expounded by Alfarabi and his Muslim and Jewish followers. What Alfarabi presents is, in a sense, an un-Platonic interpretation of Plato, at least of Plato as seen by the Hellenistic traditions (Athenian as well as Alexandrian) and their survival in the medieval period. For he presents a decidedly political Plato whose other-worldliness is accidental and whose views of the relation between this-worldly affairs and other-worldly affairs are more adequate than those of Aristotle. In short, from a historical point of view, Alfarabi's Plato or Platonic politics had not existed earlier. It was Alfarabi's own creation or re-creation, and, in any case, its framework must be sought in his understanding of political life and political science, which in turn motivated the re-creation of Platonic politics from the translations and summaries available to him.

This is true also of Aristotle's *Politics* in Latin Christianity. Aristotelian politics did not exist before the thirteenth century in any of the traditions from which the Latin West drew its scientific inspiration: the Hellenistic tradition, the earlier Latin medieval tradition, or the Arabic and Judeo-Arabic traditions. The supernatural, transpolitical end of life in earlier Christian theology; the doctrines of the Beatific Vision, Grace, and Faith; and the relative independence accorded the law of Caesar may have prepared the ground for a self-sufficient political science, which was then developed with the help of Aristotle's *Politics*. But its immediate framework is the new reformation of theology by Albert and especially Aquinas, who articulated and developed the full implications of the distinction between the supernatural and the natural, a differentiation that in some respects corresponds to Aristotle's distinction between practical wisdom and theoretical wisdom.

The Problem

We must therefore keep an open mind regarding the extent to which the Christian religious tradition in the Latin West facilitated the effort of philosophers like Albert and Aquinas to understand the intention of Aristotle's *Politics* as well as the extent to which Aristotle's *Politics* facilitated their effort to understand the Christian religious tradition's view of political life. Similarly, we must keep an open mind regarding the extent to which the Islamic religious tradition facilitated the effort of philosophers like Alfarabi to understand the intention of Plato's *Republic* and *Laws* as well as the extent to which Plato's *Republic* and *Laws* facilitated their effort to understand how Islam viewed political life.

To the extent that we turn away from the interesting but by no means always decisive questions of the availability of texts, and of antecedents and influences, to consider the intention of the philosophers themselves and what they meant to achieve through their activities as political philosophers, we tend to assume, with some justification, that the religious tradition is not only an independent factor but in some sense the fundamental and determining one: that it motivates philosophers to reinterpret earlier thinkers and philosophic traditions so as to agree with or justify their own religious tradition. It is of course true that, as a political phenomenon, a religious tradition is better established, more stable, more authoritative, and more comprehensive than the philosophic tradition developing within it.

However, this is not true of the *interpretation* of the religious tradition, whether by philosophers or the larger group of persons we call "intellectuals," who in this case are the jurists, theologians, mystics, and men of letters. Interpretations are usually presented as clarifications or reforms; this should not prevent one from realizing that a religious tradition is also susceptible to interpretations—and in a way that can affect its core—that make it agree with or justify certain philosophic points of view. One cannot, for instance, simply assume that when Alfarabi looks at Islam with Plato's *Republic* and *Laws* in mind, or when Aquinas looks at Christianity with Aristotle's *Politics* and *Ethics* in mind, either one is confined within a circle whose immovable center is religious faith or belief. It is possible that the way faith or belief is formulated as a result of such an approach is no longer the prephilosophic view of faith or belief but the result of a complex process of transformation and interpretation. This is an issue that deserves to be treated cautiously and in measured steps.

For instance, it is true that Plato's *Laws* provides a political framework for understanding divine laws, prophetic legislations, and the communities based on them; Aristotle's *Politics,* on the other hand, does not discuss these themes, and the priestly class here is part of the city, not the element defining the city. But does Plato's *Laws* suffice—that is, does Plato's analysis of the laws of Minos suffice—for the analysis of the prophets' divine laws? What Minos learned from Zeus is significantly different from what Moses, Jesus, or Muhammad learned from God. Also, Minos is not like Moses, Jesus, or Muhammad. These were men who, in broad daylight, performed miracles, promulgated new laws, and organized communities that followed their laws. And their laws are independent of place rather than being essentially connected to a given locality. They are unchangeable and their continuity is unbroken: a living chain of men constantly recovers and transmits their laws. In the case of Christianity and Islam, they are also universal, applicable to all men, using war and proselytizing as legitimate means to spread the message. The differences between Minos's laws and these divine laws are obvious enough, and philosophers in the Islamic and Jewish communities who investigated prophecy and revelation with the help of Plato's *Laws* must have been aware of them. In what sense, then, did they believe that Plato's discussion of an ancient Greek phenomenon could help them conduct their discussion—the only full-fledged theoretical discussion available to us today—of the founding acts and the founders of the revealed religions?

As for the situation in Latin Christianity, there is no political philosophy properly speaking until Aquinas. Two courses were open during the thirteenth century. The first was to follow Alfarabi, Avicenna, Averroes, and Maimonides and develop and apply the Platonic model. This was the course followed by Roger Bacon, but it did not flourish or continue in Latin Christianity. The second was to start afresh by taking Aristotle's *Politics* as the model and developing a new approach. This entailed drawing a distinction between the natural and the supernatural realms, sharply limiting the scope of political philosophy, and leaving the rest to be dealt with by theology. Political philosophy would now be limited to human laws and human affairs; and the central problem of political philosophy in the Islamic community—the relation between natural, conventional, and divine laws—would be raised and discussed in a theological, rather than political-philosophic, context. When Dante and Marsilius of Padua set about to extricate political philosophy from its presumed subservience to theology, they needed to modify and supplement Aristotle's political philosophy so as to be able to discourse on the central political question of the time: the relation between the Holy Roman Empire and the Holy Roman Church.

Jurisprudence and Political Philosophy

To understand political philosophy as practiced in the Islamic community one must begin where its authors began: with coherent reflection on political life in the Islamic community. Like his fellow citizens, a Muslim political philosopher identified himself with the Islamic religious community, the *umma*. The notion of a religious polity no longer has currency in our political lexicon, but this does not alter the fact that these philosophers lived in a religious community in which this notion was a reality that dominated men's minds, largely defined their political allegiances, and determined their social intercourse in war and peace. The Islamic religious polity in which political philosophy began its career in post-Hellenistic times was a community in which a single divine law, originally revealed to a prophet-lawgiver, regulated or claimed to regulate the lives of all its members along with ancillary legal systems (administrative, public, customary) that the divine law recognized. What are for us commonplace distinctions—such as "public" and "private," "religious" and "secular"—do not have the same weight in the divine law as in our modern legal systems.

As a citizen of such a religious polity, the political philosopher began his reflection with an attempt to understand the origin, character, and aim of the divine law, which determined what his fellow citizens regarded as true or false, virtuous or vicious, noble or base. As a good citizen he held himself bound by the legal determination of these matters and believed or acted in accord with that law's injunctions. The precise determi-

nation of these matters fell within the scope of jurisprudence, which the
Islamic community considered to be the science of the divine law par
excellence. Jurisprudence is based on certain sources handed down from
the divine lawgiver. These are things that it accepts, does not question,
and regards as axioms. From these sources, and while taking into account
the lawgiver's intention (i.e., the reasons behind his promulgation of the
law and what he aimed to achieve by it for his community), jurisprudence
proceeds to infer the legal determination of matters not explicitly determined by the lawgiver.

Now to the extent that the jurist does not reflect on these sources but
restricts himself to making inferences from them, he is not in a position
to understand them or even to justify and defend them. He restricts his
horizon and activity to the confines of his own law; he is not even able
to offer a complete account of his own legal system. (What was known
in the Islamic community as the science of the roots or fundamentals of
jurisprudence limited itself to the study of the methods of ascertaining
the sources of the law and the accepted ways of inferring particular rules
from them.) From the outset, then, the political philosopher was obliged
to widen his horizon beyond that of the jurist if he was to attain any
coherent understanding of the divine law to which he adhered.

As a good member of his own religious community, he had to accept
the opinions and perform the actions enjoined as legally binding in his
own divine law as determined by the jurist. But as a political philosopher
he needed to go beyond jurisprudence and to attempt to understand the
foundations upon which the Islamic religious community rested. He had
to ask questions that the jurist as jurist was neither required to ask nor
capable of asking: Why does a political community need to be a religious
community? Why does the ruler or legislator of the political community
need to be a prophet or the representative of a prophet? Why does a
political community need to be governed by a divine law?

These questions inevitably led him to inquire into the different kinds
of political communities, rulerships, and laws and to ascertain their relative merits. This inquiry disclosed the universal need of the human species for political association and the diversity of the possible and actual
forms of political association. It showed the diversity of opinions regarding man's end or perfection and regarding the means of achieving his
end. And it revealed that the members of various political communities
believed in opinions and performed actions that owed their origin to
three different sources: some were due to the human nature common to

all men, others were due to reason and convention, and still others were of divine origin.

The diversity of opinions about human things and the conflicting claims of these diverse opinions pointed to the need for an inquiry that could replace the opinions about these matters with knowledge of them— with knowledge available to man as man. In short, the very existence of these diverse and conflicting human opinions seemed to demand the kind of activity performed by political philosophy. This was the perspective of the political philosopher, as distinguished from the perspective of his fellow citizens. His new horizon was wider: it included and yet went beyond their (and his own) horizon as good citizens. Like them, he believed in and acted according to the requirements of the divine law. For them, belief justified and vindicated itself. They were not troubled by the claim of those who did not believe in any religion or divine law but pursued their lives according to their own light. And they were not driven by a sense of wonder that finds no rest until beliefs are vindicated or replaced by the highest knowledge possible for man.

Political philosophers discovered this new horizon in the writings of classical political philosophers, especially in the political writings of Plato and Aristotle. These writings confronted them with a fundamental and far-reaching challenge: that their religious beliefs (in this case, their religious beliefs about the end of man and the political regime that would best promote this end) be subjected to a searching inquiry, the results of which should vindicate or replace these beliefs. The political philosophers were those members of the Islamic community who took up this challenge rather than remaining satisfied with calling Greek philosophy foreign, attempting to refute it without understanding what it meant to say, or burying their heads in the sand. In so doing, they were not always understood or supported by their coreligionists.

Theology: Natural and Revealed

Political philosophy must be distinguished from theology and the political thought of theologians. To understand this distinction, one needs to go beyond the writings of the political philosophers themselves. Some of them were theologians also, but all of them, even those who were not themselves theologians or were critical of theology, were well acquainted with it and provide some of the most penetrating accounts of its principles and history. Theology of course came into being long before political philosophy in the Islamic community and, subsequently, in the Jewish community. It was the first answer to the challenges posed by Greek thought and the thought of various pre-Islamic religions. It had little to do with its namesake among pagan philosophers, notably Aristotle. For Aristotle, theology is the inquiry into divine things or the first principles as far as these are accessible to the unassisted human mind—as distinguished, that is, from the account of divine things given by mythographers, poets, legislators, and the ancestral tradition. In Latin Christianity, the inquiry into divine things that does not need necessarily to be based on divine revelation but is accessible to the unassisted human mind was called "natural" theology in contrast to "revealed" theology.

Unlike natural theology, revealed theology takes its principles from the information about divine things disclosed by God Himself to His prophets or through His own Incarnation; these principles are not necessarily self-evident to the unassisted human mind but become evident by belief or faith and only to the man who has this belief or faith. It attempts to clarify or interpret this revealed information (as embodied in the Quran and the sayings, life, and activities of the Prophet), to prove its possibility, and to defend it against those who oppose it—against skeptics and unbelievers or against those who believe in the veracity of other revealed principles. So, unlike the principles of natural theology, accessible to the unassisted human mind and therefore not limited to a particular political or religious community, the principles of revealed theology are accessible only to members of a particular religious community who believe or have faith in the original revelation and in the truthfulness of the person who transmits that information.

Like jurisprudence, revealed theology pertains to the particular religious community in which it thrives. There exists a multiplicity of revealed theologies corresponding to the multiplicity of religious communities. They may follow a rational or scientific method and even the same method or methods; this does not alter their multiplicity or the fact that their sphere of operation is limited to the religious community to which they belong. It is possible to speak of natural theology as such, that is, irrespective of the political or religious community within which it is pursued; it is not possible to do so regarding revealed theology. Revealed theology is inconceivable without a particular divine revelation, and it pertains essentially to the religious community within which it is pursued: it is in a strong sense Islamic, Jewish, or Christian theology.

One can speak of political theology as a specialized theological discipline treating political things on the basis of the revealed teaching. However, because theology is concerned with the clarification and support of the fundamental opinions and actions laid down for a religious polity by its founder, there is a sense in which all theology is political theology. Indeed, this political motive and function seem to lie at the origin of revealed theology, not in Islam alone, but in all three revealed religions. They all had to meet the challenge of Greek philosophy; each was confronted with the refusal of the members of the other religious communities to accept the new revelation and with their arguments against it; and each was threatened by internal dissensions and heresies that called into question the generally accepted interpretation of the original revelation. Jurisprudence (the science of determining what the religious community must believe in or do on the basis of inferences from the sayings and acts of the founder of a particular religious community) was neither meant nor able to meet these contingencies. Hence there arose the need for a skill or science to argue in defense of the principles embodied in the revelation forming the foundation of the religious community and to contend against all those who opposed these principles, whether on the basis of philosophy, another revelation, or internal innovations.

Political philosophy had to pay particular attention to theology for many reasons. To begin with, there was the political impetus that gave rise to theology. (Revealed theology in the Islamic community arose in response to differences concerning the legitimate ruler of the community as well as to clarify and defend God's justice and its implications for man's life on earth.) Next, theology was making every effort to offer a rational clarification of the highest and most fundamental beliefs on which the opinions and ways of life of the religious community rested and to defend them by every means at its disposal. Furthermore, theology was the religious science most open to the call of reason. All this required the political philosophers to delimit the respective spheres of theology and political philosophy, distinguish their respective principles and aims, and define the proper relationship between them.

Theology and Jurisprudence

Theology occupied an important, but definitely ancillary, place within the religious sciences in Islam. It was never considered the highest religious science or the "queen" of the sciences as in Latin Christianity. That position was occupied by jurisprudence, whose practitioners were the custodians of the divine law. The authority to ascertain the principles of the law rested with them; they determined how it should be applied in new circumstances, and, what is more important, they alone had the final authority to pronounce on what constituted true belief and right action.

When, in ninth-century Baghdad, the Muʻtazilites attempted to force judges and jurists who were not of their persuasion to confess to their theological doctrines, there was widespread resistance. Theology was not given the authority to pronounce on its own on any serious theoretical or practical matter pertaining to the Islamic community. Its function was to defend what the jurists considered the true meaning of the divine law. Jurists, like philosophers and mystics, were not particularly concerned about the kind of rational method theology used; they judged it by its practical results. They harbored and encouraged it when they needed it; they kept a close watch on it and reprimanded it whenever it seemed to be arousing doubts in the minds of the believers, drawing them to useless and dangerous discussions, or turning them away from their legal obligations.

Political philosophy showed a curious mixture of admiration for the practical utility of theology and contempt for its theoretical claims. Seen from the perspective of philosophy and logic, all revealed theology is at best dialectical—rather than demonstrative—science because its principles are not ascertainable by, or self-evident to, the unassisted human mind but are received and accepted by a particular group of people on the authority of the person to whom they were revealed. To the believer, the person of faith, revealed information is more worthy of acceptance than other kinds of information (including those principles ascertainable by, or self-evident to, the unassisted human mind). But none of this alters the dialectical character of these principles. Hence philosophers called theologians dialecticians and their science a dialectical science. Furthermore, philosophers emphasized the practical aim of theology and of its arguments for the beliefs and way of life of a particular religious community and against all those who opposed those beliefs and that way of life.

Theology could base its theoretical claim on the argument that the unassisted human mind could not demonstrate the existence of things said to be essentially beyond its power. The demonstration must, then, rest on divine revelation, that is, on information provided by the divine law. This argument crops up again and again among theologians, and it is at the basis of Ashʻarite theology and of the distinction between things "supernatural" and things "natural" in al-Ghazālī and Aquinas. The difficulty, nevertheless, is that either there is no scriptural proof for this view of theology, or ancestral tradition and the learned did not agree that this way of conceiving theology is demanded by the divine law. As a result, this understanding of what theology is and the nature of its principles could not assume the status of a valid and binding *interpretation* of the divine law. The authority to make such an interpretation rested with jurisprudence. Hence, in order to ascertain the binding character of this theological position, a Muslim needed to have recourse to jurists for a legal opinion on the matter; or, if the philosopher himself happened to be an accredited jurist, as Averroes was, he had to consider the divine law and himself determine the legal status of theological opinions as well as of the practice of theology.

Most Mu'tazilite theologians, on the other hand, assumed that everything is available to the unassisted human mind, provided the human mind is given time and applies itself to knowing them. They argued that prophecy and revelation are necessary because humans need to be instructed about things required for their well-being in this world and the next. Although some humans could know these things if given sufficient time and mental power and application, there was at the time of the coming down of revelation a disparity between what humans knew and what they needed to know. What humans know at any time is subject to a great many accidents, and in any case not all humans know what they need to know well enough to act upon it. Revelation is an act of divine grace that removes these accidental shortcomings rather than an imparting of information about things whose very nature is such that the unassisted human mind, by its very nature, has no access to them.

The question, then, is whether this interpretation of the knowledge supplied by the divine law, or the former theological position, is the correct one. The evidence of the divine law tends to support the Mu'tazilite interpretation or else leads one to suspend judgment and say that the divine law enjoins knowledge of all things but specifies neither their nature nor the method to be pursued in knowing them. Every Muslim will then have to know the nature of things as far as this is possible, using the best method available. It is, therefore, not surprising that philosophers in the Islamic community could arrive at the position that this meant knowing the highest things by using the best method—that is, by using demonstration and achieving science as far as possible. If anything theoretical in the divine law requires interpretation, this task should be assigned to the philosopher rather than the theologian. The position of philosophy in the Islamic community can therefore be formulated as follows: the divine law sets forth the principles that govern the beliefs and the actions of the Islamic community; the legal determination of what the community must believe and do is entrusted to those who are best equipped to make legal inference, namely, the jurists; the interpretation of the theoretical things in the divine law, on the other hand, should be entrusted to those members of the community who, in turn, are best equipped to perform this function, namely, the philosophers.

Having deprived theology of its claim as the best way to know theoretical things, philosophy remains nevertheless keenly aware of the practical function of theology, which gives almost all of theology an eminently political character. Being a practical discipline, political philosophy aims at a practical end: the preservation of the good achieved by the community and improving or reforming it to achieve a higher good. As an independent discipline, political theology could not perform this function adequately. To preserve what is good in a community and to improve and reform it, one needs the guidance of someone who knows or who makes it his business to know the highest perfection possible for man and society and who also develops the capacity to find out what is best for a particular community at a particular time. Hence political philosophy insists on the requirement that the philosopher train himself to perform both functions; that is, theoretical knowledge must go hand in hand with the practical virtues. Through this combination, the philosopher will be able to perform for his community the necessary function of the political theologian: help it preserve the good that is present and direct it to the good toward which it should aspire on the basis of his knowledge and prudence. Thus Islamic political philosophy considers political theology a subsidiary function of political philosophy, and insofar as philosophers address their fellow citizens with the aim of instructing them in political things—things in which they want them to believe or which they want them to do—they invariably speak and write as political theologians; that is, they defend certain beliefs and actions and argue against others. Their surviving writings, then, are not purely theoretical or scientific writings but are practical or political writings that presuppose the theoretical or scientific understanding of the issues involved while taking into account the conditions and character of the community they address.

The Foundation of Islamic Philosophy

Alfarabi established the main tradition of Islamic philosophy as we know it today. The respect with which he has been regarded by his successors has not always been matched with a clear understanding of his role as a founder or with a comprehensive appreciation of his achievement as a philosopher. Great philosophers like Avicenna, Averroes, and Mullā Ṣadrā consistently remind us that we need to know more about this towering figure. But they do not always help us grasp his central concern or the path he charted for himself. Being philosophers themselves, they had their own concerns and charted their own individual paths. We must go back to his own writings. Only then can we appreciate fully his relation to his Islamic and Hellenistic predecessors and how he went about establishing the main tradition of Islamic philosophy. Since Alfarabi's writings are still in the process of being recovered and studied, the following remarks cannot claim to be more than first impressions.

Alfarabi, al-Kindī, and al-Rāzī

Historians of Islamic philosophy usually approach Alfarabi by starting with the question of translations and the translation literature. They enumerate the books that were translated from Greek or Syriac or both, describe the techniques of translation, and summarize and paraphrase such important texts as the *Theology of Aristotle* or the so-called *Liber de causis*. What they do not usually do, and what we need to do more often, is ask what Muslim philosophers did with this translation literature. A book like the *Theology of Aristotle* was used by Alfarabi, al-Suhrawardī, and Mullā Ṣadrā, among others. Was it simply absorbed by them, or did they attempt to study, understand, modify, complete, and make use of this book in different ways? More generally, is the history of Neoplatonism in Islam a history of ideas that could not help, so to speak, but run

through the riverbed provided by Islam? Among many Muslim philosophers, at least, it is a history of conscious and many-sided use. And it was
Alfarabi who showed them how and for what purposes they could use
the Neoplatonic literature.

Next, historians of Islamic philosophy move to early Islamic theology
(*kalām*). So far as philosophy is concerned, one can say that the major
contribution of Islamic theology was to prepare the ground for philosophy, to soften up the thought and attitude of the Muslim community
and instruct it in the use of reason to the point that philosophy could
take root and begin to grow. What this means is quite simple in a way.
When one looks at the beginnings of any religious community, one finds
that it is completely taken up with revelation and a divine message. This
is not the time for quiet reflection or for working out the implications of
the revelation. It takes some time before this latter stage can be reached;
and here theology plays an important role.

Theology accepts the message, the divine law, or the revelation and
slowly moves farther and farther away from that original source. (The
history of Islamic theology, I think, is quite instructive in this respect.)
It elaborates the many problems posed by the revelation. It attempts to
harmonize apparently inconsistent statements and make explicit things
that are only implicit in the revelation. For instance, the Mu'tazilites
came to the conclusion that it is a condition of true faith that one should
on his own (by his own reason and independently from faith) know all
of the following: God's existence, essence, and attributes; the possibility
of prophecy and revelation; what is right and wrong in human action;
and the structure of the physical world and its relation to its maker. All
this, according to the Mu'tazilites, must be known by a man through his
own reason before he can call himself a true believer; otherwise, they
reasoned, he believes on the basis of authority and the imitation of others—and this is not true belief.

When one remembers the starting point—the miraculous revelation
and the power of its claim on men—it is understandable, I suppose, that
a community should need a century or two to reach such conclusions.
In traveling this road, Islamic theology prepared the way for Islamic philosophy, even though this was by no means its intention. From the very
beginning, Muslim philosophers, in turn, paid careful attention to theology. This was the religious discipline they found closest to their own
discipline, and they found it profitable to reflect on its problems, methods, and conclusions.

Finally, historians come to the two thinkers who seem to present the beginnings of Islamic philosophy and therefore to deserve a role as Alfa-rabi's predecessors: al-Kindī and al-Rāzī. In the case of al-Kindī, there is no evidence, at least not in his books that have survived, that he was a theologian or a Mu'tazilite, even though he lived in a period during which the Mu'tazilites of Baghdad were playing an important public role and was connected with the court that encouraged this theological move-ment and to some extent even sponsored and patronized it. Further, his concern with what may be thought to have been a central Mu'tazilite question—the theological question of knowledge both human and di-vine—seems to take a somewhat different form from theirs.

He seems to say that, in principle, all knowledge is accessible to man as man, even though there is another way to that same knowledge, which is the way of divine revelation. The latter cuts short the long, hard way that man has to follow when trying to acquire this knowledge by his own effort. One could say that all this seems to be quite possibly in agreement with the theological position of the Mu'tazilites. But as one looks more closely at what al-Kindī writes, it is easy to see that the spirit, inten-tion, and substance of his thought are quite different from those of the Mu'tazilites. The most important difference is his acknowledgment of what he calls the contribution to truth made by the ancients whom he sees as his predecessors, and the openness and gratitude with which he accepts their contribution.

Here we have for the first time a man who is explicitly concerned with what philosophers like Plato and Aristotle or with what the Sabians thought and contributed to knowledge. This does not mean that he ac-cepts everything given to him by these traditions. As he says in a famous passage, it is his duty to understand, assimilate, complete, and modify what is given in these traditions in terms of his own language, custom, and so forth. Furthermore, his thought differs from that of the theolo-gians in that he is concerned with and practices what we call the "hard" sciences and sciences that require special skills and practical training.

So far as we know, none of the theologians of the earlier period were proficient, or even halfway proficient, in such things as mathematics, as-tronomy, physics, or music. It is characteristic of the philosophic tradi-tion that from the very beginning it understood philosophy or wisdom as something more than an interminable disputation in which everyone is welcome and all men can sit down and figure things out by means of "right reason." Philosophy consists of a number of relatively indepen-dent sciences that had been thought through in detail and whose prin-ciples had been discussed, subjected to criticism, and commented on by a succession of classical authors whose works were available to be studied in detail and with precision; and it is concerned with the relation among these sciences and the problem of the organization of knowledge.

Already in al-Kindī, the atmosphere and the literary genealogy are quite distinct from anything we know among the theologians of this period, for whom philosophy is a collection of largely anonymous doctrines. For instance, they would say: we do not believe X as the philosophers—en masse—believe. This is not what al-Kindī does. On the other hand, and perhaps because al-Kindī poses the question of the parallelism between human and divine knowledge and sees divine knowledge as a more direct way to the knowledge of everything, he bequeaths to later philosophers a number of questions that persist in Islamic philosophy. (1) The creation of the world: what it means; how it differs from emanation on the one hand and natural causality (say, the four causes in Aristotle) on the other. (2) The immortality of individual souls: what it means; how it can be proved. (3) Divine knowledge of particulars: whether it has anything to do with astrology; how it takes place, whether through the stars or directly. (The stars, by the way, begin suddenly to play a much greater role as we move away from theology to philosophy. Theologians were not particularly concerned with the stars or the heavenly bodies. But for the philosophers—whether in connection with some sort of pagan star worship, understanding the principles of the physical world, or the attribution of souls and intellects to them, the reasons may vary—the question of the nature of the heavenly bodies becomes important, if not central.)

When one considers al-Rāzī, one finds that questions like the creation of the world or the immortality of the soul are by no means the special concern of the theologians or of so-called religious philosophers. Even a man who presumably did not believe in revelation and reportedly considered prophecy to be a hoax is still concerned with defending the creation of the world and the immortality of individual souls, in his own fashion. More generally, most of the questions raised by al-Kindī—questions that appear to be of special concern to a Muslim philosopher or a religious philosopher so called—were in fact raised (and quite analogous stands regarding them were taken) by pagan philosophers in pre-Islamic times as well as by nonreligious philosophers in Islamic times. Whether a philosopher took his stand for or against what is commonly believed to be the standard biblical or Quranic view of creation, for example, does not seem to be closely related to whether or not he was a believer in revelation. (This question is treated in a complex yet illuminating fashion in Maimonides' *Guide*.)

Unlike al-Kindī, however, al-Rāzī took a somewhat novel stand in relation to the philosophic and scientific tradition. Like al-Kindī, he was concerned with the thought and the writings of the major ancient authors. But whereas al-Kindī was content to pick and choose among those writings, selectively adapting them to what he saw as the new needs of his own time, al-Rāzī saw his relation to earlier thinkers as one of continuity and progress. In the process, he did not single out any ancient author—be it Aristotle, Plato, or Galen—for the honor of having found *the* truth, so that philosophy or science would forever consist of commenting on this author, understanding him, explaining him, and defending his ideas. (This kind of dogmatism is almost never found in Islamic philosophy. The only possible exception is thought to be Averroes, but even here I doubt very much that what is generally said about his relation to Aristotle is in fact borne out by a careful study of his works.) Thus al-Rāzī held a number of important doctrines (regarding time, place, and so forth) in opposition to Aristotle. His criticisms of Aristotle were ignored for a while, but reemerge soon thereafter as part of a non-Aristotelian and anti-Aristotelian tradition in Islamic philosophy.

Finally, al-Rāzī held a rather strict (and apparently scandalous) view regarding the difficult problem of the relation of divine revelation, the divine law, and the religious community to science and philosophy. He seems to have radicalized the theological doctrine that all knowledge is in principle accessible to man as man. He is reported to have said that human reason is the only way to knowledge of the physical world and of what is good and bad and that every other source of knowledge is simply pretension and deceit.

One must remember, however, that we possess only a small portion of the philosophic works of these two philosophers and that we are forced therefore to reconstruct their thought on the basis of fragmentary evidence. It is of course uncertain whether their works were as complete or thorough as their titles suggest to us, who think of the contents of books with similar titles by later philosophers; a number of the works that have survived appear to have been hastily written epistles. Still, there is no way of telling what a book that we do not possess may or may not have contained. Alfarabi is the first Muslim of whom we have in our hands a substantial number of complete philosophic books. We do not have all of them. If we think in terms of sheer bulk, we do not have even half of them. But compared to al-Kindī and al-Rāzī, much more has survived, especially in the fields of politics and logic.

Just as it is not possible to explain the thought of al-Kindī and al-Rāzī as an extension of Islamic theology or of the Muʿtazilite movement, it is impossible to explain Alfarabi's thought as an extension or simple development of the thought of al-Kindī and al-Rāzī. Alfarabi wrote a book in refutation of al-Rāzī's metaphysics that is not extant. Normally, he ignores al-Kindī completely; and in this he was followed by al-Ghazālī, Avicenna, Averroes, and many other philosophers. In a book on music (Mahdi 1976, 76–78), where he does speak of al-Kindī, Alfarabi accuses him of discussing musical theory and musical practice without knowing what he is talking about.

In general, later historians of Islamic philosophy followed the lead of Alfarabi and Avicenna in criticizing al-Kindī and al-Rāzī; and their criticisms are largely derived from judgments passed by these philosophers or their students. In the case of al-Rāzī, these historians say that he was a naturalist rather than a metaphysician or general philosopher. In the case of al-Kindī, they say that his knowledge of logic was incomplete. These and similar criticisms became part of the lore handed down by historians of Islamic philosophy in later times. But the point is not just that Alfarabi adds metaphysics or logic to the philosophic syllabus or that he is a better student of metaphysics or logic. The texture of his thought is more coherent and distinctive, and the quality of his knowledge of Plato and Aristotle is on quite a different level. All three philosophers had the translation literature and access to some of the same primary sources. Alfarabi and al-Rāzī were contemporaries (Alfarabi outlived al-Rāzī by about twenty years), so that Alfarabi did not have the advantage of significant advances in translations or scientific inquiries beyond al-Rāzī. Therefore, we must look for the explanation elsewhere.

Alfarabi's *On the Rise of Philosophy*

There are a few details of a historical nature that appear to be crucial for understanding the origins of the new tradition in Islamic philosophy. The surviving fragments from Alfarabi's lost book *On the Rise of Philosophy* are our primary source for reconstructing this important episode in the history of philosophy, but there seems to be no good reason to doubt its main features. Alfarabi explains that he belongs to a particular philosophic school. This school, according to him, is a direct continuation of a tradition of philosophic learning that existed in Alexandria in the fifth and sixth centuries A.D. He gives an account of the movement of that school from Alexandria to Antioch, to Carrhae (Ḥarrān), and then farther east to Iran and down to Baghdad. He provides some information about the teachers, students, and books that represent this line of scholarship. The school became almost extinct except for two or three students who kept the tradition alive. He gives the name of his own teacher, Yūḥannā Ibn Ḥaylān, a Christian cleric, who is otherwise unknown as a teacher, scholar, or writer.

It seems certain that neither al-Kindī nor al-Rāzī, nor any other earlier philosopher in Islam, had access to this school tradition, which does not mean access just to men but also to books and conversely does not mean access just to books but also to men: it was a dual tradition, both oral and written. An important part of that tradition was the reading of Aristotle's *Posterior Analytics,* the logical work of Aristotle that deals with the question of science and the method of science. Alfarabi relates that church authorities had forbidden the study of various books, especially this one, because they were thought to be dangerous; the church had limited the study of logic to certain parts (i.e., to formal logic up to certain chapters of the *Prior Analytics*) and had forbidden study of the rest in public. Presumably, this means that one could obtain permission to study these other chapters in private, so that some sort of a tradition of studying the rest did continue.

Alfarabi then states that he was the first (Muslim) to have studied the *Posterior Analytics.* What Alfarabi perhaps means here is that he was the first to read this book with a man who had spent years, perhaps a lifetime, studying and trying to understand it with a master, who in turn had done so with an earlier master, and so on. There is, then, the connection with the school at Alexandria. This connection was evidently very important. More important, however, is what Alfarabi learned from this Alexandrian tradition and how he in turn understood and interpreted it.

The connection with the school of Alexandria reveals itself in many ways in Alfarabi and his colleagues, students, and successors. One can see it, for instance, in the writing of so-called great, or large, commentaries (we have two of them by Alfarabi), in the care with which Aristotle's text is analyzed and interpreted, and also in the continuity of the scholarly tradition. Aristotle had written the book. Earlier thinkers expressed their own ideas about the subject; all of these are discussed. There were significant disagreements among them. These are explained. Earlier commentators are cited and their explanations are approved of, criticized, or developed in detail. The commentary becomes a depository of a thousand years of thought and reflection on the questions discussed in Aristotle's text. It pays a great deal of attention not just to the text but also to the recently translated writings of earlier commentators.

Here, again, paying attention to earlier commentators does not mean that one accepts the views of these commentators or tries to synchronize these views. One can accept the view of one commentator, reject the view of a second, discuss the view of a third, and show that this one is superficial or that the other one is profound. It is an open field in which the thinker inquires into all the alternatives and considers the possibilities embedded in the tradition. In the end, he has to make up his own mind. Such, at least, are the external features of the tradition of Alexandria.

In contrast, al-Kindī may be connected with the Hellenistic-Roman Athenian school rather than the school of Alexandria. The great name that is usually mentioned in connection with the Athenian school is that of Proclus. People who talk about Neoplatonism sometimes do not realize that they are referring to a long, complex, and many-sided tradition. In a way, all philosophy since Plato is Neoplatonic. But there are Neoplatonists and Neoplatonists.

There were, for instance, the Middle Platonists, who paid some attention to Plato's political teachings and who incorporated much of Aristotle's logic and metaphysics into the Platonic tradition. There was also the Neoplatonism of Plotinus, who tries on almost every page to tackle problems that had been posed by Plato and Aristotle—the two great masters. When we talk about Neoplatonism, we should not think of it as necessarily syncretic or necessarily anti-Aristotelian or anti-Platonic. Then there was the Neoplatonism of Plotinus's successors, especially the Neoplatonism of the scholars who were at the head of the philosophic schools in Athens and Alexandria. As heads of these philosophic schools, they were primarily teaching the works of Plato and Aristotle. The notes they wrote for, or the notes their students took from, their lecture courses are in the form of large or middle commentaries on works by Plato or Aristotle. Most of their own ideas, different as they may have been from those of the two great masters, are contained in these commentaries and take the form of developments of certain notions in the Platonic and Aristotelian texts.

Now the Athenian school, at least in some periods of its long life, was characterized by the teachings of Proclus and others who seem to have gone wild in developing a cosmology consisting of many layers of angels or spirits, which is not present in Plotinus. They were concerned with the interpretation of things like magic and oracles and alchemy, with which other Neoplatonists were not concerned. The Alexandrian school seems to have been particularly sane and moderate in this respect. It tried to meet the challenge of the time, which was Christianity, and succeeded in harmonizing some of the basic differences between philosophy and Christianity. The Athenian school, on the other hand, seems to have gone to extremes in trying to support the pagan religious movement against Christianity, and its members wrote pseudophilosophic, pseudo-scientific works on things like magic and pagan religious practices of various kinds. Broadly speaking then, it makes sense to say that there was a difference in attitude in the way the two schools looked at such questions as the relation between philosophy and religion, at least during a certain period in the history of the two schools— when one compares Athens and Alexandria in, let us say, the period from the fourth to the sixth century A.D. I say "broadly speaking" because there was a great deal of movement between the two schools. A bright young man from Alexandria would go to Athens, study under Proclus, then return to become the head of the school or the successor to the chair of philosophy at Alexandria, and vice versa; the two schools did not represent two traditions hermetically sealed from each other.

The Alexandrian scientific and philosophic traditions are historically crucial to everything that happened later on in science and philosophy in the Islamic world, in Byzantium, as well as in the Latin West. These philosophers, commentators, and thinkers—"Alexandrine" though they were in certain respects—were the ones who handed down to the Muslims the books and the tradition of reading or studying these books and interpreting them; this took the form of a clearly defined scholarly tradition, not vague connections with earlier thought as was the case in the first stages of Islamic theology. But although this Alexandrian connection between the Muslims and classical Greek thought is extremely important, we must realize that the tradition of Alexandria (and Athens) was available to Byzantium and later to the Latin West from the renaissance of the eleventh–twelfth century onward. Yet these three heirs to the Alexandrian tradition and, through Alexandria, to the classical Greek tradition did not understand or develop philosophy in the same way. Alfarabi, who was the first philosopher to claim that he represented this Alexandrian tradition in Islam, was not a translator or a historian of philosophy, not merely a carrier of a philosophic tradition, but a philosopher in his own right; and if one is to believe such men as Avicenna, Averroes, and Mullā Ṣadrā, he was a philosopher who must be ranked next to Aristotle himself. It is therefore important that we begin to understand how Alfarabi himself understood, interpreted, and presented the tradition of philosophy to his Muslim readers.

Political Philosophy and Metaphysics

The vast majority of Alfarabi's surviving writings fall into two major divisions: logic and politics. (There are of course also his writings on music, which are substantial and not without philosophic interest.) Political science or political philosophy is absent from the works of al-Kindī and al-Rāzī that we know. Both deal with something called ethics, but not with political science. In fact, when al-Kindī mentions political science, he seems to be thinking of an ethical work by Aristotle. There is thus no preparation in earlier Islamic thought for the emergence of political science as a major philosophic discipline. But, curiously, in the earlier traditions in Alexandria and Athens also, there is no preparation for the appearance of political science as a major philosophic discipline, or for the introduction of Plato as primarily a political thinker. For the most part, the earlier so-called Neoplatonists had looked at Plato's *Timaeus* as a mystical work and had shown no interest at all in any of Plato's political writings—for instance, the *Republic* and the *Laws*—as political writings; their interest in these works centered on the myths, metaphysical doctrines, and supposed mystical notions.

All of a sudden Alfarabi presents to us a Plato who is neither mystical nor metaphysical but who is primarily and massively political. Here is a Plato whose *Timaeus* is not a work on cosmology but a political work meant to instruct the citizens in correct opinions. And then this account of Plato, which is presented in a book called the *Philosophy of Plato,* is followed by an account of Aristotle, in a book called the *Philosophy of Aristotle,* in which again metaphysics seems to be absent. And these two accounts are preceded by an account of philosophy in Alfarabi's own name, in a book called the *Attainment of Happiness,* whose main theme is the dilemma or tension and even conflict between theoretical knowledge and realization— a description not only of practical knowledge or knowledge of practical things such as virtue and happiness but also of how to realize or attain virtue and happiness.

To know is one thing; to realize what is known—that is, what is known to be possible or realizable—to bring it about, to have it actually exist among humans and cities and nations, that is something else. Or, to know is to realize a thing in a certain way, to realize it in the mind; but realization has yet another dimension, which is to see the thing exist in others and in cities and nations. This is not attained by knowledge alone. How does one realize things outside one's own mind? And what kind of additional knowledge and action is required for this? "Do you suppose," Alfarabi asks his reader, "that these theoretical sciences have also given an account of the means by which these four [virtues] can actually be realized in nations or cities, or not?" How do you bring into being in cities and nations the things you know? Can you bring them into being outside your mind exactly as they are known, or do they have to be modified according to certain conditions? What are the conditions that make realization possible?

All of a sudden, theoretical knowledge and knowledge in general become a prolegomenon to action, ethics, and politics. In the book called the *Enumeration of the Sciences* one again finds the same scheme. One moves from language to logic, mathematics, and physics and metaphysics, and then one finds a break within metaphysics. Metaphysics does not simply crown the sciences. It does this, to be sure, but it also becomes a preface to political science; and political science studies everything that is necessary for realization, preservation, and reform. It is in this sense that political science includes jurisprudence and theology and deals with questions like prophecy, the divine law, and revelation, for these are seen in terms of realization rather than simply as theoretical matters.

One must admit that this is a wholly new and radical perspective on metaphysics on the one hand and revelation, the divine law, and prophecy on the other. Alfarabi seems to urge his reader to make the question of realization the central question of philosophy and to pose and try to resolve the questions "What is philosophy?" and "Why philosophy?" in the perspective of realization rather than in the perspective of knowledge simply, although the perspective of knowledge is never really absent. The simple and perhaps simplistic way in which people nowadays pose the question of realization is in terms of the relation between what is revealed and what is known by reason. Alfarabi, too, is concerned with this relation.

But the question as he poses it is not that simple; he urges us to understand also the context within which we must look at this relation. For if prophecy, revelation, and the divine law are in fact the primary nexus between knowledge and realization, one will have to understand them, not simply as another way of achieving the same kind of knowledge that can be achieved by reason or even a higher kind of knowledge than can be achieved by reason (as al-Kindī, e.g., understood it), but as a special kind of knowledge that already embodies the conditions necessary for realization, for making what is known exist among men and cities and nations. In this way one can understand more fully the miraculous character of the divine law, its mode of communication, its concreteness, and its concern with various types of opinions and actions. This is why one can say that with Alfarabi we have for the first time an adequate or a more adequate philosophic approach to the divine law, perhaps the central question in Islamic philosophy.

City, Soul, and Cosmos

There are various ways in which one may proceed with the study of political philosophy in the context of a revealed religion. One may think that the proper way is to start with an elaborate discussion of political science, look at the human condition, and try to understand and explain what is needed to improve the lot of human beings on earth and why improving their lot should take this particular form. Or one could start with psychology and ask how it is that a human, the prophet, has special powers that enable him to receive a revelation and give a divine law. Or one could start with cosmology and ask how the universe is structured, from the highest principle down to man, and how this structure makes possible such phenomena as prophecy, revelation, and the divine law. But these three approaches are not independent from each other. Political science, psychology, and cosmology seem somehow to be related; one needs to work out the structure of the city, the structure of the soul, and the structure of the universe and see how they are related to each other. This leads to what one may call a comparative structural study of the city on the one hand and the soul and the cosmos on the other, a study that must be concerned with the question of whether these three are identical, similar, or comparable in their structure. This kind of study is at the same time political, psychological, and cosmological.

The fact is that, of these three structures, the only one that we know well is the structure of the city, the political structure. You cannot penetrate a man's heart and see the way his soul is structured. You can observe it through human action; and since action takes place in the city, one can say that the structure of the soul is projected into the structure of the city as its larger image, and therefore that it can be studied best by observing this larger image. As to the third structure, that of the universe, it cannot for the most part be observed directly; it is too vast and too distant to be seen or experienced as a whole. Now if we follow the advice of Aristotle that we are better off if we move from what we know to what we do not know, or from what is better known to us to what is less known to us, we must in effect move from the structure of the city, which we experience directly and in which we live our lives, to the structure of the soul, which again we experience directly to some extent and indirectly in the city—that is, to what we do not see but experience—and from there to the structure of that third thing, the whole universe, which for the most part we neither see nor experience, or which we see and experience only to a limited extent. This approach may not lead us very far, but it at least has the advantage of being based on a solid foundation: not jumping into the unknown but moving carefully and step-by-step from what is known toward the unknown.

However, the ordinary citizen would rather have things arranged the opposite way—that is, first be told what the universe is like and how it is structured, then be told how the soul is structured and what is going to happen to it in the future if one does the right things and avoids the wrong things, and finally be told why he ought to become a member of a particular community and be advised as to how he can become a member in good standing of such a community. This is the direction that is more desirable and convincing so far as the citizen is concerned. For this reason Alfarabi's political writings move in this way. They begin with a cosmology, with the structure of the universe, the character of each of its main parts, and how they function together, given to the reader as a preacher would give an account of the universe to his audience— this is how it is! Then he gives an account of the structure of the human soul and the human body, their parts, and how they function together. Finally, he proceeds to give an account of the structure of the city, its parts, how they ought to be organized and the various ways in which they are in fact organized in actual cities and nations, and a description of the opinions and actions of each of these cities.

Ever since Alfarabi wrote these political works (and this includes the last hundred years, in which attempts have been made to revive these works and study them), they have baffled and mystified their readers. Nobody could ever figure out easily what they are. Here is a book that begins with metaphysics or cosmology, goes into psychology and physiology, and ends up with politics. During the past ten centuries, philosophers and scholars must have looked at books such as the *Virtuous City*, whose full title is the *Principles of the Opinions of the Inhabitants of the Virtuous City*, and the *Political Regime* and asked themselves, what kind of books are these? Their structure appears to be unique.

No one before or after Alfarabi has written a philosophic book with such a structure. They are not treatises on logic or physics or mathematics or psychology or metaphysics or even politics, they are not dialogues, and they are not strictly speaking philosophic investigations. No Muslim philosopher attempted to imitate him. His successors must have somehow suspected that one could not take what is said in these books as philosophic investigations or doctrines—that one could not, for instance, consider that anything said in these books forms part of Alfarabi's psychological or metaphysical doctrine. And because they did not fully understand the nature and purpose of these writings, Muslim philosophers referred to them with a great deal of caution. Even today, one cannot quote any portion of these books as representing Alfarabi's philosophic doctrines without first explaining why they are presented in this strange manner.

Fortunately, Alfarabi himself wrote an explanation, in a book called the *Book of Religion,* which is a programmatic indication as to how and why such books should be written and for what purpose. Perhaps the best way to characterize these political works is to say that they are "letters" addressed to the enlightened citizens in the Muslim community, to potential philosophers and potential rulers. During his long and colorful life, Alfarabi traveled to many strange and wonderful lands to which his fellow Muslims had not traveled, opened many gates locked to them, and entered many delightful places that they had never entered. The political works are his letters to the folks back home—simple, straightforward accounts that do not even mention the long journey, let alone its perils; concise descriptions couched in the language of those who had never left their homeland but whose ears were not sealed and whose sense of wonder had not been completely dulled. Let me now conclude with a few remarks on the importance for contemporary Islamic thought of Alfarabi's central concern, the question of realization.

The Question of Realization

Alfarabi's concern with realization is not confined to personal salvation but directed to the salvation of the community at large, to social or political salvation. Even here Alfarabi's concern is not just with one city or nation or with a particular community but with humanity at large, with civilized men everywhere. These are the central subjects of his political science or political philosophy. The very fact that Alfarabi makes political philosophy, which deals with man's public life in cities and nations and religious communities, one of the central concerns, and ultimately perhaps the central concern, of his philosophy means that he was not satisfied with the alternative approach prevalent among earlier Muslim philosophers and their Neoplatonic predecessors in Hellenistic and Roman times: the concern for personal or private salvation as against public salvation, for private virtue as against public virtue, and for only such public action as leads to one's private virtue and salvation.

The philosopher who concerns himself only or primarily with his private salvation is a man who has given up on the body politic, on the community at large. He may think that he understands it, but he does not think that he can contribute to improving or reforming it. But public life does not lose its importance merely because the philosopher neglects it or turns away from it. It is always there. It determines everyone's life, including everyone's—even the philosopher's—private life. Furthermore, the urge to live in a virtuous, decent, honorable, and humane city and community and to contribute to improving the quality of public life is not a perversion or an unnatural urge. It is, on the contrary, a most natural human urge. It is an expression of man's concern, his philanthropic spirit, and his delight in living in a good community. Such publicspiritedness is to be expected of every good citizen.

So the question is whether the philosopher is to be more or less public-spirited than the good citizen. It may be true that the philosopher's main contribution to the quality of public life takes the form of improving public understanding of the nature and purpose of public life. This means that he must first understand it as a philosopher and then communicate this understanding in an effective way to the citizenry at large. This is precisely what is at the center of Alfarabi's political philosophy. And it is a mystery that his followers did not carry forward the brilliant beginning that he bequeathed to them and instead turned philosophy back into the concern with private, personal salvation. Theologians and jurists continued to struggle with the problem of the leadership of the community and other questions of public law. But theology and jurisprudence, as is made clear by Alfarabi, are not substitutes for political philosophy. They lack the necessary breadth of vision, freedom of spirit, and ability to confront and understand radically new situations.

The neglect of political philosophy is damaging to the quality of philosophy as well as to the quality of public life. It leads to a narrowness in the community's horizon, to the impoverishment of public discussions of the aims and alternative forms of public life, to resignation, to the absence of rational discourse on public issues, and ultimately to narrowing the choice before the citizen to crusty conservatism or blind faith in tradition on the one hand and the destructive pursuit of change for its own sake on the other. The community is deprived of the necessary enlightenment regarding various forms of government, the way they change one into the other, and the way they can be improved. This is the price the community pays when philosophy turns away from public life.

There have always been philosophers who think that they can pursue wisdom as private men regardless of the quality of public life; that they should tend exclusively to their own private gardens; and that their task as philosophers is to explore the depths of their own souls, imaginations, and intellects. Perhaps there are times and places that necessitate these views. Yet one need not make a virtue out of necessity. Alfarabi was aware of a fundamental tension between the pursuit of private and public salvation. But he is almost the only Muslim philosopher who chose to explore this tension and in the process brought to the fore philosophy's philanthropic spirit and the philosopher's high-minded devotion to the true welfare of his community. In this he performed an immense service to the Islamic community.

Unfortunately, there were many others, great and famous men in their own right, who, out of ignorance or despair, turned their backs on public life and on their communities. Even today there are respectable thinkers among us who cannot understand what the expression "political philosophy" means and therefore cannot write it down without placing it in quotation marks, as if to say that these are meaningless words or that the expression represents the frivolous pursuit of men who have not yet discovered true philosophy. These thinkers may teach us many things, but they will never teach us how to reason well about public issues, how to improve the lot of our fellow men, or how to establish and preserve a polity in which philosophy and science can be pursued without grave danger to the seeker of knowledge or the rest of the community.

PART TWO

The Virtuous City

Science, Philosophy, and Religion

One of the striking features of classical Islamic philosophy is the prominence of political philosophy and the incorporation of jurisprudence and theology into philosophy by subordinating them to political philosophy. During the ten centuries that separated Cicero from Alfarabi, one cannot point to a single great philosopher for whom the problem of philosophy was inseparable from the problem of political philosophy or in whose writings political philosophy occupies a massive, central, or decisive position. Political philosophy may not be totally absent from pagan and Christian Platonism in the Hellenistic-Roman period, but it remained marginal and subterranean, or else overwhelmed by metaphysics, theology, and mysticism.

One can speak profitably, perhaps, about the Hellenistic-Roman background of Alfarabi or the external history of the transmission of Greek learning through Syriac into Arabic, the early history of Islamic philosophy, Alfarabi's account of his philosophic genealogy, and his critique of his predecessors and contemporaries. One should also remember his impact on later Muslim, Jewish, and Christian philosophers, and especially the fact that, until the recovery of Aristotle's *Politics* in the second half of the thirteenth century, he remained the political philosopher par excellence. But to speak about any of these topics intelligently and profitably presupposes an understanding of Alfarabi's philosophy in general and the place he assigns to political philosophy in particular, and this in turn presupposes understanding his writings. This is where we must begin.

Of Alfarabi's political works, chapter 5 of the *Enumeration of the Sciences,* entitled "On Political Science, the Science of Jurisprudence, and the Science of Theology" ("De scientia ciuili . . . et de scientia iudicandi, et de scientia eloquendi" or "De scientia ciuili et scientia legis et scientia elocutionis"), is perhaps the earliest and best-known statement on political science in the Middle Ages. It was available in Arabic as well as in

Hebrew and Latin translations. And it was known through summaries, paraphrases, and quotations in all these languages. It was intended as an introductory statement and forms part of a book intended for the beginner, a contribution to general education, as it were. It is a good text with which to begin.

Since Alfarabi wrote a few other introductory statements of this sort, it is worthwhile to look first at his introduction, where he states what he intends to do in this book in particular. Alfarabi's intention is to enumerate the "generally known" *(mashhūra)* sciences and make known their content, parts, and the content of each part (43.4–6). The book is divided into five chapters, covering (1) the science of language, (2) the science of logic, (3) the sciences of mathematics, (4) natural science and divine science (metaphysics), and (5) political science, the science of jurisprudence, and the science of theology.

The uses to which one can put the content of the book are also five in number. First, the student who wants to learn and inquire into any one of these sciences will know to what he should turn and into what he should inquire, and also the benefit of learning or inquiring into that science. Second, one can use the book to compare the sciences as to their excellence, utility, precision, and so on. Third, it can be used to test the claim of an ignorant man who pretends to know a science by asking him to enumerate its parts and give its content. Fourth, it can be used to test someone who knows a certain science so as to find out how much of it he knows. Finally, the book can be used by someone who is after a quick education and likes to learn the outline of every science, imitate the men of science, and be thought to belong to them. The five uses are thus intended for different kinds of readers.

The first two are for the student who wants to learn. He will make use of the book to know, first, what he is about to engage in. But the book is also meant to be useful to the student who wants, not just to "learn" a science, but to "inquire into" it, compare it with other sciences, and learn the relative excellence, utility, precision, and so on of all the sciences. This seems to be the highest positive use of the book. So far as the genuine student of science is concerned, this book is a beginning and an end: he begins with it before he goes on to study the individual sciences, and he comes back to it after having studied them to learn what he should "inquire into" and about their relative rank and excellence. The next two uses are meant for testing others, both those who merely claim to know and those whose knowledge is incomplete. Alfarabi does not state the qualities of the man who will do the testing. The assumption is that it will be someone who himself is ignorant of these sciences but likes to test others and will therefore read this book for that purpose. The last use, too, is somewhat problematic. Merely to learn the outline of every science and to appear to be learned do not seem particularly worthy objectives. All one can say is that, at this initial stage, it is difficult to distinguish between the genuine and spurious student or between the potential philosopher and the potential sophist.

Alfarabi's enumeration of the sciences is not conventional or haphazard. The book consists of five chapters and has five uses (43–44). Attention is drawn to the third, or central, chapter on the sciences of mathematics, whose seven divisions are enumerated in the introduction (43.7–9; cf. 75.3). Chapter 4 includes, not one, but two sciences (natural science and divine science [metaphysics]). And chapter 5 includes three sciences (political science, the science of jurisprudence, and the science of theology), which are simply listed without indicating what they have in common.

When we turn from the introduction to the divisions and subdivisions of the book's five chapters, we find the following arrangement. (1) The science of language is divided into seven "major" parts; the seventh, the science of the rules that govern poems, is subdivided into three parts. (2) The science of logic is divided into eight parts, the first three of which deal with the rules of syllogism in general and its parts, and the rest with the rules of the five modes of reasoning proper. (3) The science of mathematics, like the science of language, is divided into seven "major" parts, of which the second, the science of geometry, is subdivided into two parts and the fifth, the theoretical science of music, is subdivided into five "major" parts. (4) Natural science, like the science of logic, is divided into eight parts, but these are eight "major" parts; and divine science is divided into three parts. (5) Political science, the science of jurisprudence, and the science of theology, finally, are each divided into two parts.

So, the five chapters cover a total of eight sciences, divided into thirty-nine parts, of which twenty-two are "major" and seventeen are not "major." Three of the thirty-nine parts (the seventh, the seventeenth, and the twentieth, all of which are "major" parts) are subdivided into a total of ten parts, of which five are "major" and five are not "major." In the center of both the thirty-nine and the forty-nine parts stands the theoretical science of music, the fifth part of the book's third, or central, chapter; and, like the book as a whole, it is divided into five major parts. Finally, three of the eight sciences (natural science, divine science, and political science, which have a total of thirteen parts) are set apart from the other five (and their twenty-six parts or, with their subdivisions, thirty-six parts) by Alfarabi's emphasis on the substantive "science" rather than its subject matter, with the consequence that one cannot easily separate the "science" from its subject matter—one cannot, for instance, say "natural" instead of "natural science" as one can say "language" instead of the "science of language."

Even without going into fancy numerological notions, the numerology of the *Enumeration of the Sciences* calls attention to a number of peculiarities for which there are no ready or conventional answers. Why is the science of mathematics so central? Why are the science of the rules that govern poems, the science of geometry, and the theoretical science of music emphasized by giving them subdivisions? Why is divine science (metaphysics) combined with natural science in the same chapter? And why is political science combined with the science of jurisprudence and the science of theology?

One way to see how Alfarabi puts his building blocks together is to compare their arrangement with other generally known arrangements of the sciences. These are basically two. The first is the Aristotelian classification of the philosophic sciences into theoretical sciences (mathematics, physics, and metaphysics) and practical sciences (ethics, politics, and economics). The second is a more comprehensive classification of all the sciences, both philosophic and nonphilosophic, which existed in the Islamic community. The principle of this latter classification is not the distinction between theoretical and practical philosophy or science but rather the distinction between philosophy (or science as defined by philosophy) and other disciplines that are not philosophic or scientific in the sense that they owe their principles, methods, and conclusions (but especially their principles or premises) to unaided human reason. Depending on how one looked at the source of the principles or premises of these sciences, they were called Arabic, traditional, legal, or Islamic sciences. They included two main branches: the sciences of language (i.e., the Arabic language), which were considered instrumental or propaedeutic, and the religious sciences (i.e., the Islamic religious sciences), which included the Quranic sciences and the sciences of the Tradition of the Prophet (these being the primary sources of religious doctrine and practice) and such ancillary sciences as jurisprudence and theology. All these sciences were also considered indigenous because their subject matter was originally given or articulated by the convention of a particular nation or by revelation and were distinguished from the foreign sciences or the sciences of the ancients, whose subject matter is given or articulated by nature or human reason.

Broadly speaking, the difference between the traditional or religious and the rational or philosophic sciences was understood in the following way. To find out whether a linguistic expression or religious belief is correct, one must go back to linguistic usage or the revealed texts, which are the final authority in such matters; whereas to know whether a mathematical or natural law is correct, one observes and thinks, and this is the final authority. Now, compared with these two classifications, Alfarabi's classification was judged by the eleventh-century Andalusian cultural historian Ṣāʿid (*Classes of Nations,* 53) as "unprecedented" and following a "method which had not been followed by anyone else." It ignores the principle underlying the classification of the philosophic sciences into practical and theoretical as well as the principle underlying the classification of all the sciences into rational or philosophic and traditional or religious. His "generally known" sciences encompass more than the philosophic sciences. They include the sciences of language, the science of jurisprudence, and the science of theology, which no one before had classified as philosophic sciences. These traditional or religious sciences are integrated into the philosophic sciences. Yet their integration is not effected on the basis of the principle underlying either of the two generally known classifications.

Science, Art, and Philosophy

Looking again at the five chapters that make up the *Enumeration of the Sciences,* one notices that in a number of places Alfarabi departs from the program announced in the introduction. Indeed, almost one-third of the book consists of digressions in which Alfarabi discusses subjects that fall outside the enumeration of the generally known sciences and their parts and subparts and content. As I see it, there are seven such digressions. (1) The first occurs at the beginning of chapter 1 where Alfarabi defines "rules" *(qawānīn)* and their relation to "arts" *(ṣanāʾiʿ)* and "instrument" *(āla)* (45.6–46.8). The second, third, and fourth occur in chapter 2, whose arrangement is curious in that only a small part of it (70.6–72.10) enumerates the parts of the science of logic. It begins with (2) a lengthy "report" on the utility of logic, its subject matter, and the meaning of the title "logic" (54.16–63.13). This is followed by (3) an exposition of the classes of syllogism, syllogistic arts, syllogistic statements, and the major and minor parts of syllogistic statements (63.14–

70.5). And after the enumeration of the parts of logic, the chapter concludes with (4) a defense of the primacy of the "fourth part" in relation
to the other seven parts of logic (72.11–74.13). In the enumeration of
the eight parts of logic, this fourth part was said to contain "the rules of
the affairs that make up philosophy and everything by which its [philoso-
phy's] activities become more complete, excellent, and perfect" (71.3–
4). (5) The fifth digression occurs in chapter 3, after arithmetic and
geometry have been enumerated; it comments on the principles and
methods of these two sciences and on Euclid's exclusive use of synthesis
in the *Elements* (79.5–12). (6) The sixth occurs at the beginning of chapter 4 and consists of an extended discussion of natural and artificial bodies (91.7–95.11). (7) The last occurs at the end of chapter 5 and details
the ways in which theologians defend their religions (108.10–113.7). I
will try to show that the general purpose of these digressions is to clarify
the relation among "science," "art," and "philosophy" and contribute to
an understanding of their ranks of order (cf. 44.1–4 with 113.8).

In the expression "the science of language" the term "science" is initially used in a broad sense: it includes the ability to memorize and recite
and, in general, all powers and occupations that are useful or necessary
conditions for possessing knowledge or perfecting it but are not themselves knowledge. Next, it is restricted to knowledge as distinguished
from these ancillary conditions. For instance, the "science" of simple utterances (lexicography) may require one to memorize the simple utterances in a particular language, but in a stricter sense the lexicographer's
science is knowledge of the meaning or signification of each of these
utterances (45.3–4). Further, only two parts of the science of language
(the science of simple utterances and the science of compound utterances) consist of knowledge of the significations of utterances. The other
five parts are sciences in a still more restricted sense in that they deal with
the "rules" that govern these utterances.

While originally and according to the ancients a rule meant any instrument or practical device used to protect the practitioner of an art
against error (e.g., the plumb line), to encompass everything in his art
so that nothing escapes him (e.g., arithmetical tables), or to facilitate an
overview of the content of his art (e.g., the outline of a long book),
Alfarabi uses the term in a more general way. A rule is a "universal, that
is, comprehensive statement," that embraces many individual things belonging to an "art." It is only when a number of such rules are formed
and brought together in the mind according to a definite order that an
art with a particular subject matter is formed; it is only through these

rules and their proper ordering that an art stakes out a field of its own and excludes what belongs to other arts, discovers its own errors, and facilitates its own learning and preservation. This is true of "all the arts, whether practical or theoretical" (45.15).

To return to the parts of the science of language, the first two parts (the science of simple utterances and the science of compound utterances) can be said to consist of direct knowledge of their subject matter, which is made up of many individual things (words, speeches, poems). This is not true of the last five, that is, the science of the rules of simple utterances (phonetics and morphology), the science of the rules of compound utterances (prefixes and suffixes, and syntax), the science of the rules of correct writing, the science of the rules of correct reading, and the science of the rules of poetry (metrics, verse-endings, proper usage). Unlike the first two, these last five parts consist, not of direct knowledge of individual utterances, but of knowledge of the general rules that govern these utterances, arranged in an orderly manner so as to encompass the behavior of certain parts or aspects or groups of utterances under certain conditions, for example, when spoken, written, or used in poems.

Occasionally, Alfarabi calls what appears to be one or another of the last five parts (e.g., writing and grammar) an "art," as when he lists "writing" along with "medicine, husbandry, and carpentry" (45.14–15) or when, in chapter 2, he compares the "art of logic" with the "art of grammar." But in such cases "art" does not necessarily mean the same thing as "science," for one may have the "science of the rules of correct writing" without being able to write correctly, let alone elegantly or artistically. Alfarabi argues that the "science of the rules" is useful and even indispensable for the correct practice of the art but is not sufficient for practicing it well. In any case, Alfarabi persists in calling each one of the last five parts of the science of language the "science of the rules of" whatever these rules govern; he does not identify any of them as "art," nor does he explain how any of them may serve or are related to a corresponding art. Finally, and unlike the direct knowledge of the utterances of a particular language, which makes up the first two parts of the science of language, the sciences of the rules of these utterances afford Alfarabi the opportunity to compare various languages and indicate the common subject matter of many of these rules, even though the names given to linguistic phenomena and to linguistic habits may be different in different languages. Still, the science of language in all its parts deals with a particular language, its utterances, and their rules. Even where it deals with rules that are analogues in or common to a number of or all languages, it is concerned with these rules insofar as they apply to a particular language and with the manner in which they do so. The treatment of what is common to the languages of all nations belongs to logic.

In the chapter "On the Science of Logic" Alfarabi speaks of "logic," the "rules of logic," the "science of logic," the "science of the rules of logic," and the "art of logic." Unlike the seven parts of the science of language, however, none of the eight parts of logic is called a "science." Strictly speaking, none of them is called an "art" either. Each part is said to be made up of "rules" or "statements," which means that the distinction between the two kinds of science that obtained in chapter 1 is no longer relevant; all of logic is of the "science of the rules of" type, and no part of it deals with individual things. Logic deals with the rules of intelligibles.

These rules, like the rules of grammar and prosody and such instruments as balances, rulers, and the pairs of dividers, are meant to test the intelligibles in which one is subject to error, that is, the ones apprehended by reflection and inference and reasoning *(qiyās)*. It is argued that logic is necessary for whoever does not wish to base his convictions on mere opinion but on knowledge and insight. As for the argument that logic is not necessary, or that experience in dialectical arguments and discussions, experience in mathematics (geometry and arithmetic), or a perfect innate disposition may be enough to ensure correctness in any of the sciences—this argument is said to deserve the same answer as the argument that experience or a perfect innate disposition is a substitute for the rules of grammar as a means for testing correct language.

Unlike grammar, which tests the correctness of utterances in a particular language, logic tests the correctness of utterances insofar as they designate the intelligibles in any language; it gives rules regarding such utterances insofar as they are common to all languages. Further, it gives rules for the correctness of the intelligibles themselves as they are in the mind, as inner speech. In doing these two things, logic aims at the correct development of the innate power that distinguishes man as man, so that this power may perform its activity (inner thought and the expression of thought) in the most correct manner possible. This power can be described as the ability to make a statement (an inner speech or an external expression) with which one corrects or verifies an opinion, which the ancients (Aristotle) call *qiyās:* reasoning or syllogism. When properly selected and compounded and arranged, the intelligibles and the rules that govern them form the subject matter of the science or art of logic.

In chapter 1, Alfarabi referred in passing to the distinction between practical and theoretical arts. In the sense that they do something or perform an activity, all arts are of course practical. In chapter 2, when speaking of the innate power of reason or speech, Alfarabi says, "it is the power by which man acquires the intelligibles, the sciences, and the arts, by which deliberation takes place, and by which he distinguishes noble from base actions." Here, the "arts" are grouped together with the "sciences" and the acquired intelligibles and separated from the deliberative and moral—that is, the two practical— faculties. Since the aim of logic is the correct development of this innate power or reason or speech as a whole, the "art" of logic would appear to be the overarching art, the so-called art of arts. But as we turn to consider the eight parts of logic, we learn that none of them is an "art." Each is made up of a set of rules employed in what are called the "syllogistic arts."

On first view, one may get the impression that these arts are "logical arts," and that the first three parts of logic (dealing with the rules of single intelligibles, of propositions, and of syllogisms common to the five syllogistic arts) contain rules that are employed by the "arts" of logic, which are presumably the last five parts of logic: demonstration, dialectic, sophistry, rhetoric, and poetics. But this impression is false. Each of the last five parts of logic, too, is said to consist of rules, but now they are said to be rules by which one examines or tests special kinds of statements, the ones that belong to the "arts" of demonstration, dialectic, sophistry, rhetoric, and poetics, respectively. One must, then, distinguish between, for example, the rules by which one examines dialectical statements and the dialectical statements themselves or the "affairs that make up the art of dialectic and by which its activities become more perfect, excellent, and effective" (71.6–8).

Alfarabi does not say that there are five logical arts; what he says is that there are five "syllogistic arts"; and when he expounds the character of each of these arts in the third digression, he is speaking, not about the (logical) rules by which one examines what makes up each of these syllogistic arts, but about the syllogistic arts themselves. The distinction between syllogistic and nonsyllogistic arts is not based on whether an art does or does not employ reasoning or syllogism but on the character of the ultimate activity of the art (the activity that proceeds from it after it is perfected). Only demonstration, dialectic, sophistry, rhetoric, and poetics are arts whose ultimate activity consists in the employment of reasoning or syllogism in speech or argument. Other arts, for example,

medicine, employ reasoning and syllogism, too, but this is not their ultimate activity; when the art of medicine is perfected and moves on to
perform its ultimate activity, it heals the sick. In turn, this does not mean
that the arts whose ultimate activity is to employ reasoning or syllogism
may not lead to practical activities or abstention from practical activities.
Indeed, they all do. However, as syllogistic arts, they produce this practical activity by means of the kind of reasoning or syllogism they employ
rather than by doing or making anything else. Two of these arts, rhetoric
and poetics, are arts in this sense as well as crafts *(ṣinā'a* as well as *ṣan'a),*
that is, arts of making various classes of speeches and poems (71.12–
13, 72.5–6).

Finally, Alfarabi says that each one of the eight parts of logic is to be
found "in a book" and proceeds to give an account of what is "in" each
of these eight books (the traditional six books of the *Organon,* plus the
Rhetoric and the *Poetics*). This account makes it clear that, although each
one of these eight books includes the rules of the respective part of logic,
it may include other things as well, for example, in the case of the *Rhetoric* and the *Poetics,* an account of the arts of rhetoric and poetics and an
account of the craft of making rhetorical speeches and poems. Then, all
the content of these eight books is identified as the subject of the "art"
or "science" of logic, resulting in the kind of ambiguity that has bedev-
iled historians of logic.

To resume, each one of the eight parts of the "science" or "art" of
logic contains certain rules (i.e., universal statements) governing the
parts of the syllogism (1–2) or by which one tests the syllogisms common
to the five syllogistic arts (3) or by which one tests only the particular
kind of syllogism employed by the art of demonstration (4), dialectic (5),
sophistry (6), rhetoric (7), or poetics (8). They are, strictly speaking,
instruments of the five arts of reasoning. Historians of logic need not
therefore be puzzled about Alfarabi's incorporation of the "practical
arts" of rhetoric and poetics into the *Organon.* The arts of rhetoric and
poetry are no more logical arts or parts of logic than the arts of sophistry,
dialectic, or demonstration. Whether and to what extent any of these
arts is "practical" or "theoretical" is an independent question that the
traditional arrangement of the *Organon* (as can be seen from the ambiguous status of the arts of sophistry and dialectic) did not answer either.

Chapter 2 culminates in a digression in praise of the fourth part of
logic as the part that is "most emphatically prior in dignity and superiority" and as being the "primary intention" of logic, while the other parts
are either preparatory or introductory to it (parts 1–3) or else are aids

and, as it were, instruments that are more or less useful for the fourth part or whose exposition is meant to alert the one who seeks the "certain truth" against the danger of falling, unawares, into the use of one of the four methods (parts 5–8). The exposition of the latter (parts 5–8) for their own sake and for the service they render the practitioners of the art corresponding to each is only a "secondary intention" of logic. According to its primary intention, logic as a whole is said to provide the "certain methods," to aim at the "certain science," and to help one guard against the use of methods that lead to mere opinion or an image of the truth.

Now, the fourth part of logic corresponds to the first syllogistic art, the art of demonstration or the art that employs demonstrative statements that produce the "certain science." Alfarabi's account of this part is as follows:

> In the fourth [part of logic, or the book that contains it] are (a) the rules by which one examines demonstrative *(burhāniyya)* statements and (b) the rules of the affairs that make up philosophy and everything by which its [philosophy's] activities become more complete, excellent, and perfect. (71.3–4)

Our first impulse is to identify "demonstrative statements" or the art of demonstration with "philosophy," especially in view of the fact that in at least two other (logical) works, Alfarabi appears to use the utterances "art of demonstration" and "art of philosophy" interchangeably (*Introductory "Risāla" on Logic*, 227; *Utterances*, 107–8), and the fact that he "translates" the titles *Prior Analytics* and *Posterior Analytics* as "Syllogism" and "Demonstration," respectively (71.1–2, 71.5). Further, in these other two works "philosophy" or the "art of philosophy" is said to contain certain "parts" or "arts" or "sciences," which are four in number (the science of mathematics, natural science, divine science, and political science; this last called also "political philosophy" and "practical philosophy"), which seems to explain the arrangement of the remaining chapters of the *Enumeration of the Sciences*. The primary intention of logic, then, is to provide rules for the art of demonstration or philosophy, which consists of four parts or arts or sciences; and these will be treated, in the order just enumerated, in chapters 3–5.

But we must also consider the following difficulties. This view leads us to expect a "demonstrative" political or practical science. Alfarabi's account of the fourth part of logic is explicit about the fact that it contains two sets of rules; and the rules by which one examines demonstrative statements are clearly separated from the "rules of the affairs that make up philosophy." (We may believe that these "affairs" include demonstrative statements, but we have no reason to assert that they include nothing more. In any case, Aristotle's *Posterior Analytics* will not support such an assertion.) Finally, the two other works to which I have just referred do not give an account of the parts of philosophy but merely mention them. It is therefore useful to see whether the suggestion of a thoroughly demonstrative philosophy is borne out by Alfarabi's account of the sciences in the remaining part of the *Enumeration of the Sciences*.

Like the seven "major" parts of the science of language, each of the seven "major" parts of the science or sciences of mathematics (cf. 75.2–3 with 43.7) is called a "science." In the case of four of them, Alfarabi explains "what is [generally] understood by this name"; and it turns out that in every case the name is ambiguous.

In the case of arithmetic (1) and geometry (2), the name "science" covers two "sciences," one "practical" and the other "theoretical." Only theoretical arithmetic and theoretical geometry, which investigate their respective subject matters as such, absolutely, or without qualification, are "to be included among the sciences." Practical arithmetic and practical geometry, though generally called "sciences," are not in fact sciences. They investigate their subject matters as applied to bodies "in which the multitude deals in market transactions and political transactions" and bodies that are the materials of various artisans (carpenters, blacksmiths, builders, and farmers), that is, in each case the material of a special "practical art."

In the case of the science of the stars (4), the name "science" covers two things, which are not distinguished by Alfarabi as practical science and theoretical science. They are judgments of the stars (astrology), which is merely a power or vocation that enables man to foretell the future, and mathematical astronomy, which is "the one to be counted among the sciences and included in mathematics."

In the case of the science of music (5), finally, the name "science" covers two sciences, one "practical" and the other "theoretical." However, practical music is not called an art. The theoretical, on the other hand, is called an "art"; but it is not said to be "the one to be counted among the sciences." Theoretical music covers the principles and causes of notes and melodies, their composition, adaptation to musical instruments, the manner of their production, etc., up to, but not including, their actual production in natural or artificial instruments, which is the work of the practical musician. (The uncertainty regarding the place of theoretical and practical music among the arts and sciences invites comparison with political science and political activity.)

The names of the remaining three parts of mathematics do not seem to present serious problems. The science of aspects (optics [3]) is a special field of (theoretical) geometry and is called an "art." And the science of weights (6) deals with the principles governing two kinds of instruments (balances and lifts); while the science of (mechanical) devices (7) deals with the applicability of mathematical knowledge to natural bodies, the production of instruments, and in general the "principles of practical, political arts."

To summarize. There appear to be two purely theoretical mathematical sciences: theoretical arithmetic and theoretical geometry. Optics and mathematical astronomy seem to be more specialized mathematical sciences or arts. And weights and mechanical devices merely apply some of the things discovered in other mathematical sciences or arts and serve specialized practical, political arts. Theoretical and practical music form a parallel structure that descends from theoretical knowledge (knowledge of notes and melodies as intelligibles) to the actual production of melodies. The generally understood name "science" covers all of these things: it covers theoretical sciences that are sciences in the genuine sense, theoretical sciences that are also arts (but not practical arts), and practical sciences that give the principles of the particular practical, political arts.

This should make it clear already that the science or sciences of mathematics cannot be a single, thoroughly demonstrative, art. Demonstration in the highest sense—that is, giving the causes and explaining the "why"—is mentioned twice only, in connection with geometry and optics, which is a special field of geometry (78.8, 80.10–11). (When "demonstration" is mentioned again in connection with mechanical devices [88.12–13, 89.3], it refers to things whose "existence" only is demonstrated in mathematics.) Otherwise, mathematics for the most part "inquires," "investigates," etc., but does not demonstrate, which means that there are inquiries or investigations that are theoretical and lead to "certain science" but are not demonstrative.

After enumerating theoretical arithmetic and theoretical geometry, Alfarabi interrupts his exposition to remind the reader that geometry consists of foundations and principles, which are limited, and other things derived from these, which are unlimited. Then he adds:

There are two methods of inquiring into it [geometry]: the method of analysis *(taḥlīl)* and the method of synthesis *(tarkīb)*. The ancient practitioners of this science used to combine in their books both methods, except Euclid, who organized the content of his book [the *Elements*] according to the method of synthesis alone. (79.9–12)

(In the *Harmonization*, 8.20ff., the "affair" of division [*qisma*] and synthesis [*tarkīb*] with respect to giving a complete account of definitions is compared to climbing and descending from the same ladder; and the two are said to be quite different.) Here, then, we have one of the important "affairs that make up philosophy"—the method, indeed, that leads to the discovery of the principles of theoretical science in general—that is not covered by demonstration.

In the *Enumeration of the Sciences*, Alfarabi confines himself to hinting at the importance of this method and at his view that theoretical science and philosophy include more than demonstrative statements. The view of theoretical science or philosophy that restricts it to demonstrative statements is, in a sense, a generally known view of science, too. Since the *Enumeration of the Sciences* enumerates the generally known sciences, the structure of each of its chapters imitates Euclid's *Elements*, starting, as it were, from the top of the ladder and descending to the ground, to the principles of the practical, political arts employed by the multitude in the marketplace and the city.

Natural, Divine, and Political Science

The sixth and seventh digressions introduce chapter 4 and conclude chapter 5, setting the two chapters and the five sciences they include apart from the rest of the book. The exposition of natural science has the following features in common with the exposition of the science of logic. Both are preceded by relatively long introductions. Both are divided into eight parts. None of the parts has subdivisions and none is called a science or an art. Logic was seen as the counterpart of grammar; natural science is seen as the counterpart of the practical arts. The subject matter of natural science is natural bodies presented as the counterparts of the artificial bodies produced by art and the human will, to which frequent references were made in the practical sciences of mathematics, especially the science of devices (mechanics), which immediately preceded chapter 4. Nevertheless, the digression on natural and artificial bodies, which is almost as long as the enumeration of the parts of natural science and divine science taken together, does not assume the sciences of mathematics in the way that logic assumed the sciences of language. Instead, the reader is invited to consider artificial bodies, the products of the practical arts, as analogues of natural bodies.

Such things as "body" (e.g., a garment) and "attributes constituted by the body" (its smoothness), the "agent" that brings it about (the weaver), "purpose" and "end" (warmth), and "form" (interweave of warp and woof) and "matter" (the yarn) are said to be more apparent in artificial bodies. Most of them can be observed directly by sense perception, and the rest (e.g., the intoxicating power of wine and the healing power of medicines) can be seen indirectly through observing the activities of artificial bodies. Because the principles of artificial bodies and of their attributes are better known to the "multitude" *(jumhūr)* than the principles of their natural counterparts, the multitude give the names of the principles better known to them to the natural principles and treat the two sets of principles as though they were the same. "It is customary in the arts," on the other hand, "to transfer to the things contained in them the names that the multitude apply to the likenesses of those things" (95.7–8).

The principles of natural bodies are less apparent than the principles of artificial bodies, most of their forms and matters cannot be observed by sense perception, and "for us, their existence can only be verified by reasoning and certain demonstrations" (94.1–2). Yet Alfarabi gives no reasoning or demonstration to prove the existence of any of the principles of natural bodies, let alone the cause of their existence. The eight "major" parts of natural science (arranged in a descending order, from the principles common to all natural bodies to stones, plants, and animals) "inquire" and "investigate"; they do not "explain," "make evident," or "demonstrate" anything at all. Natural science is an exclusively "inquisitive" science. And its inquiries appear to be confined to the principles of bodies as such, rather than their ultimate causes or their practical uses. Nothing is said about God or the unmoved mover, intellect, or even the soul, although soul and intellect must at least be inquired into in the parts that deal with plants (7) and animals (8).

Unlike the mathematical sciences, which have so-called practical sciences or practical arts as their counterparts, and some of which study the principles of the practical, political arts, there is no such thing as a "practical" science or an art that corresponds to any of the parts of natural science, and none of these parts is said to have anything to do with any practical, political art, not even where we might expect a certain relation, such as between the study of minerals (6) and the art of mining, the study of plants (7) and the art of agriculture, or the study of animals (8) and the art of medicine. There is no such thing as a practical or applied *natural* science or art. Indeed, Alfarabi goes so far as to avoid the terms "practical" and "theoretical" altogether in connection with natural science and its parts.

All this is true of natural science. But it is not true of chapter 4 as a whole; for we must still consider divine science and its three parts. Now, divine science (like political science, the science of jurisprudence, and the science of theology) lacks the kind of introduction that indicates the fact that the enumeration has been completed. The result is that the part dealing with this science (like those dealing with the three sciences that make up chapter 5) becomes purely enumerative, free of any connective tissue that may explain possible ranks of order or the direction governing the enumeration. This is all the more strange in view of the fact that the connection between natural science and divine science is a commonplace in traditional introductions to divine science. Its absence indicates one of two things. Divine science may be simply a continuation of natural inquiry under a different name; but this would imply that "beings as beings," into which divine science inquires, are nothing more than natural bodies and their principles. Or there is no special connection between the two sciences, which is what Alfarabi's exposition seems to indicate, but which makes one even more baffled as to why the two sciences are treated together in one chapter and without any explanation.

Divine science is divided into three parts. The first investigates beings as beings and their attributes. Nothing further is said about this part. The second investigates "the principles [or premises] of the *demonstrations* in the particular theoretical sciences," verifies and makes known their substances and special attributes, and enumerates and criticizes the corrupt opinions held about them by the "ancients."

A "particular" theoretical science is defined as a science that inquires into a "special" kind of being. The principle of the independence of the particular theoretical science is, then, the "particularization" of beings into kinds or genera. Three such sciences are listed: the science of logic, the sciences of mathematics, and natural science. Logic, which was never called a theoretical science in chapter 2, is now explicitly counted as one of the three particular theoretical sciences; it is assumed that the "intelligibles" with which logic deals are a special "kind of being," different from mathematical and natural beings.

This means that, except for chapter 1 (which dealt with the science of language), the book has been enumerating nothing but "theoretical" sciences so far: three "particular" theoretical sciences (logic, mathematics, and natural science), which study the intelligibles or intelligible beings, mathematical beings, and natural beings, respectively. And now we have a divine science, which is not itself called a theoretical science, yet its second (or central) part investigates the principles of the three particular theoretical sciences. It would seem that we have covered all the theoretical sciences. If their subject matter is being as being, the principles of particular kinds of being, and the particular kinds of being themselves, we have accounted for all of it.

The third part of divine science investigates "the beings that are neither bodies nor in bodies." This last (or eleventh) part of chapter 4 does eleven things, which are ordered as follows. In the first five, it demonstrates the existence of these beings that are not bodies or in bodies (the so-called intelligences); explains that they are many; demonstrates that their number is finite; demonstrates that they form a hierarchical order with respect to perfection and that this order terminates in a being that is simply perfect, one, first, and prior; and explains that it bestows being and so forth on every other being—all this without the benefit of revelation. Then, as its sixth (or central) activity, the third part of divine science explains that the supreme being thus far described is that which one ought to "believe" God to be—that is, presumably, the God of revelation—and whose names are to be sanctified (100.13–14). In the last five, it delves into and fully enumerates God's attributes; makes known the generation of beings through or by God; investigates their order; delves into, fully enumerates, and explains the goodness of God's activities; and, finally, refutes all the false views about God's activities that impute imperfection to Him and the beings created by Him:

> it refutes them all by demonstrations that provide certain science, such that it will be impossible for man to have any misgiving or entertain a doubt about it and impossible for him to abandon it at all. (101.8–10)

Unlike the ten preceding parts of chapter 4, none of which demonstrated anything at all (the "investigation" of principles of demonstrations in the tenth part—the second part of divine science—was of course not demonstrative), the eleventh begins and ends with demonstrations. It is the most demonstrative of all the sciences. Indeed, it contains more demonstrations than all the sciences in the book. We have, it would appear, finally found a science, or one part of a science, that, if not thoroughly demonstrative, is at least largely demonstrative.

But against this, we must weigh the evidence of Alfarabi's more philosophic works (the commentary on Aristotle's *Metaphysics* known as the *Book of Letters,* the short work *On the Purposes of Aristotle's "Metaphysics,"* and the *Philosophy of Aristotle*), where he argues directly or indirectly against the inclusion of what corresponds to this third part of divine science in metaphysics or against the view that it has an important or central place in metaphysics. (Since he also says that it is elaborated by Aristotle in book Lambda of the *Metaphysics,* he indicates, in effect, that book Lambda is an exoteric work and does not represent Aristotle's doctrine of being.) The only way to explain this discrepancy is to take seriously Alfarabi's statement in the introduction to the *Enumeration of the Sciences* that his purpose is to enumerate the "generally known" sciences and their parts—that is, generally known to the multitude who understand the principles of natural bodies in terms of the principles of artificial bodies and apply the same names to both.

However this may be, Alfarabi's enumeration of the theoretical sciences (logic, mathematics, and natural science) culminates in a divine science, which in turn culminates in an account of the universe that is orderly, hierarchical, and free of injustice, imperfection, conflict, disharmony, or evil of any kind. This account of God and the universe is made into a part of divine science, placed in the same chapter as natural science, and followed immediately by political science, jurisprudence, and theology, which are placed in the next chapter. This arrangement is quite different from the arrangement that emerges from Alfarabi's more extensive accounts of divine science and political science in which what is here called the third part of divine science is joined to political science. The *Virtuous City* and the *Political Regime,* which are clearly political works, begin abruptly with an account of God and the universe (in exactly the same fashion as in the third part of divine science in this book) and proceed without interruption to give an account of man and of what is produced by human will and art: human associations, the principles and forms of political life, and the particular, political arts.

The fusion of divine science and political science can be interpreted in two ways. In Alfarabi's political works, it must be interpreted as a "political" theology and cosmology. In Avicenna, on the other hand, politics becomes an appendage of divine science. The *Enumeration of the Sciences* separates divine science from political science and yet enumerates them in the same order in which they appear in Alfarabi's political works. Even more important, perhaps, is the distinction between divine science and so-called revealed theology, which belongs to a separate chapter with political science and jurisprudence. Divine science is separated from theology by political science and jurisprudence, which means that, in order properly to arrive at so-called revealed theology, one must first go through political science and jurisprudence.

Political Science 1 and 2

Alfarabi's political science (which he also calls political philosophy) is the political science of the ancients, of Plato's *Republic* and Aristotle's *Politics*. It speaks of rulership and kingship, cities and nations, and science and philosophy, but says nothing about prophecy or divine lawgivers, religion, or theology. His jurisprudence and theology, on the other hand, are decidedly "modern." The very terms *(fiqh* and *kalām)* employed to designate these two sciences are specifically Islamic. They are sciences that follow in the footsteps of prophecy, the divine lawgiver, and divine revelation. They have to do with the opinions and actions of a religious community. They contain no reference to philosophy or kingship or the city. A deliberate effort is made to create two different and contrasting atmospheres: ancient and modern, a prereligious or nonreligious political science and religious sciences that assume revelations, divine laws, and a number of religious communities. The account of political science avoids the name of God altogether. The account of jurisprudence and theology is saturated with such utterances as God, divine things, divine revelation, divine intellects, divine mysteries, and miracles.

There is one apparent exception to all of this. When investigating human activities and their ends, political science

> explains that some of them [the ends] are true happiness, while others are presumed to be happiness although they are not. That which is true happiness cannot possibly be of this life, but of another life after [or beyond] this, which is the life to come [or the other life]; while that which is presumed to be happiness consists of such things as wealth, honor, and pleasures, when these are made the only ends in this life. (102.9–13)

This statement recalls the religious view of happiness as the happiness of the next life, of paradise or the beatific vision, which is said to be true happiness, as against the happiness of this life, which is said to be presumed and not genuine happiness. Yet it also recalls the philosophic view that man should not confine his ends in this life to such things as wealth, honor, and pleasures but seek a higher end, such as virtue or knowledge: he should lead "another" life in "this" life. Alfarabi appears to be using the Aristotelian and Platonic distinction between this life and the other life.[1]

The central theme of political science is what Alfarabi calls "virtuous rulership" or the "virtuous royal craft"—that is, the art of the ruler who establishes, rules, and preserves the virtuous city or nation and whose end is true happiness, which is attained by good, noble, and virtuous deeds. It is distinguished from ignorant rulerships, which establish ignorant cities and nations whose ends (such as wealth and honor) are only presumed to be happiness. To the question "What constitutes the virtuous royal craft?" Alfarabi gives two answers, which occur in two slightly different accounts of political science.

1. In the first account (102.4–104.15), political science performs seven functions, which cover the subject matters of what Aristotle calls ethics and politics, without explicitly distinguishing between ethics and politics. In the first four, political science investigates actions, ways of life, and moral habits, without reference to the city or the nation. In the fifth, it explains that these cannot exist in man except when "distributed in cities and nations according to a certain order and are practiced in common" (102.16–103.1). This leads to what political science does next, which is to explain the necessity of rulership, that one becomes a ruler by virtue of a craft and a positive disposition, that this is called "royal craft," "kingship," or whatever one chooses to call it (103.5–6), and the divisions of rulership. The seventh and last step is to explain what constitutes the "virtuous royal craft." The virtuous royal craft is said to be composed of two powers or faculties: (1) the faculty for general rules and (2) the kind of competence or expertise *(ḥunka)* acquired through long experience, observation, and practice in particular situations—actions, men, and cities. This is explained by the analogy of the art of medicine: the physician becomes a perfect practitioner by knowing the general rules he learns from medical books and, in addition, a power acquired from long experience, observation, and practice.

Thus the subject matters of the virtuous royal craft and of political science are not coextensive. Political science gives two things: the general rules and the general patterns of their determination or application in particular cases and times. Like medical books and medical science, political science provides only the first power or faculty required by the virtuous royal craft. It leaves the actual determination or application to another faculty, which cannot be acquired through science. Furthermore,

1. Cf. *Book of Religion*, 52.18, 55.7–8, where the goods (and the happiness) of this world are said to be the things that are called good by the multitude—that is, they are vulgar goods.

according to this first account, political science and political rulership (including the virtuous royal craft) are self-sufficient and concerned exclusively with practical or political matters. They are not in any way dependent on, or in need of, the theoretical sciences.

The horizon of the virtuous royal craft is defined by political science as the general rules of political life as such. It is true that the royal craft requires "another faculty, other than this science" (104.13), but this is a faculty that can be acquired through "long practice in political deeds" (104.1–2), that is, dealing with the particular cases encompassed by the general rules given by political science. In this respect, this political science corresponds to the last five parts of the science of language and the last five parts of the science of logic. It provides the rules necessary for the correct practice of the art of politics.

2. The occasion for giving a second account of political science is the division of this science into two parts (104.16ff.). (A quick look at the way Alfarabi presents the other sciences in this book is sufficient to show that it was by no means necessary for him to repeat a full-fledged account of political science just because he needed to indicate its divisions. He could have started his account of political science, as he frequently does in the case of other sciences, by saying, "this science consists of two parts," and then presented the content of the science under the two headings; or else he could have finished his account with a short indication of the way in which it divides itself.) According to the second account of political science, the two parts of this science perform four and fourteen functions, respectively.

The four steps in the first part correspond to the first four steps of the first account; they are summarized and reordered, and the new order, broadly speaking, recalls Aristotle's *Nicomachean Ethics,* even though the distinction between ethics and politics is again absent. The second part elaborates and adds substantially to the last three steps of the first account. (It is stated at this point that the matters discussed here are to be found in Aristotle's *Politics,* but that "this [second division of political science] is [to be found] also in Plato's *Republic* and in books by Plato and others" [105.5–6]. Almost the entire section that follows next corresponds to parts of Alfarabi's *Philosophy of Plato.*)

There are a number of new elements in this second account that are specifically Platonic. The most important of these is the explanation of the things that go into making up the "virtuous royal art." These are no longer the two faculties given in the first account—that is, the faculty for general rules (given by political science) and the competence acquired through long practice in political deeds. Instead, their exact number is now left open; only some of them are mentioned; and the implication is that other things may be added. "They include," he says, "the theoretical and practical sciences" (106.1), to which the faculty acquired through experience should be joined.

The experiential faculty is the same in both accounts. But for the general rules provided by political science alone in the first account, Alfarabi now substitutes "the theoretical and practical sciences" (both in the plural), and possibly other things as well. The establishment and preservation of the virtuous city are made contingent on a man who possesses this "virtuous royal craft" and on the uninterrupted succession of such princes or kings. This political science also explains the proper selection, upbringing, and education of future kings, so that they come to possess this kind of royal craft and become "fully" or "completely" accomplished kings. Unlike these true kings, those whose rulership is ignorant should not be called kings at all; they do not need "either theoretical or practical philosophy" but can run their cities or nations by the experiential faculty alone, provided they are clever or perceptive and good imitators of earlier ignorant kings.

In contrast to this second account, the first account of political science was much more sober and practical. It gave a classification of regimes and rulerships, confined the task of political science to the formulation of general rules of political life and general patterns of their application, confined the powers or faculties of the virtuous royal craft to knowledge of these general rules and to what can be learned from experience, and did not even raise the question of the nonvirtuous royal crafts or how they operate. On the crucial question as to what kind of knowledge and competence the virtuous ruler needs in order to establish and rule a virtuous city, the answer was clear: political experience and political science are enough.

While political experience is, of course, one of the requirements in the second account also, it is mentioned as a matter of course, does not occupy as important a place as it did in the first account, and is debunked at the end as the hallmark of ignorant rulers. This is especially significant if we remember that in a parallel work (*Book of Religion*, 58.15–59.1), Alfarabi says of this experiential faculty that it is the faculty that "the ancients [i.e., Aristotle] call 'prudence.'" As to the higher faculty for the general rules given by political science, neither this faculty nor political science is mentioned as such. They are included in something much larger, which comprehends the theoretical and practical sciences, or theoretical and practical philosophy, as well as perhaps some other, unspeci-fied things; and the place of political science (or of the faculty for the general rules of political life), which was clear and circumscribed in the first account, is not specified in this larger whole.

The first account of political science or political philosophy is not criticized directly. It is silently replaced by an account of political science whose central theme—the things that constitute the royal virtuous craft and the selection and training of the kings who will be able to establish and preserve the virtuous city—cannot be provided by political science as such. And because the regime in this second account is constituted by the operation of the virtuous royal craft (103.6), political science cannot (either by itself or in cooperation with political experience) establish or preserve the virtuous city.

It is time to ask why nowhere in this book is political science or politi-cal philosophy called either a practical or a theoretical science. Since Alfa-rabi knows of this distinction and makes use of it in the second account in connection with the virtuous royal craft, we can surely ask whether his political science is a practical or a theoretical science. So far, we have encountered the distinction between theoretical and practical arts, which was not elaborated, and theoretical and practical sciences, where the the-oretical were included among the sciences proper, and the practical were excluded from the sciences proper and said to be practical arts or the study of the principles of the practical, political arts. Then we have been presented with his accounts of political "science" or political "philoso-phy," which is not one of the practical or political "arts" mentioned pre-viously. Finally, we are told that its central or highest theme is a positive disposition or craft whose activity consists in the production and preser-vation of the regime, the political regime, which in turn establishes and preserves all the particular actions and positive dispositions and crafts in the city. This seems to be the supreme or ruling science or art, which includes and transcends all the arts and sciences practiced in the virtu-ous city.

In the first account of political science, on the other hand, where the royal art is said to be made up of two elements, the general rules of political life provided by political science and the experience acquired in political life itself, we have a political science that does not deal with any of the theoretical sciences mentioned so far, nor is any of the themes treated by it constituted by these theoretical sciences. We can, therefore, safely call this first political science a practical science or art, in the sense that it deals exclusively with things done and made by man, his activities

and ways of life whose principles are human will and choice; and call
the royal craft the supreme practical craft or art, since it establishes and
preserves the regime that makes possible what the citizens do and make.
This would be practical science or art or philosophy as against theoretical
science or art or philosophy (logic, mathematics, natural science, and
divine science).

The difficulty we encountered in the account of true happiness (which
was said to be possible in "another" life, meaning a life beyond or higher
than the life dedicated to such things as wealth, honor, and pleasures, to
vulgar goods or ends) can be resolved by identifying the "other" life with
the virtuous life (the life dedicated to virtue for its own sake) and by
calling the "other" city the "virtuous" city, its rulership the "virtuous"
rulership, and the craft that establishes and preserves it the "virtuous"
royal craft. For all intents and purposes, this first account of political
science must identify the good, the noble, and the virtuous with the
moral virtues, which fall within the class of things whose principle is human will and choice and which are isolated from theoretical science. The
"virtue" or the "art" of the "virtuous royal craft" in the second account
of political science, in contrast, is not exclusively a practical virtue or a
practical art, for it is constituted by (1) the theoretical and practical sciences and (2) political experience. We saw that political experience is the
same in both accounts.

As for the "general rules" of political life given by political science in
the first account, Alfarabi now substitutes the "theoretical and practical
sciences" or theoretical and practical philosophy: the theoretical sciences—that is, logic, mathematics, natural science, and divine science—
and the practical sciences, perhaps the parts of the first account of political science and the arts subordinate to it. This interpretation is confirmed
by the parallel passage in the *Book of Religion* (60.6–7), where the full or
complete operation of this virtuous royal craft requires "knowledge of
the general rules of this art [politics], which is to be coupled with theoretical philosophy, and to which prudence is to be joined." (Thus, the
theoretical sciences = theoretical philosophy; practical sciences = the
general rules of this art [given by political science]; the experiential faculty = prudence.)

It is plain that a political science whose central theme is the virtuous
city established and preserved by this royal craft and the education of
kings who are "completely" kings is not strictly a practical science or
strictly a theoretical science. It is not any of the theoretical or practical

arts or sciences enumerated so far. This political science must cover and order all of them, not as enumerated in this book, but as they must exist in the soul of the king who is completely king—that is, in their proper ranks of order. It is thus a political science or philosophy that includes, transcends, and rules all the "theoretical and practical sciences" or "theoretical and practical philosophy" (utterances that occur only in this account of political science and nowhere else in the book). In this sense, the upward movement from the science of language to the science of logic, to the science of mathematics, and to natural science and divine science has as yet little momentum. The first account of political science as a mere practical science was only an interlude that made possible the account of a political science that in a way includes more and is therefore more comprehensive than all the theoretical and practical sciences enumerated so far.

Jurisprudence and Theology

Jurisprudence and theology are each called both a "science" and an "art." But the name science occurs only in the titles of the two sections and in the remark concluding the first. The brief exposition of the two disciplines concerns the "art of jurisprudence" and the "art of theology" exclusively. Unlike any of the theoretical and many of the practical sciences or arts mentioned so far, the arts of jurisprudence and theology about which Alfarabi speaks here exist and are practiced in certain nations only and at a certain stage in their development.

There ought to have existed a lawgiver who had legislated a divine law *(sharī'a)* or a religion *(milla)* for a particular nation (the city, in the singular, now disappears from view; cf. 107.13). Religion consists of two broad classes of things, which are defined and determined by the lawgiver: opinions and actions. Opinions are legislated about such things as God, His attributes, the universe, and so forth; and actions are legislated about such things as prayers and civic transactions. So long as the lawgiver is on the scene, he will be the one who defines and determines what ought to be believed or done and supports or defends these beliefs and actions by persuading his followers and others to accept them. After the lawgiver or the founder of the religion leaves the scene, there will remain opinions and actions that he did not have time, or did not consider important enough, to attend to himself; and new issues and situations arise that will require new determinations as to what one should believe or do. Also, the opinions and actions that the lawgiver had determined will require support and defense against new objectors and new objections.

It is at this point that Alfarabi's exposition begins. The art of jurisprudence is the "positive disposition" *(malaka)* that enables man to make the new determinations, and the art of theology is the "positive disposition" that enables man to defend the religion. Since the things that need to be determined or defended in the religion are either opinions or actions, jurisprudence and theology each has two parts, dealing with opinions and actions, respectively. Jurisprudence proceeds as follows. It learns the "purpose" of the lawgiver from the religion he had legislated for that particular nation and the things that the lawgiver had already determined in his religion. On the basis of these two things, it discovers or infers what determinations are to be made about things of which the lawgiver had not spoken explicitly or things that did not exist in his time. Theology, on the other hand, does not make new determinations. It takes what the lawgiver had determined, defines them, and refutes what disagrees with them.

Alfarabi's account of theology is followed by an extensive exposition of the opinions of various theological schools as to what methods and opinions should be employed in supporting one's religion, all of which belong to the rules of the syllogistic arts enumerated in the science of logic. (He does not explain the methods employed by the art of jurisprudence, but there are indications that jurisprudence applies some of the same rules of logic.) This is the last of the seven digressions to which I have sought to draw attention. It is also the most dramatic part of a somewhat undramatic book, highlighting the proclivity of the defenders of religions for shining armor and sharp weapons. Its main effect, however, is to draw attention away from the question of the manner in which jurisprudence and theology are related to political science and conversely.

One notices, first, that like the science of language—and unlike logic, mathematics, natural and divine science, and political science—jurisprudence and theology are not single universal sciences. There are as many arts of jurisprudence and as many arts of theology as there are religions or divine laws. (The terms "nation" and "nations," whose frequent use was a hallmark of chapter 1 on the science of language, are replaced here by the terms "religion" and "religions.") Alfarabi states what all these arts do, their ends, and the methods they employ to achieve their ends. Only in this formal sense does he speak of the science or art of jurisprudence or theology. To know what each does in particular, one must learn the particular opinions and actions legislated by a particular lawgiver and the purpose of his religion and then see either how the jurists of this religion employ the methods described by Alfarabi in making new determinations or how the theologians of this religion employ the methods he describes in defending the religion's particular opinions and actions. On the surface at least, Alfarabi seems to be resigned to the multiplicity of lawgivers and religions and juridical disciplines and theologies. Moreover, he abstains from praising or condemning any of them as good or bad, virtuous or vicious. Religion is defined in a perfectly neutral manner, and so are the religious sciences.

Second, jurisprudence and theology are not substitutes for political science or alternative approaches to the study of political life. They are not religious or sacred political sciences as against a "secular" political science. They do not conduct any of the investigations conducted in political science, give any of the explanations given in it, or make any of the distinctions made in it.

Third, they are not parts of political science. The two parts of political science were stated and explained earlier. Neither jurisprudence nor theology corresponds, either wholly or in part, to either of those parts.

Fourth, and more generally, jurisprudence and theology do not investigate the truth or falsehood of the opinions given in any religion about God, His attributes, and the universe. This is the function of the theoretical sciences enumerated earlier, especially the third part of divine science. Nor do they investigate the nobility or baseness of the actions demanded in any religion, distinguish the kind of happiness achieved by performing these actions, or judge the purpose or end the lawgiver had in view in giving this religion. All this is the function of political science, which has been completed already.

Jurists and theologians perform certain defined practical tasks within an established religious community. Their success or failure is not contingent on their ability to conduct an independent inquiry or attain direct knowledge of things, either theoretical or practical. Their knowledge, in particular, is derivative. They learn what their lawgiver had in mind (his purpose) and his statements as transmitted through written or oral reports. For the rest, the power or faculty they employ in performing their task as jurists or theologians has to do with particular cases. Should this opinion be accepted or that action be performed? Or, how can I best support this opinion or defend this action, convince this man or this group of men, or take care of this objection or ward off that criticism?

At best, the jurist makes use of a limited kind of experiential faculty or prudence that functions within a framework established by the lawgiver, and the theologian makes use of certain dialectical and rhetorical arguments.

The Lawgiver, Religion, and Political Science

This manner of juxtaposing political science to jurisprudence and theology, without providing an explicit transition from political science to the religious sciences and without stating explicitly the connection between them or their ranks of order or how they form a single whole, mirrors the initial situation in which the student of these sciences who is a member of, or lives in, a religious community finds himself. On the one hand, he finds himself before a rational, philosophic science that claims to be *the* science of practical life, to encompass the entire range of the human ends in this and the other life, and to explain what man ought to do to achieve these ends. On the other hand, he is confronted with jurisprudence and theology, which claim that they are the sciences that determine what he must believe and do to achieve what appear to be the same ends.

To understand why Alfarabi is able to present these two claimants side by side without stating the relation between them, we must realize that the above situation is neither universal nor necessary. It does not represent the condition of man as man. Philosophy and political science can exist and did exist in nations that did not possess revealed religions, jurisprudence, or theology. And revealed religions existed and could continue to exist without philosophy or political science. The coexistence of these claimants can, therefore, be said to be an accident, a historical accident. Still, once they have come to coexist in the same community, the relation between them becomes a problem. Yet it is not an essential theoretical problem for political science in the sense that political science as political science must necessarily raise and answer the question of revealed religion plus jurisprudence and theology. It is, of course, also not a problem that must or even can be discussed by jurisprudence or theology. But although historically and theoretically the relation between political science and the religious sciences is accidental, this does not mean it should not or could not be understood or clarified.

Since the claim of jurisprudence and theology is more urgent from a practical point of view, let us begin here. This claim is not based specifically on the methods of these disciplines but on the assumption that they follow in the footsteps of a divine lawgiver, understand his purpose, and supplement his activities. They are admittedly subordinate arts, subordinate to the original, greater, and more comprehensive art of the divine lawgiver. We must, then, go back or ascend to the divine lawgiver whom the jurists and theologians follow and understand his art. To do so, we must follow in the footsteps of the jurists and the theologians and study all the things that the divine lawgiver declared or determined by speech or deed. This is the divine law or the religion he legislated. (The religious sciences necessary for a better comprehension of the principal sources or roots of the divine law, whether written or oral, are assumed by Alfarabi in this context.) And we must try to understand the divine lawgiver's purpose or intention in legislating his religion in the nation for which he legislated it.

As we look at these three things (the divine law, the purpose of the lawgiver, and the nation for which he legislated this divine law), we perceive a possible link with some of the things we learned in political science. The divine lawgiver is a kind of ruler or king; at least he performs some of their functions. For instance, he defines and determines particular actions that he asks a particular nation to perform in common so as to attain a certain end. He is not necessarily a theoretical man or a political scientist, but a leader of men. He decides what this particular group of men must do or believe in, here and now, so as to achieve a designated end in this life and/or the next. Minimally, then, he is a ruler who possesses what Alfarabi called the experiential faculty (or prudence). But the fact that he possesses this faculty does not, by itself, prove that his purpose is to lead men to genuine happiness rather than some spurious kind of happiness, or whether he does or does not possess what Alfarabi called the virtuous royal craft. The fact that divine lawgivers establish religions does not in itself prove that their religions are good or bad, true or false. The multiplicity of religions that claim divine origin, their conflicting claims, and interreligious theological controversies point in the same direction.

The question, then, is whether one must be satisfied with learning the purpose of the divine lawgiver and the divine lawgiver's particular determinations, which is what jurists and theologians do; or whether one can go further and judge the character of the divine lawgiver's purpose. Jurisprudence and theology are constitutionally unfit either to raise or to answer this question. Political science, on the other hand, while it does not claim right here in this chapter that it can raise and answer this question with respect to divine laws and the communities based on them, does in fact claim that it can give an account of all classes of ends, actions, regimes, rulerships, and purposes and distinguish between the true and the false, virtuous and nonvirtuous, among them—that it provides a standard and measure by which all past and present and future regimes and their founders can be investigated and judged. It is not, then, necessary to repeat this claim in connection with any particular kind of polity.

The only difficulty is this. Political science as presented in this book says nothing about lawgivers and laws, of which divine lawgivers and divine laws are one species; or about the relation between the art or craft of the lawgiver and the art or craft of rulers who are not lawgivers; or about the relation between the regimes based on laws and the regimes not based on laws. This serious omission can be shown, however, to be intentional and deliberate. It has the practical consequence that the book avoids the necessity of even enumerating certain delicate and controversial problems, which is perhaps not incompatible with the introductory character of the book or with the fact that it did not promise to enumerate all the sciences but only the generally known sciences (43.4). Unlike political science, jurisprudence, and theology, the science or the division of the science that is omitted here and that we may call the philosophic and political science of divine laws and revealed religions, was surely not generally known to Alfarabi's readers. It was in many ways a new science invented or established by Alfarabi himself.

The Philosophic Science of Religion

The origins or the germs of the new science, however, are contained in the "ancient" science of politics, especially in the second account of political science given by Alfarabi in this book. What distinguishes divine laws is the fact that they include both opinions about God, His attributes, and the universe, as well as actions. What Alfarabi called the virtuous royal craft in the first account included, besides the experiential faculty, only the faculty for the general rules given by a political science that had nothing to do with the theoretical sciences. This means that this ruling craft can establish and preserve a regime that contains only actions, not opinions. This limited kind of political science will not, obviously, be able to investigate divine laws.

Recall, however, that in the second account, this same virtuous ruling craft was, in addition to the experiential faculty, constituted by the "theoretical and practical sciences." Therefore, unlike the former, this ruling craft is prepared to establish and preserve regimes that contain actions as well as the opinions contained in divine laws. That is, this ruler possesses the craft that includes both the theoretical sciences (including the third part of divine science, which deals with God and His attributes) and the practical sciences. In addition, he possesses the experiential faculty through which he can discover or define and determine the specific form in which both knowledge and action can be presented to a particular group of men under given conditions.

It is true that Alfarabi does not say all this in so many words. But his silence here (106.1–4) is more telling than his explicit speech. He says that the experiential faculty must be joined to both the theoretical and the practical sciences and proceeds to say that the experiential faculty determines the particular "actions, ways of life, and positive dispositions." Now "positive disposition" can, of course, include knowledge and opinions. In fact it must. Otherwise, it would be hard to understand why the experiential faculty should be joined, not only to the practical sciences, but to the theoretical sciences as well.

But now comes the difficulty. For Alfarabi also says that the regime founded by such a ruler cannot be preserved unless there is an uninterrupted line of rulers who possess the very same qualifications as those of the founder, which is why the question of the education of future rulers who are "completely" kings becomes an important theme. This is so because a regime will inevitably degenerate in the absence of such a ruler. Yet one of the main reasons for laying down laws is that they be followed after the death of the lawgiver, when the community is no longer ruled by a man who possesses his qualifications. And we know by now that the main reason for the existence of jurisprudence and theology is to preserve the regime of the divine lawgiver after his death, when the religious community no longer has a divine lawgiver at its head.

During his lifetime, in fact, there was no law in the sense that jurists and theologians understand and practice it. What the divine lawgiver said or did was the living law, and he could change or abrogate it to meet new circumstances as they arose. No follower of a divine law or a revealed religion would take exception to the proposition that the best time was the lifetime of the divine lawgiver, or that the best arrangement would be to have an uninterrupted line of divine lawgivers. There is, then, no disagreement regarding the desirability of a state of affairs in which men do not follow the law, even the divine law, of a dead legislator but are ruled continuously by living philosopher-kings or divine lawgivers.

Nor, I believe, is there disagreement that this is a state of affairs that is unlikely to obtain because such men are very rare; or that, in their absence, the best alternative is to follow their intention as embodied in what they said and did. So the question of the laws or of the regime ruled by laws remains an important theme of political science. Alfarabi leads the reader to this theme in the *Enumeration of the Sciences* without discussing it explicitly.

What the *Enumeration of the Sciences* does, however, is to pose the problem and express an intention. Political science now coexists with jurisprudence and theology: this is a massive historical fact that it cannot ignore. The first account of political science, which is strictly practical, cannot coexist with jurisprudence and theology without being subordinated to or absorbed by them. Their subject matter is wider. It includes opinions about practical things and actions (e.g., prayers) that are related to theoretical things. This practical political science, on the other hand, deals with a special kind or one division of actions.

The only way this practical political science can preserve its independence and superior claim over its companions is to show that all these so-called theoretical opinions and all these actions that are related to so-called theoretical opinions are in fact practical. But then this practical political science will have to do two things. First, it has to prove this claim, which it cannot do if it remains a purely practical science. It must broaden its concern and somehow encompass all the theoretical sciences. It will need a theoretical dimension.

Second, it must develop a new branch or part of political science to deal with these theoretical opinions and with theoretically oriented actions. This will be a practical or political divine science or theology that keeps one eye on the theoretical sciences and another on human ends and actions. In this way, it will broaden its scope and deal with opinions as well as actions. This is now demanded by the facts of political life. Alfarabi will do this in the *Book of Religion,* which is the counterpart of chapter 5 of the *Enumeration of the Sciences.* What the *Enumeration of the Sciences* has done is to show that the strict division of sciences into practical and theoretical is no longer *practically* tenable. In the second account of political science there are two kinds of rulers: those who possess the "theoretical *and* practical sciences" (106.1; emphasis added) and those who "do not need . . . theoretical or practical philosophy" (106.15–16).

Political Philosophy and Religion

*M*edieval political philosophy is by and large a philosophy of religion, just as classical political philosophy is by and large a philosophy of the city and modern political philosophy is by and large a philosophy of the state. In chapter 5 of the *Enumeration of the Sciences,* Alfarabi juxtaposes the political philosophy of the ancients, that of Plato in particular, to jurisprudence and theology. In this way, he points to the unfinished task of political philosophy, namely, the need to develop a philosophy of religion. The relation between religion and philosophy in general and political philosophy in particular is the subject of the *Book of Religion,* the counterpart of chapter 5 of the *Enumeration of the Sciences* that fills in the gap in this latter work.

It presents religion as the central theme of a new political science or political philosophy—a theme that forces political philosophy to reconsider its relation to theoretical philosophy and to broaden its framework to include opinions about theoretical things in addition to opinions about practical things and actions. Thus one notices the Platonic character of the entire book. One notices, in addition, the point in the *Book of Religion* (46.22) where the expression "philosophy" is introduced and that the earlier distinction between theoretical and practical things in religion (secs. 2–3, 44.14–46.10) is said to be similar to the distinction between theoretical and practical philosophy.

Thus the distinction appears first in the description of religion even though it is now (sec. 5, 46.22–47.17) said to be similar to a distinction in philosophy. The origin of this distinction seems to be religious or political rather than philosophic. The *Enumeration of the Sciences* (105.15–106.2) includes the theoretical sciences in what makes up the excellent royal craft, but it does not discuss the legislation of opinions about theoretical things by the supreme ruler. It does refer to theoretical opinions, however, when giving an account of jurisprudence and theology (107.10–11, 107.16–108.2).

To this end, the *Book of Religion* (52.10ff.) repeats the account of political science given in the *Enumeration of the Sciences* (102.4ff.) but with certain omissions and additions. The most significant addition is an enumeration of all the beings, offered in a second account of political science (59.3ff.) as forming part of political science. The nearest thing to this political cosmology or theology in the *Enumeration of the Sciences* is the third division of divine science (99.14ff.), presented there, not as part of political science, but as the last part of metaphysics and the concluding part of the theoretical sciences. The new version of political science is presented in the *Book of Religion*, not in the beginning but after an account of religion and its relation to philosophy (theoretical as well as practical or political) on the one hand and jurisprudence on the other. Theology as a religious science, of which an elaborate account was given in the *Enumeration of the Sciences*, is silently dispensed with. The *Book of Religion* can therefore be said to substitute a political theology derived from theoretical and practical philosophy for theology as a religious science.

What Is Religion?

The *Book of Religion*, unlike the *Enumeration of the Sciences*, focuses directly and immediately upon religion. It begins with the following definition:

> Religion is opinions and actions, determined and limited by certain conditions, prescribed for a community by their supreme ruler, who seeks to achieve by their practicing them a definite goal with respect to them or by means of them. (43.3–4)

Broad and neutral, this definition sets forth no particular opinions about God, angels, prophecy and revelation, rewards and punishments in the hereafter, or morality. It consists of four elements that answer four questions. (1) What is religion? A set of opinions and actions determined and delimited by certain conditions. To use the analogy of medicine, religion is not like medical science but like the doctor's orders: do this and do not do that; when you feel pain in this spot, take two of these green pills. (2) What agent brings it about? The first or supreme ruler who is the founder, the being—human or whatever—who prescribes these opinions and actions. (3) For whom are these opinions and actions prescribed, or what is the material upon which the founder impresses these opinions and actions? A community, a multitude of human beings. The founder does not prescribe the religion for himself or merely for a few disciples, but for a community of a certain size. (4) What is the end, or why does the founder want the community to accept the opinions and perform the actions? He has a definite purpose in mind: either he wants them to achieve, or he himself wants to achieve, something by their practicing what he prescribes for them. Alfarabi takes up these four elements in the following order: the community (3); the founder (2), together with his purpose (4) and his art; and, finally, the content of the religion (1)—that is, the opinions and actions themselves. (Consider the relation between the four elements in the initial definition of religion in the *Book of Religion*, 44.3ff., and Aristotle's four causes.)

The Size of the Group

As soon as we look at religion as the medieval counterpart of the ancient city and the modern state, we begin to wonder about the size of the community that constitutes a religion. Are there any limits? Or does religion, unlike the city or the state, extend all the way from a very small community or even a private person, a family religion or private religion, to the largest conceivable community of human beings, a universal or world religion? There are limits, according to Alfarabi, but they extend beyond the city, and in both directions.

Four possible communities are mentioned (43.4–6): (1) the tribe; (2) the city or the region, that is, the city and its region or perhaps a number of independent cities in one region; (3) the "great" nation comprising a large number of cities or regions; and (4) many nations. A tribe can have its own religion. But a tribe is not a complete or perfect political community. It lacks certain elements—perhaps a permanent dwelling place, a minimum of diversity, or most of the arts—indispensable for a complete human community. With the city, the religious community becomes—at least with respect to size—the same as the political community.

The upper limit is a number of nations, but not all nations in the entire inhabited world. This limitation seems rather strange; the idea of a universal or world religion, one very much alive at the time, is either ignored or rejected. Alfarabi expresses, not what the followers of any particular religion believe the size of the religious community ought to be, but what the extent of actual communities is. That he neglects to mention universal or world religion is due either to his not believing a world religion in the strict sense possible or feasible, or to his deeming it impossible to obliterate, overlook, or overcome differences among human beings by any type of political community; and religion, beginning with the civic community, is a type of political community.

Now, we moderns find it strange to think of religion as a political community. Though we readily admit that there were times and places where political community did not take the form of the modern sovereign state, we tend to identify the complete political community with the state. We speak of city-*state* and of religious-*state*, almost as if we can understand and express the idea of a complete political community only through the state. For us, city and religion have lost the political connotation they had for the ancients and the medievals. Indeed, they would have to say something like state-*city* or state-*religion* in order to understand and express our notion of political life.

There are specific differences between the city, religion, and the state as forms of political community. But they have in common that each in its own way represents the whole or the constitutive element—the constitution—of political life. The question of the size of the political community is crucial for understanding the character of each of them. To be sure, the city is defined, not by its walls, but by its constitution or regime; and the state is defined, not by its borders, but by its form of government.

Still, there cannot be a city or a state without walls or borders. What are the walls or borders of religion or of a religious community? Since religion can extend beyond the city and the state—or since, as Alfarabi says, the religious community can be a city, a great nation, or many nations—then religion must comprehend a variety of possible sizes, and one must try to understand what happens to the quality of political or religious life as the community grows larger and larger. Though not discussed in the *Book of Religion*, we meet this question again and again in Alfarabi's other political writings and in the writings of his successors among the Muslim philosophers. Here, Alfarabi is willing to consider extending the community beyond the city to, at least, many nations. (But see *Book of Religion*, 53.20ff., where only the city and the nation are mentioned explicitly.)

The Founder: His Purpose

As we turn from the community to the founder and his purpose, we find that this, too, requires an extension of the classical classification of rulers

and ruling. The classification adopted by Alfarabi in his accounts of political science in the *Enumeration of the Sciences* (103.7–17) as well as in
the *Book of Religion* (54.17–55.16) is based on Plato's *Republic*. It divides ruling into two broad classes: (1) a virtuous or excellent rule whose
aim is that both the ruler and all the ruled attain true happiness; and (2)
an ignorant rule whose aim is that the ruler alone, the ruled alone, or
both ruler and ruled attain some lower good. The latter class is further
subdivided, according to the particular good pursued, into *(a)* indispensable (necessities of life), *(b)* vile (wealth), *(c)* base (pleasures), *(d)* ti-
mocratic (honor), *(e)* despotic (victory), and *(f)* democratic (freedom
and equality) regimes.

The classification of the founders of religions and of their religions
in the *Book of Religion* (43.6–44.6) includes the above classification of
regimes, with the important omission of the democratic regime. As a
consequence, one notices the absence of freedom and equality from the
aims pursued by the founders of ignorant cities (43.9–15). Then, two
new classes are added to the classification found in the political science
that Alfarabi attributes to the ancients. These are (3) the religion based
on error and (4) the religion based on falsification or falsehood.

In the first, the founder thinks himself to be excellent and wise and
his followers think and believe him to be excellent and wise, when in fact
he is not. The aim is for both the founder and his followers to attain
what he thinks is ultimate happiness, which is not in fact ultimate happiness. Both the founder and his followers are sincere believers who seek
to deceive neither themselves nor anyone else, but they are wrong in
their belief.

In the latter class, to the contrary, the ruler is not excellent or wise
and knows perfectly well that he is neither one nor the other. Yet he
deliberately induces his followers to believe that he is excellent and wise
and succeeds in fooling them. Unlike the founder who is in error, this
founder is not wandering in the dark. He knows exactly what he wants—
one of the lower goods of the ignorant rulers, such as wealth or pleasure
or honor. The deception he perpetrates among his followers—namely,
that both he and they will attain ultimate happiness—is meant to help
him use his followers to obtain that lower good for himself alone.

The addition of these last two classes of religion—ones Alfarabi also
lists elsewhere, notably in the *Virtuous City* (71.1ff.) and in the *Political
Regime* (104.3ff.), as classes of political regimes to indicate that in his
new political science political and religious regimes are more or less coex-

tensive—is not easy to explain. Error and willful deception have always been known as important elements in political life. Have they acquired added importance now that religion has come to dominate political life? And have they become so important that they characterize two whole new classes of regimes?

As far as their aims are concerned, the two new classes of religion are in fact variants of ignorant religion. Whatever the founder and his followers think about his virtue and wisdom, he definitely lacks virtue and wisdom; and his aim is one of the lower aims of the ignorant regimes. But there is a difference. Both the founder of an ignorant regime and his followers think that wealth or honor is the highest end of life. Either they have not even heard of virtue and wisdom; or they have heard about them but refused to listen; or, finally, they have heard about them but thought they were new gimmicks for making more money or having more fun. Blissful in their ignorance, they proclaim openly and proudly that happiness is the particular lower end they pursue.

With the advent of revealed religion, this state of happy ignorance—which neglects or openly rejects the claims of virtue and wisdom—has become difficult to sustain. In a world where so many founders and their followers claim to be in possession of virtue and wisdom, to be knowledgeable of the truth about all the beings, to be performing all the right actions, and, by dint of these opinions and actions, to be marching straight to ultimate happiness in the next world—in such a world, it is extremely difficult to remain immune to the temptations of virtue and wisdom, especially since their possession is now equated by most human beings with the highest claim to rule. Under these conditions, a potential ruler can hardly expect to gain followers by simply proclaiming wealth or honor as the highest end of his regime. Rather, he must jump on the bandwagon of the higher religions and either deeming or claiming himself to be excellent and wise succeed in making his followers believe as much of him. In this sense, the political situation has changed radically from pagan times. Plain, healthy ignorance is no longer respectable. The widespread use of self-deception and deliberate falsification reflects how important it has now become to be excellent and wise and to possess the necessary qualifications of the founder of a virtuous or excellent religion.

The Founder: His Art

In order to accommodate the new type of ruler and founder Alfarabi wishes to present here, this individual's qualifications are redefined in the

immediate sequel (44.6–13). The qualifications of the excellent founding ruler consist of (1) the royal craft together with (2) a revelation from
God to him. This position appears to be perfectly orthodox. Alfarabi
neglects to elaborate on the qualifications of the rulers or founders of
ignorant, erring, and false religions, and this gives the impression that
their craft is merely royal—that they are in fact mere worldly kings—
while the excellent founding ruler is both king and prophet: he possesses
the royal craft that others possess and, in addition, receives revelation.

But this is only a first impression. Alfarabi has a much more elevated
royal craft in mind. He will explain that, although one can speak of royal
in connection with all kinds of ruling crafts, only the craft that encompasses practical and theoretical philosophy is truly royal (54.13–14,
55.10–11, 58.7ff., and 60.5ff.). That is, the royal craft of the founder of
the excellent religion is not one of the run-of-the-mill variety possessed
by every worldly king but the craft that is truly royal: it combines practical and theoretical philosophy with revelation. But this position is still
somewhat orthodox, for it implies both that the founder of the excellent
religion possesses the highest qualifications of a worldly king—the king
who is not merely a king but a philosopher-king—and that he possesses,
in addition, a revelation from God.

It is therefore crucial that we understand the specific function assigned to revelation in the operation of this ruler-founder's craft. By revelation, says Alfarabi, the excellent founding ruler only determines the
actions and the opinions in the excellent religion. This is obviously a
crucial equation: revelation equals determination. Actions and opinions
as universals and as general rules are not said to have anything to do with
revelation; they remain the preserves of practical and theoretical philosophy.

Determination, further, is done through the experiential faculty (see
Enumeration of the Sciences, 104.1–3), which is identified here as prudence or practical judgment (59.1).[1] Determination is made through
revelation in one of three ways (43.7–12). First, all the opinions and actions are revealed in determined forms, and the founder merely communicates them as revealed. Second, through revelation, the founder acquires a power or a faculty with which he himself determines the opinions
and the actions; in this case, revelation consists of his acquiring the faculty that reveals to him how to determine the opinions and actions, and

1. On the metaphorical use of "wisdom" *(ḥikma)* for "prudence" *(taʿaqqul)*, see *Selected
Aphorisms,* aphorism 52 (61.10 and 62.1) and passim.

the founder himself does the actual determination. Third, some opinions and actions are determined in the first manner and others in the second.

The first two meanings of revelation seem to correspond to direct and indirect revelation—for example, the Quran and the Traditions of Muhammad—or to revelation and divine inspiration or intuition. Considered in isolation, they would describe the common view of prophecy and of the founding of divine religions. But Alfarabi joins them to the royal craft. If royal craft denotes simply the ability to rule, the combination would again describe the common view of a prophet who is also a king. Difficulty arises when we learn that by royal craft he means theoretical and practical philosophy and that revelation is in fact a substitute, *not* for theoretical and practical philosophy— that is, the common view of revelation—but for practical judgment or the experiential faculty normally acquired through long experience in political life. In the first meaning cited above, everything is determined by revelation; and practical judgment can be dispensed with. In the second, practical judgment is acquired through revelation rather than through long experience in political life.

Let us look at the analogy of medicine cited in chapter 5 of the *Enumeration of the Sciences* (104.3–8). In the second case, the physician will need to know medical science and will be given the ability to determine particular remedies for particular cases by revelation instead of long experience. In the first case, however, revelation will tell him directly what particular remedy to prescribe for particular cases. But why does this physician need to know medical science at all? Correspondingly, why does a prophet need to know theoretical and practical philosophy? This question cannot be considered without going into Alfarabi's view of how revelation takes place and how a power or faculty is attained through revelation.

He does not speak of these matters here but limits himself to saying that they "have been explained in theoretical science" (44.12). We do not come across them in chapter 5 of the *Enumeration of the Sciences* either, which indicates that the science of revelation—like the science of religion of which it is the theoretical counterpart—is not a generally known science. I assume that by theoretical science Alfarabi means the science of the soul or psychology and its faculties or powers, that is, the domain within Aristotelian inquiry where the question of revelation is normally discussed. In the *Book of Religion*, Alfarabi merely assumes the theoretical or philosophic explanation of revelation, namely, that revelation "passes through" the theoretical and practical faculties to the imaginative and motive faculties, which are to be controlled by practical judgment. The agent of revelation par excellence is the divine mind called active intellect, which is generally thought to come into contact with the human theoretical intellect.

At issue here is, again, the autonomy of practical judgment and of Aristotle's practical science. Practical judgment has been subordinated and joined to the theoretical and practical faculties. Through revelation, one may even be able to dispense with it or acquire it effortlessly. That is merely another way of saying that practical judgment cannot be the supreme faculty that grasps the principles of practical or political science. On the other hand, Platonic political science, which debunks practical judgment and insists on the necessity of theoretical and practical philosophy informing practice, is supported by the idea of revelation in which the ultimate source of political life (of the opinions and actions in the city) is not the human being who truly knows—the philosopher-prophet—but the revealer.

Yet we must not underestimate the close connection between revelation and practical judgment. Both intimate the idea of an immediate grasp of what ought to be said or done under particular conditions, of almost miraculously hitting the mark in the face of innumerable alternatives, something no theoretical or practical science can do. By drawing our attention to additional things in which revelation and practical judgment are related, Alfarabi widens the range of activity of practical judgment. It is now expected to determine opinions as well as actions.

Opinions

Although the opinions set forth in the excellent religion concern in part the same objects as the ones investigated in the theoretical sciences, they are to be distinguished with respect to the knowledge and certainty pursued in the latter. Not the result of speculation or *theoria*, these theoretical opinions are determined and delimited descriptions of theoretical things presented to the community by the founder with a definite aim in mind. Further, not restricted to theoretical affairs, the opinions in religion cover practical affairs as well. Theory and practice merge so imperceptibly into one another that the sharp distinction between theoretical and practical knowledge based on the distinction between things one can know but not do and things one can both know and do cannot always be applied to these opinions.

Alfarabi divides religious opinions into two groups, one encompassing descriptions of theoretical things and the other voluntary, practical

things (44.14–45.24). The first group consists of descriptions of the following: God's attributes; the spiritual beings—that is, the intellects of
the heavenly bodies and the divine mind called the active intellect— their
ranks of order, their relation to God, and the activity of each; the generation of the universe and all its parts, the ranks of order of its parts, their
interconnection, and their relation to God and to the spiritual beings;
the generation of human beings, the soul, and the intellect, as well as
the intellect's place in the universe and its relation to God and the spiritual beings; what prophecy is and how revelation takes place; and death
and the life to come, plus the happiness of the virtuous and the misery
of the vicious in the hereafter.[2] The second group of opinions, meant
to be concerned with voluntary, practical things, consists exclusively of
descriptions of past and present, excellent and base (ignorant and erring)
prophets, kings, and rulers; their good and bad deeds; the fate of their
souls; and the fate of the souls of their followers.

It is plain that these two groups of religious opinions correspond to
the matters investigated in theoretical science and in political science, as
can be seen from a cursory look at chapters 4 and 5 of the *Enumeration
of the Sciences*. Together, they form a comprehensive, detailed, and specific description of the universe and of political life. A striking difference
between the theoretical opinions and the corresponding investigations
in theoretical science is that theoretical science is analytical and seeks to
know the relations among the parts of the universe (including human
beings, the soul, and the intellect) as concurrent phenomena, while opinions consist of descriptions that emphasize the genetic, almost temporal,
descent in the universe step-by-step from God to human beings. The
cosmic structure discussed in theoretical philosophy is now presented as
a cosmogony or cosmic history. The difference is even more striking
when we compare the way political science investigates the classes of rulers and regimes with the descriptions in the second group of religious
opinions: these descriptions are presented as a political history of prophets and kings, of good and bad rulers and communities past and present,
and of their rewards and punishments in this world and the next.

These and other features make it clear that while such religious opinions may concern the same things as the ones investigated in theoretical
and political science, they are not scientific opinions. They are descriptions the community receives from the prophet, who in turn receives

2. Avicenna includes these topics in the part devoted to the "branches of divine science"
in *Divisions of the Rational Sciences*, 114–16.

them through the operation of the royal craft. They presuppose theoretical and practical science—included in the royal craft—but they are a religious version of theoretical and practical science, transformed by the royal craft for a practical end.

This transformation is described by Alfarabi at the end of his statement on religious opinions (45.20–24). The contents of religious opinions, he says, ought to be

> so described as to make the citizens imagine everything that is in the city—kings, rulers, and servants; their ranks, the relation between them, and their subordination to one another; and everything else prescribed for them—so that these descriptions become similitudes, or examples, for them to follow in their respective ranks and activities.

The universe and theoretical things in general, as well as political things, are to be transformed by the royal craft into descriptions that present images of the city and its parts and the relation between its parts in such a way that the citizens see in the universe and in political history something like their city, examples that can be actively imitated by them in everyday life. Theoretical science is thought to engage in investigations whose aim is to know the universe and human beings; it is not concerned with the city and the practical life of the citizens, or with the question whether the universe is an image of the city in general, let alone of any particular city. The royal craft, on the other hand, is concerned with determining the opinions of the citizens of a particular regime, and the opinions must be such as to present images of their city and provide them with examples to imitate in their activities; that is, the founder must determine these examples in such a way that, by imitating them, the citizens will perform certain activities but not others.

Clearly, the entire process of transformation that results in religious opinions is guided by the practical aim of the founder, by what he wants the citizens of his city to think and do as citizens. (One has to imagine a cross where theoretical stands at the top and practical at the bottom of the vertical line, and activity at the left end and opinion at the right end of the horizontal line. The four parts thus produced will be theoretical-activities at the upper left side and theoretical-opinions at the upper right side, while practical-activities will be at the lower left side and practical-opinions at the lower right side.)

Actions

The other part of religion consists of actions. Alfarabi's description of religious activities (46.1–9) is not as elaborate as his description of religious opinions. Religious activities seem to follow from religious opinions. For the most part their function is to establish these opinions firmly in the soul through ritual activities and ritual speeches that express praise or blame—glorifying and praising God, spiritual beings, angels, prophets, and excellent kings and rulers; and condemning vicious, erring, and ignoble kings and rulers, past and present. This is the first group of religious activities, which are a practical supplement to, or an application of, religious opinions about theoretical and practical things. Through the repetition of such activities in speech and deed, the citizens express their attachment to religious opinions. Just as the religious opinions themselves were meant to have a practical, political use, so must this group of religious activities be determined with a view to presenting images of the city and providing the citizens with examples to follow in their respective ranks and functions.

The second group of activities, to which Alfarabi pays only limited attention, consist of activities by means of which the citizens deal with one another; the things one must do by oneself and the things one must do when dealing with others. Alfarabi does not describe these activities. He limits himself to saying that they ought to be determined and that justice, which is a practical virtue, must be defined in connection with each one. The limited attention paid to these practical activities is somewhat puzzling, especially in view of the practical orientation of Alfarabi's account of religion as a whole. It may be inferred that these practical activities are not the hallmark of religion, which is characterized by opinions and the first group of activities, the basic elements that hold the religious community together and make it almost unnecessary to pay excessive attention to purely practical matters. Belief in God and the angels as well as in rewards and punishments in the hereafter and the right view of past and present good and bad rulers and communities, confirmed by the constant practice of the rituals in speech and deed, make it easier for human beings to do what is right.

Definitions

So far, Alfarabi has presented his own account of religion. He turns next to the common view of religion or, rather, to what the names used to designate a religion commonly signify. These are *milla* and *dīn,* on the one hand, and *shariʿa* and *sunna*, on the other (46.11–14). *Milla* and *dīn*, he says, are almost synonymous.[3] *Shariʿa* and *sunna*, he adds, are also almost synonymous.[4]

There is also the question of the relation between the two pairs, or between religion and law. The second pair, he says, is for the most part applied to determined activities, that is, to the second of the two parts which constitute religion, to ritual activities and speeches and to transactions. Yet one of the terms that make up the second pair, *shariʿa*, may designate the determined opinions or the first part of religion also. Thus, *shariʿa*, *milla*, and *dīn* are truly synonymous; or, the differences among them are not significant and can be ignored. *Sunna* is left out, apparently because it does not designate opinions.

Common usage reflects the common understanding of religion and seems to presume the distinction between religious opinions and religious activities as well as between opinion-oriented and action-oriented religions. But activities alone no more suffice to make up a religion than do opinions alone. Broadly speaking, Alfarabi's account and the common view of religion are in agreement. However, the common view tends to see religion more as a law *(shariʿa)*, as determined activities and defined opinions to be accepted and followed. Of course, the common view is not unaware of the lawgiver, the community, and the aim of the lawgiver, but it is aware of these things in the context of the determined opinions of the religion received from the lawgiver. This is also true of how the followers of a particular religion view other religions, earlier or contemporary.

All these considerations are included by Alfarabi among the determined opinions of the religion. What the followers of a particular religion believe to be excellent or wise in general—their views about the excellence and wisdom of other religions and their lawgivers as well as about the excellence and wisdom of their own religion and their own lawgiver—originate in their own lawgiver. To the extent that they are faithful believers who merely accept what he says, they are in no position to judge whether he was in fact excellent or wise. This is obviously a vicious circle: commitment, faith, and unquestioning obedience are es-

---

3. As I understand it, the difference between them in common usage is that for a Muslim, *dīn* denotes *the* religion, while *milla* denotes religion in general. Books by Muslims about the doctrines of all or most religions are books not about *adyān* (the plural of *dīn*) but about *milal* (the plural of *milla*). Alfarabi calls his treatise *Book of the Milla;* and *milla*, not *dīn*, is the term he has used thus far.

4. Again, as I understand it, *shariʿa* is more properly the divine law, while *sunna* is the more general term designating any law or tradition.

sential for the functioning of a religion; detachment, a certain rebelliousness, and free questioning are essential for understanding religion and judging its true excellence.

Alfarabi suggests the following formula for distinguishing between an excellent and an erring religion (46.15–21). One should look primarily at the first class of opinions in religion, the ones concerning theoretical things. These opinions are expressed in one of two ways: through a name that pertains to something in particular and habitually signifies the thing itself, or through the name of a similitude that imitates or resembles it. Every opinion in an excellent religion must be either the truth or a similitude of the truth. Otherwise the religion is a religion of error.

So far Alfarabi has said nothing unacceptable to the followers of any religion. The opinion about God's oneness can be expressed by the name "one," a name that habitually signifies the idea of oneness itself, not some other idea similar to, but not identical with, oneness. However, the opinion about God's power may be expressed by the name "hand," and the opinion about His knowledge may be expressed by the names "seeing" or "hearing"—similitudes, not identical with, but imitations of, power and knowledge.

To the question how we can tell in each case whether the opinion has been expressed in one or the other of these two ways, the answer is: we cannot tell for certain unless we ourselves know the truth. For how could we know that God does not have a hand unless we know the truth about God's corporeality or incorporeality? And "truth in general," says Alfarabi, "is that which a human being ascertains by himself by way of primary knowledge or by way of a demonstration" (46.18–19). This does not mean that in every case we first learn the truth and then judge religious opinions, or that we need to know the whole truth at the outset. But it does mean that religion contains opinions whose truth can be ascertained (i.e., the truth is potentially or in principle ascertainable) by a human being either through primary knowledge or through demonstration, or else opinions that can be ascertained as being similitudes or resemblances of the truth. A religion that contains opinions whose truth is *impossible* for a human being to ascertain in one of these two ways under any circumstances is, according to Alfarabi, a religion of error (46.19–21).

With respect to these theoretical opinions, ignorance and the regimes based on ignorance are not at issue. Here an assertion is being made about a being or about what ultimate happiness is, and it must be the truth, a similitude of the truth, or an error. Ignorance means that one does not know and does not say anything about such matters, and the ignorant regimes are regimes in which it is asserted that a human being's end consists in pleasure, for example. This is a practical, not a theoretical, assertion, although it may of course assume a wrong view about a theoretical matter, for instance, that God does not exist.

The difficulty seems to be this: if we keep an open mind about religion and take a large comparative view of religions, we find that there are various types of religion. When we look at the contents of certain high, advanced, or older religions, we are particularly impressed by the presence of opinions or views regarding the world as a whole. We are also faced by the assertions made by the believers in, or the defenders of, these views that they are true or are *the* true views about the world. Correspondingly, we are faced with science or philosophy, a discipline that makes a systematic effort to understand the world's nature and structure. It, too, seeks true views, especially *the* true view about the world. Philosophy and religion cannot be brought face to face directly. This can only lead to conflict and misunderstanding.

The philosopher must first attempt to understand what religion is, and he cannot do so by engaging in theological controversies or by attacking or defending this or that religion on the basis of the views of the philosopher's own religion. Whatever its merits, this approach is not scientific. In order to understand religion, the philosopher must first understand that religion is not science or philosophy and not expect religion to be or do what it is not and what it cannot do. Religion as Alfarabi defines it consists of the four constitutive elements into which he divides opinions and activities: theoretical opinions, theoretical activities, practical opinions, and practical activities. One point at which philosophy and religion converge seems to concern opinions about theoretical things: both are concerned with the world as a whole and especially with the highest things. There is a fundamental difference, however. Religion expresses the truth, not in scientific terms, but in common, habitual terms. Of course, it does not restrict itself to these but employs–and must employ—expressions that signify the resemblances of things in addition. This is a fundamental difference that the philosopher must understand and accept. The hope for a philosophic or scientific religion is based on misunderstanding the fundamental character of religion.

The crucial question or alternative is whether it is possible to relate the expressions employed in religion—designating either the things themselves or their images—to what science or philosophy considers the truth to be; or differently stated, whether there is a path leading from religious views to philosophic or scientific truth. Alfarabi does not enter into detail here regarding what the truth is. He speaks in general terms: generally speaking, truth is what a human being can ascertain, either through primary knowledge as self-evident or through demonstration. He does not say that science or philosophy already possesses such a truth. Religion, on the other hand, claims it possesses the truth. Alfarabi seems to be asking the question "Is this a claim that a human being by himself, unaided by revelation, can possibly ascertain as true—either as self-evident or as demonstrated—or else as an image of the truth?" To this question Alfarabi gives no positive answer. Yet it seems that if religion is virtuous or excellent, a positive answer ought in principle to be forthcoming. That he gives a negative answer suggests the following: if it is *impossible* to ascertain the truth of the theoretical views of a religion, it is an errant religion.

Cautious as this view of religion is, it reflects a fundamental position regarding the relation between science or philosophy and religion. It implies, first, that the two are related or that it is legitimate to ask about the truth of the theoretical views in a religion and, second, that the theoretical views in religion contain nothing inherently supernatural or suprarational in the strict sense. There are other possible answers, given by theologians of various persuasions. They may say that the two are not related but are concerned with two different worlds. Or they may say that the two are related but that religion communicates truths inherently and eternally hidden from, and beyond the reach of, human beings: they are mysteries a human being can only accept and perhaps seek to understand but can never hope to know.

Alfarabi's view requires him to explore further the mysterious relationship between religion and science or philosophy. To be sure, that science or philosophy and religion are not related can mean that the truths of religion are beyond human intellectual grasp, but it can also mean that the world of religion can be apprehended by a human being and the truth of religious opinions—opinions referring to things directly as well as opinions presenting images of them—can be found out, not by reason or science or philosophy, but only through exercise, activity, the heart, or taste. This is the mystical view, where *ergon* rather than *logos* is the way to the mysterious One-Beyond-Being-and-Nonbeing, a view held by pagan thinkers such as Plotinus and Muslim thinkers such as al-Ghazālī.

We are not now considering the further view that all religions are ignorant, wrong, or base—that is, made up of lies meant to deceive the

ignorant multitude, divide them into warring sects, and exploit them—
a view attributed to the great physician al-Rāzī and held in modern times
by Marx. But it is a view useful to recall if we are to have a sensible appreciation of Alfarabi's position. Alfarabi's quest for the virtuous or excellent
religion indicates not only that he did not hold such a view but that he
had the highest regard for religion compatible with the practice of science or philosophy. He saw in religion *the* alternative to science or philosophy, an alternative whose claim to be the true way had to be given the
most serious consideration.

Religion and Philosophy

Alfarabi proceeds to deduce the similarity between the excellent religion
and philosophy (46.22–47.17, where the expression "philosophy" is introduced for the first time) and then to divide both—in part on the basis
of the analogy of philosophy to religion—into theoretical and practical
parts. This seems to call for changing the expressions "opinions" and
"actions" into "theoretical things" and "practical things," respectively, a
change that leads to important consequences. The two pairs of expressions appear to be coextensive when applied to religion. Thus Alfarabi
says that the theoretical things in religion are the things a human being
may know but cannot perform.

Nevertheless, matters seem somewhat more complicated. For there is
the apparent identification of the theoretical faculty with the "theoretical
calculative," or "theoretical deliberative," faculty.[5] The practical things,
too, are not mere activities but things that a human being can perform
when he knows them. Thus the practical things involve knowledge, and
the theoretical things involve calculation or deliberation. A preliminary
surface impression is that the resemblance between philosophy and religion applies to each of the two parts of religion and philosophy, respectively, whereas a subsequent, deeper impression is that what is essentially
practical (religion) resembles what is essentially theoretical (philosophy)
in the way that what is essentially particular resembles or exemplifies what
is essentially universal, or in the way that what is essentially determined
and limited resembles or exemplifies what is not determined or limited.

5. For the curious expression "theoretical calculative" or "theoretical deliberative" *(nazariyya fikriyya)*, see *Book of Religion*, 46.23, where it is defined as what one may know but not
do. Calculation or deliberation results in (practical) knowledge. See the meaning of *fikriyya*
in *Selected Aphorisms*, aphorisms 7 (29.15–30.2), 33, 94 (96.8–10), and 95; and *Attainment
of Happiness*, 2.4, 20.11ff. The expression *nazariyya fikriyya* is not repeated in *Book of Religion*.

Further, resemblance recalls image. Yet instead of elaborating on the statement that the excellent religion resembles philosophy as its image, that it takes philosophy as the example and model in prescribing opinions and activities, or that it is the practical, determined, and limited embodiment of philosophy, Alfarabi abandons the question of resemblance and image. He turns instead to a complicated discussion of the relation between part and whole, subordinate and superior. The discussion seems to aim, not at explaining how the excellent religion resembles philosophy, but at preparing the declaration that the royal art is subordinate to philosophy.

Thus the practical things in religion have their universals in practical philosophy. Such universals are limited or qualified with determinations in religion. The similarity between the practical part of religion and the practical part of philosophy is qualified by the subordination of religion to the practical part of philosophy. In the case of the theoretical part, the distinction is not between unqualified and qualified but between what is demonstrated and what is taken without demonstration. Hence the situation here is reversed: it is in philosophy that the theoretical things are demonstrated, whereas in religion they are taken without demonstration. The practical part of religion is both subordinate to and part of practical philosophy. The theoretical part of religion is subordinate to but not part of theoretical philosophy. Philosophy, without reference to parts, gives the demonstrations of what is in religion, again with no reference to parts. Finally, the royal art giving rise to religion, in both of its parts, is subordinate to philosophy; nothing is said about its being part of philosophy, and so far nothing is said regarding its need of theoretical or practical philosophy.

One part of religion, the practical, is both part and subordinate; another part of religion, the theoretical, is simply subordinate. Hence both parts together are subordinate to philosophy as a whole. The royal art, which brings about both parts of religion, is, similarly, subordinate to philosophy. This does not contradict the assertion that one part of religion and one part of the royal art, the practical in both cases, are also parts of practical philosophy. But the royal art as a whole, being a practical art, should have been said to be both part of and subordinate to practical philosophy, not subordinate to philosophy as a whole. Here again, the problem of the relation between calculation or deliberation and the two parts of philosophy is left in the dark.[6] The statement raises also

6. But see *Selected Aphorisms,* aphorism 7 (29.15): "the *fikriyya* is that [faculty] with which we deliberate *(nurawwī)* about the thing we want to do."

the question of the difficulties involved in the distinction between the theoretical part and the practical part in both philosophy and religion, which in turn raises questions regarding the ultimate tenability of the similarity between philosophy and religion and of the subordination of the one to the other, throwing a dark shadow on the earlier reference (44.6) to the royal art and its relation to revelation.

Earlier, the art of the supreme excellent ruler was said to be royal conjoined to a revelation, not to philosophy, as in the *Attainment of Happiness,* in the *Political Regime,* or even in the *Virtuous City.*[7] Revelation was said to do two things: either reveal all opinions and actions as determined or qualified (cf. *Virtuous City* on revelation) or provide the ruler with the power or faculty to do the determinations himself or do some in one way and others in the other way. Unlike in the *Virtuous City,* nothing is said anywhere in the *Book of Religion* about the revelation of unqualified opinions and activities or of universals. Now, however, the royal art is mentioned alone without revelation; philosophy takes the place of revelation and the royal art is subordinated to philosophy, not to revelation. The division into practical and theoretical refers primarily to religion. When Alfarabi mentions the expression "practical philosophy" for the first time, he does so by noting that "all the excellent laws[8] are subordinate to the universals in practical philosophy" (47.5–6). This is what he attempts to show in the rest of the *Book of Religion.*

Dialectic and Rhetoric

The legislation or institution of religion by the supreme ruler through his royal art seems to be complete now. Dialectic and rhetoric appear to perform the subordinate functions of correcting and defending the opinions and establishing them more firmly. Dialectic is presented as having a field wider than that of demonstration. It provides "strong opinion" in those things regarding which, or regarding most of which, demonstration gives certainty. Rhetoric has a still wider field: it persuades regarding things that are not such as to be demonstrated or looked into by dialectic.

The excellent religion is not meant for philosophers or those whose

---

7. *Virtuous City* (58.20) is closer in this respect to the initial account of the supreme ruler in *Book of Religion* (44.6–7), while *Political Regime* is closer to the accounts of political science in *Book of Religion* (secs. 11ff., 52.10ff.).

8. That is, *sharāʾiʿ*. Alfarabi took pains in the immediately preceding paragraph to widen the meaning of this term to include actions as well, that is, to make it coextensive with excellent religion.

rank is such that they can be addressed by way of philosophy only. Most of those who learn the opinions of the religion are of a lower rank, either by nature or because they are too occupied with other things to reach the higher rank. However, most of them are not so low as not to understand the generally known *(mashhūrāt)* and the objects of persuasion *(muqniʿāt)* (48.1–3)—hence the great use of dialectic and rhetoric. The reference here is clearly to the postlegislative relevance of dialectic and rhetoric. Poetics seemed more relevant to the legislative moment. Yet that referred to the opinions themselves, not to the methods of communicating them. The latter are said in the *Attainment of Happiness* to be persuasive.

Jurisprudence, Religion, and Philosophy

The true successor of the founder of the religion who can change the law is not discussed in chapter 5 of the *Enumeration of the Sciences,* at least not in connection with jurisprudence. Therefore the *Enumeration of the Sciences* does not point to the alternative to jurisprudence or to the fact that jurisprudence is a second-best alternative, the best being a true successor.[9] The art of jurisprudence is an art that becomes necessary due to the absence of a true *imām* and king. The characterization of this art in the *Book of Religion* resembles that which is stated in chapter 5 of the *Enumeration of the Sciences* and so does its division into two parts; but the exposition of its principles is much more elaborate in the *Book of Religion* and includes details not found in chapter 5 of the *Enumeration of the Sciences.* This elaboration has to do precisely with the method of jurisprudence and with what the jurist must know: laws, language (rhetoric), the generally known *(mashhūr),* customs, traditions—either generally known *(mashhūrāt)* or persuasive *(muqniʿa)*—and so forth.

Jurisprudence is concerned either with practical particulars whose universals are contained in political science or with scientific matters. With respect to the first, it is part of political science and subordinate to practical philosophy (cf. 48.14ff.). The latter are either particulars whose universals are contained in theoretical philosophy or images of things *subordinate* to theoretical philosophy (cf. 46.22, "theoretical calculative," or "theoretical deliberative"). Therefore, it is a part of theoretical philosophy and *subordinate* to it. This is the link between jurisprudence and political science that is missing in chapter 5 of the *Enumeration of the Sciences.* (In both content and form, the account of the relation between

9. This is clear from *Book of Religion,* sec. 8, beginning. Cf. the dimensions of this problem in *Virtuous City, Political Regime,* and *Selected Aphorisms.*

jurisprudence and philosophy presented at 48.14ff. and especially at 52.4–9 is a repetition of the account of the relation between religion and philosophy set forth at 46.22–47.17.)

With respect to the practical part of jurisprudence, its universals are now said to be contained in political science, not in practical philosophy. And the practical part of jurisprudence is said to be part of political science, not of practical philosophy. It is, however, said to be subordinate to practical philosophy. There is, apparently, a distinction to be made between political science and practical philosophy, and it goes along with Alfarabi's allusion to the possible subordination of political science in all its parts to practical philosophy. (This distinction and subordination seem to be connected with the problem of knowledge as one and fractioned discussed in Plato's *Sophist*, 257c7–d3. See Klein 1965, 84–86.)

In addition, we have now a bipartite division of things theoretical in jurisprudence. First are the particulars whose universals are contained in theoretical philosophy. This can mean the God of theoretical philosophy compared to the God of this or that religion. These are, of course, not the particulars of a universal in the strict sense, but neither was "writing human being" the particular of the universal "human being" (it would have to be *this* and *that* human being as against "human being"). By particulars, Alfarabi has meant "determined" or "qualified" in the sense of his example, in which case God with the attributes assigned to Him in various religions as opposed to God without attributes will be what is meant. Similarly, the cosmos, angels, and so forth as "demonstrated" would be "universals," whereas without demonstrations and with qualifications, they would be particulars. Second are the images of things subordinate to theoretical philosophy. "Subordinate," or "part," was defined (47.8ff.) to mean either taking without demonstration what is demonstrated in the higher science or containing determinations (particulars) whose "causes" are given by the higher science. Hence the phrase here means "images of particulars (determinations) whose causes or the demonstrations of whose universals are given in theoretical philosophy."

The whole question is whether it makes sense to speak of particulars and determinations of theoretical things and still call them theoretical things rather than opinions. It is assumed that theoretical things in religion equal opinions. Is Alfarabi simply trying to magnify these opinions by calling them "theoretical" in order to point to a certain similarity and relationship? (See Klein 1965, 85.) The distinction between the first and the second is this: the first entails particulars versus universals, whereas the second entails images versus particulars versus universals. "Contained" means the same as subordinate to: for it is in theoretical philosophy that the universals, and only the universals, are either known by primary knowledge or demonstrated.

This division silently contradicts the apparent meaning of section 4 of the *Book of Religion,* where Alfarabi seems to say that theoretical opinions as determined in excellent religions are either true or the image of what is true, "true" defined as that which a human being can ascertain by primary knowledge or by demonstration. This distinction is now repeated, but we have come far enough to know that the theoretical opinions in religion and in jurisprudence cannot be true in this sense, since only the universals of theoretical things—not the opinions that have to do with particulars, for example, God as believed in by this or that nation—can be true in this sense. We know also that the images are direct images, not of what is true, but of the particulars of what is true (cf. *Virtuous City* on the imagination). Both must be subordinate to theoretical philosophy in the sense that what is particular and determined is subordinate to what is universal and unqualified, not in the sense that the higher science gives demonstrations of this or that particular God. If there is a demonstration at all to be given, it must be given by political science.

To return to the first, or practical, part, it makes sense to say that it is part of political science and subordinate to political philosophy only if political science is understood to contain the universals *and* to give the causes of the particulars (cf. the definition of human and political philosophy in *Enumeration of the Sciences,* chap. 5, 104–7). Hence political science becomes the link between religion and philosophy. Since political science is both part of and subordinate to philosophy, religion can be said to be part of and subordinate to philosophy, for it is part of political science. By introducing political science as the pivot for the practical part of religion or jurisprudence, the relationship is now made clear. The thesis will be completed when political science is made to intervene in the theoretical part as its functions unfold. One needs to imagine three circles—philosophy, political science, and religion—each inside the other.

Political Science: The City, the Universe, and Human Beings

The *Book of Religion* answers the questions raised by chapter 5 of the *Enumeration of the Sciences* about the way jurisprudence and religion or the divine law are related to political science. The distinction between things theoretical and practical first appears in the *Book of Religion* in the way religious opinions are distinguished from actions with respect to jurisprudence. Philosophy, too, is divided into theoretical and practical parts. The practical, or action, part of religion and jurisprudence is said to be part of and subordinate to practical philosophy; and the theoretical, or opinion, part of religion and jurisprudence is said to be part of and subordinate to theoretical philosophy. However, this explicit answer is too broad. It obscures the way jurisprudence and religion are related to political science or political philosophy as distinguished from philosophy in general or from theoretical *and* practical philosophy. As one looks at the end products—religion and jurisprudence—one sees that the opinions and actions they contain or are concerned with resemble, are part of, or are subordinate to theoretical and practical philosophy, respectively. Jurisprudence is clearly subordinated to lawgiving or the founding of religion, and the founding of religion is described as the product of the activity or operation of the royal craft, which is said to be subordinate to philosophy (47.16–17). But to which philosophy? And is it subordinate to both parts of philosophy or to political philosophy in particular?

Like the *Enumeration of the Sciences* (102.3ff. and 104.10ff.), the *Book of Religion* (52.10ff. and 59.3ff.) presents two accounts of political science. In the first, the royal craft covers the "general rules" and the power of actual determination, which is identified with what the ancients called prudence or practical judgment. The general rules are given by the political science that is *part* of philosophy and is concerned exclusively with activities and voluntary matters (58.7ff.); that is, it corresponds to political science as it is treated in Aristotle's *Nicomachean Ethics* and *Politics*. In the second account, the *Enumeration of the Sciences* had said that the excellent royal craft is made up of many things, including the theoretical and practical sciences and, in addition, the experiential faculty. The *Book of Religion* (56.8–19) distinguishes between the "first," or founding, excellent royal craft and a royal craft that is subordinate to the first and applies the founder's law. The latter, Alfarabi says later, "does not need philosophy by nature" (60.14). The best arrangement, then, is a succession of rulers who possess the royal craft of the first, or founding, ruler, who needs philosophy by nature.

In the second account of political science, the *Book of Religion* says that

> it [political science that is part of philosophy] explains that the first excellent royal craft cannot operate in a complete or perfect manner except by knowing the universals of this art [i.e., the political art] in [such

a way] that theoretical philosophy be joined to them [the universals
of this political art] and prudence or practical judgment be added to
them. (60.5–7)

Here, then, the first excellent royal craft is essentially a political craft.
First and foremost, it must know the universals of the political art. Theoretical philosophy is not one of the two constitutive elements of this royal
craft but must be joined or attached to the universals of the political art
because the royal craft must have access to theoretical philosophy in order to perfect its operation, just as prudence or practical judgment is not
part of the royal craft but must be added to the royal craft so that it can
make the particular determinations.

The *Book of Religion* is not concerned with accounting for or enumerating the sciences but with religion. After discussing what religion is, it
proceeds to give an account of political science to explain how regimes
are produced or founded. It has now reached the point of describing the
perfect operation of the royal craft that produces the opinions and actions that constitute the excellent religion. Alfarabi had already said that
revelation—what the ancients had called prudence or practical judgment
and what Alfarabi himself now calls prudence or practical judgment—is
not enough; first and foremost, the founder needs to possess the royal
craft. To operate perfectly, the royal craft requires knowledge of that political science which is part of philosophy as well as knowledge of theoretical philosophy, which is the rest of philosophy according to the *Enumeration of the* Sciences—it *requires* knowledge of all of philosophy. Yet
Alfarabi also says that it is subordinate to philosophy (47.16–17). This
refers to the royal craft in its activity or operation, which produces religion. But the operation of the royal craft is the operation of prudence or
practical judgment—that is, the actual determination of opinions and
actions. In what Alfarabi calls "this [political] art" (60.6) one can distinguish between theoretical philosophy and political science but cannot
separate the one from the other or both from prudence or practical judgment. (This question is discussed in detail in *Attainment of Happiness.*)

The final question is whether prudence or practical judgment is related directly to theoretical philosophy or directly to political science and
only indirectly to theoretical philosophy through the mediation of political science; and how it requires theoretical philosophy or political science. The *Enumeration of the Sciences* and the *Book of Religion* up to
the place where it presents an account of political science (52.10ff.) give
the impression that prudence or practical judgment, which determines

the opinions and activities in religion, has direct access or is joined to both theoretical science and practical or political science. The account of political science in the second part of the *Book of Religion,* on the other hand, suggests an alternative scheme. The *Book of Religion* repeats the two accounts of political science given in the *Enumeration of the Sciences,* with the following major differences. It omits the discussion of jurisprudence and theology and goes on to describe a wholly *new* function of political science not found in the *Enumeration of the Sciences.* Here political science itself—not physics, metaphysics, or any other theoretical science—proceeds to describe (1) the structure of the universe, its parts, and the ruling-ruled relations among its parts, until it ascends to its Supreme Ruler. (2) Then it descends to show how all other things are ordered under His governance; then it seizes upon the corresponding things and structures in (3) the human soul, (4) the human body, and (5) the excellent city—placing the king in the same position in the excellent city as the position occupied by God in the universe. Then it (6) orders the parts of the city down to the ones that are merely subservient and (7) describes the structure of the city until it reaches back to the rank of the king. After that, it (8) ascends from the king to the Trusted Spirit (the name given to the angel Gabriel), who is the agent of revelation, the being through which God reveals things to the founder of the city. Finally (9), it ascends from the agent of revelation to God and explains how revelation comes down step-by-step, through the mediation of the spiritual beings, to the founder of the city, shows that God governs the city as well as the universe—but in different ways, which nevertheless bear a certain resemblance to each other—and explains the correspondence between the universe and the city and that the king needs to follow in God's footsteps in founding and preserving the city. Therefore, the founder of the excellent city must have a comprehensive knowledge of theoretical philosophy so as to understand how God governs the universe and to be able to imitate Him.

This description of the universe, the soul, the body, and the city—this cosmology, psychology, physiology, and structural account of what we call the political system—is an integral part of a practical political science, not of a theoretical physics or metaphysics. It is based on the assertion that there is a certain correspondence or similarity between the structure of the universe as a whole and the human soul, the human body, and the city, between what is by nature and what is by nature plus will. The first impression is that the city is to be organized on the analogy of the universe. But the universe to which the city is to correspond is itself made known and described by political science, by the science of the city, and seems to be thoroughly political or politicized: the parts of the universe rule and are ruled, the higher ones govern the lower while the lower serve the higher.

This explicit extension of the domain of political science beyond Aristotelian ethics and politics to encompass a political cosmology and theology, a political psychology, and a political physiology was unheard of before Alfarabi. Henceforth, we cannot avoid making a distinction between a theoretical and a political metaphysics or theology, between a theoretical and a political psychology, and between a theoretical and a political physiology.

The result is that what Alfarabi calls the universals or general rules of this new political science include not only actions but opinions as well: political science itself contains the rules for the practical and theoretical things that the royal craft must know in order to found the excellent city. One difference between the practical and theoretical components of this new political science seems to be that, whereas the principles of the practical rules that govern the organization of the city and the practical activities of the citizen are to be found in political science itself, in what Alfarabi calls the "first part" of political science, the principles of the theoretical things the citizens ought to believe about the universe are to be found in physics and metaphysics: they are political-religious images or similitudes of things properly known only in physics and metaphysics. To operate perfectly, the royal craft must know both the principles and the general rules based on them or the general opinions that reflect them; for the royal craft is constantly called upon to adjust these rules and opinions to particular situations, and unless it knows the principles, it will not know whether a particular adjustment is good or bad.

Nevertheless, for all practical purposes, political science provides a total framework within which practical judgment operates and determines particular actions and opinions for a particular city. Practical judgment as such has no access to the principles, whether practical or political, but only to the general practical rules and the general theoretical images or arguments given by political science. We have three concentric circles, as it were, which encompass the realms of theoretical science, political science, and practical judgment, respectively.

Alfarabi's Political Corpus

The *Enumeration of the Sciences* concludes with an account of postprophetic religion and gives an account of the religious sciences, jurisprudence and theology, as they existed in Alfarabi's time. It shows what kind of "ancient" political science can potentially cope with religion. The *Book of Religion* begins with a comprehensive account of religion, analyzes its elements, and traces its foundation and development into a postprophetic religion, into jurisprudence and theology. Then it proceeds to present a detailed program for a new political science that can actually cope with religion and contribute to the improvement of religious communities. The most striking feature of the new political science is that it concerns itself with opinions, with what human beings believe about the structure of the universe, the human soul, the human body, as well as the city. This is the new element.

Plato and Aristotle had given two accounts of political science, which Alfarabi presents in the *Enumeration of the Sciences* as generally known. These accounts of ethics and politics as combined and supplemented by Alfarabi in the *Attainment of Happiness,* for instance, continue to be valid. Yet Alfarabi makes substantial additions to them. With regard to opinions, Plato had given various political accounts of opinions in such writings as the *Laws* and the *Timaeus.* These were admittedly images or resemblances of the truth, models to guide future legislators in establishing new cities. Models of this kind mediate between the truth and what human beings can imagine or believe. They are artful productions created by the teacher of legislators with an eye to general habits, character, opinions, and conditions, and these the legislator will adjust further with a view to a particular city under particular conditions.

But times have changed. Opinions about the universe have changed in basic ways because of the spread of the revealed religions on the one hand and the spread of the philosophic sciences on the other. These two traditions now form the general education of the thoughtful men of Alfarabi's time. No one in his right mind can expect the new societies to revert to pagan cosmologies and cosmogonies, not even in the most refined Aristotelian or Platonic form. There is need for new models that take into account the temper of the times and what people believe in here and now. These models must be substantially new and different from the Platonic models.

Alfarabi creates two such models in two of his well-known political works: the *Principles of the Opinions of the Inhabitants of the Virtuous City* and the *Principles of the Beings,* or the *Political Regime.* Both works are confined to a particular aspect of his new political science: that concerned with the opinions or the general rules of the opinions of the city, which he added in the *Book of Religion* to the "ancient" political science presented in chapter 5 of the *Enumeration of the Sciences*. In each of these two political works he presents a political cosmology and cosmogony as well as a corresponding description of the parts of the human soul, the parts of the human body, and the parts of the city. I have said enough about this subject to forestall the mistake of confusing these models with what is wrongly called Alfarabi's cosmology—by which one usually means Alfarabi's theoretical or scientific physics and metaphysics. These models are parts of political science. They are meant to serve future legislators and rulers, human beings who must possess the royal craft, which should encompass the theoretical and practical sciences and practical judgment. The models are partial syllabi to be used in the education of future princes.

The Virtuous City

$\mathcal{A}$lfarabi was the first philosopher who sought to confront, to relate, and as far as possible to harmonize classical political philosophy with Islam—a religion that was revealed through a prophet-legislator (Muhammad) in the form of a divine law, that organized its followers into a political community, and that provided for their beliefs as well as for the principles and rules of their conduct. Unlike Cicero, Alfarabi had to face and solve the problem of introducing classical political philosophy into a radically different cultural atmosphere; unlike Augustine, he did not have a relatively free sphere of this-worldly life in the organization of which classical political philosophy could apply unchallenged but had to face and solve the problem of the conflicting claims of political philosophy and religion over the whole of human life.

The importance of Alfarabi's place in the history of political philosophy consists in his recovery of the classical tradition and in making it intelligible within the new context provided by the revealed religions. His best-known writings are political works concerned with the political regimes and the attainment of happiness through political life. They present the problem of the harmony between philosophy and Islam in a new perspective: that of the relation between the best regime, as Plato had understood it in particular, and the divine law of Islam. His position in Islamic philosophy corresponds to that of Socrates or Plato in Greek philosophy insofar as their chief concern may be said to be the relation between philosophy and the city. He was the founder of a tradition that looked to him, and through him to Plato and Aristotle, for a philosophic approach to the study and understanding of political and religious phenomena. His works inspired men like Avicenna, Averroes, and Maimonides. They admired him as their "second teacher" after Aristotle, and he was the only postclassical thinker whose authority commanded their respect alongside that of the ancients.

Divine and Political Science

There are a number of striking resemblances between many of the fundamental features of Islam and the good regime envisaged by classical political philosophy in general and by Plato in the *Laws* in particular. Both
begin with a god as the ultimate cause of legislation and consider correct
beliefs about divine beings and the world of nature as essential for the
constitution of a good political regime. In both, these beliefs should reflect an adequate image of the cosmos, make accessible to the citizens at
large (and in a form they can grasp) the truth about divine things and
about the highest principles of the world, be conducive to virtuous action, and form part of the equipment necessary for the attainment of
ultimate happiness. Both consider the functions of the founder and legislator—and, after him, of his successors in the leadership of the community—of absolutely central importance for its organization and preservation. Both are concerned with the giving and the preserving of divine
laws. Both are opposed to the view that mind or soul is derivative from
body or is itself bodily and to the timorous piety that condemns humans
to despair of the possibility of ever understanding the rational meaning
of the beliefs they are called upon to accept or of the activities they are
called upon to perform. Both direct the eyes of the citizens to a happiness
beyond their worldly concerns. Finally, both relegate the art of the jurist
and that of the apologetic theologian to the secondary position of preserving the intention of the founder and of his law, and of erecting a
shield against attacks (*Enumeration of the Sciences,* chap. 5, 107.5–108.9;
Book of Religion, secs. 8–10, 49.9–52.9).

Alfarabi's important political works *(Virtuous City, Book of Religion,*
and *Political Regime)* are a meeting ground between Islam and classical
political philosophy where these affinities, and not possible differences
or conflicts, occupy the foreground. By laying the stress on such affinities, and by encouraging or even forcing both Islam and philosophy to
take a step in the direction of the other, he intends to make visible the
common elements in both and to encourage and guide his Muslim
reader to understand the characteristic features of classical political philosophy. This is revealed first of all in the very style of these works and
in the way in which they are composed. Stylistically, they bear as much
resemblance to legal codes as to philosophic treatises. They consist mainly
of positive statements about the attributes of God, the order of the
world, the place of man within it, and how a good society is to be organized and led.

Following a pattern common to Plato's *Laws* and the Quran, many of these statements are preceded by preludes preparing the way for the promulgation of sound laws that regulate the conduct of rulers and prescribe the beliefs and the actions of the citizens. Although not philosophic or political treatises or specific legal promulgation in the strict sense, these works contain the results of philosophic and political investigations presented in a practically useful way—as a basis for formulating a plan to order a good political regime. They are works whose form and intention could be readily understood by a Muslim reader committed to the acceptance of a true view of the world at large and to obedience to laws that promote virtue and lead to ultimate happiness. But they also conform to the intention of classical political philosophy in that they aim at presenting a rational and persuasive account of the world, couched in terms understandable to the citizens. They perform an important practical task insofar as they indicate by their appearance the possibility of a rational understanding that does not destroy, but preserves and explains, the beliefs and actions prescribed by the revealed law; and they achieve a preparatory task inasmuch as they indicate the direction in which such a rational understanding can be sought.

Alfarabi's political works form a new genre of writing in Islamic political literature. With habitual caution, he discreetly abstains from directly quoting, expounding, or even referring to the Quran, Muhammad, or specifically Islamic religious issues. Yet the first impressions that Alfarabi's works leave on his readers are unmistakable: the author intends to enable his coreligionists, and indeed all communicants of revealed religions, to see the wide area of harmony that exists between their divine law and the practical intention of classical political philosophy. These readers could now see in their divine law a practical fulfillment of the doctrines of the most prominent wise men of antiquity. They could turn to the study of these philosophers, not merely for the limited purpose of defending their own beliefs and practices or the negative purpose of assuring themselves that rational understanding is powerless before the higher authority of revelation and the divine law, but for rising above the slavish state of blind believers and for penetrating into the secret intentions of revelation and the divine law—to enlighten themselves, through the understanding of the most respectable tradition of human wisdom, about the wisdom of their religion.

Alfarabi gives them in these works the possibility of gaining a new disposition toward the study of the works of Plato and Aristotle. He encourages them to cease considering these philosophers as the originators of a foreign tradition that might undermine their beliefs and social virtues, a tradition that they ought to study with a view to refuting and combating. He makes them see that this tradition belongs to them no less than to the Greeks, and that they must make it their own because it is concerned with matters closest to their minds and hearts. They are made to hope for a fuller understanding of their highest political and religious concern—the things that constitute the essence of their religion and their way of life, distinguish them from their heathen ancestors, and give them their unique claim to superiority over other communities.

The Virtuous Regime

The central theme of Alfarabi's political writings is the virtuous regime, the political order whose guiding principle is the realization of human excellence or virtue. He conceives of human or political science as the inquiry into man insofar as he is distinguished from other natural beings and from divine beings, seeking to understand his specific nature, what constitutes his perfection, and the way through which he can attain it. Unlike other animals, man is not rendered perfect merely through the natural principles present in him; and unlike divine beings, he is not eternally perfect but needs to achieve his perfection through the activity proceeding from rational understanding, deliberation, and choosing among the various alternatives suggested to him by reason. The initial presence of the power of rational knowledge, and of the choice connected with it, is man's first, or natural, perfection, the perfection he is born with and does not choose. Beyond this, reason and choice are present in a human being to use for realizing his end or the ultimate perfection possible for his nature. This ultimate perfection is identical with the supreme happiness available to him:

> Happiness is the good desired for itself; it is never desired to achieve by it something else, and there is nothing greater beyond it that a human being can achieve. (*Virtuous City*, 46.14–16; cf. *Political Regime*, 72.15–75.3 and 78.1–8)

Yet happiness cannot be achieved without being first known, and without performing certain orderly (bodily and intellectual) activities useful for, or leading to, the achievement of perfection. These are the noble activities. The distinction between noble and base activities is thus guided by the distinction between what is useful for and what obstructs perfection and happiness. To perform an activity well, with ease, and in

an orderly fashion requires the formation of character and the development of habits that make such activities possible:

> The forms and states of character from which these [noble] activities
> emanate are the virtues; they are not goods for their own sake but goods
> only for the sake of happiness. (*Virtuous City*, 46.17–19; cf. *Political
> Regime*, 73.9–74.12)

The distinction between virtue and vice presupposes knowledge of what
human perfection or happiness is as well as the distinction between noble
and base activities.

The virtuous regime can be defined as the regime in which human
beings come together and cooperate with the aim of becoming virtuous,
performing noble activities, and attaining happiness. It is distinguished
by the presence in it of knowledge of man's ultimate perfection, the distinction between the noble and the base and between the virtues and the
vices, and the concerted effort of the rulers and the citizens to teach and
learn these things and to develop the virtuous forms or states of character
from which emerge the noble activities useful for achieving happiness.

The attainment of happiness means the perfection of that power of
the human soul that is specific to man: his reason. This, in turn, requires
disciplining the lower desires to cooperate with and aid reason to perform its proper activity and also acquiring the highest arts and sciences.
Such discipline and learning can be accomplished only by the rare few
who possess the best natural endowments and who are also fortunate
enough to live under conditions in which the requisite virtues can be
developed and noble activities performed. The rest of men can only attain some degree of this perfection; and the extent to which they can
attain that degree of perfection of which they are capable is decisively
influenced by the kind of political regime in which they live and the education they receive.

Nevertheless, all the citizens of the virtuous regime must have some
common notions about the world, man, and political life. But they will
differ with regard to the character of this knowledge and, hence, with
regard to their share of perfection or happiness. They can be divided
broadly into the following three classes: (1) the wise, or the philosophers, who know the nature of things by means of demonstrative proofs
and by their own insights; (2) the followers of these, who know the nature of things by means of the demonstrations presented by the philosophers and who trust the insight and accept the judgment of the phi-

losophers; (3) the rest of the citizens—the many—who know things by means of similitudes, some more and others less adequate, depending on their rank as citizens. These classes or ranks must be ordered by the ruler, who should also organize the education of the citizens, assign to them their specialized duties, give their laws, and command them in war. He is to seek, by persuasion and compulsion, to develop in everyone the virtues of which he is capable and to order the citizens hierarchically so that each class can attain the perfection of which it is capable and yet serve the class above it. In this manner, the city becomes a whole similar to the cosmos, and its members cooperate toward attaining happiness.

The virtuous regime is a nonhereditary monarchical or an aristocratic regime in which the best rule, with the rest of the citizens divided into groups that (depending on their rank) are ruled and in turn rule—until one arrives at the lowest group, which is ruled only. The sole criterion for the rank of a citizen is the character of the virtue of which he is capable and that he is able to develop through his participation in the regime and obedience to its laws. Like the regime itself, the citizens are virtuous, first, because they possess—or follow those who possess—correct similitudes of the knowledge of divine and natural beings, human perfection or happiness, and the principles of the regime designed to help human beings attain this happiness; and, second, because they act in accordance with this knowledge in that their characters are formed with a view to performing the activities conducive to happiness.

Once the main features of the virtuous regime are clarified, the understanding of the main features and the classification of all other regimes become relatively simple. Alfarabi divides them into three broad types. (1) The regimes whose citizens have had no occasion to acquire any knowledge at all about divine and natural beings or about perfection and happiness are the *ignorant* regimes. Their citizens pursue lower ends, good or bad, in complete oblivion of true happiness. (2) The regimes whose citizens possess the knowledge of these things but do not act according to their requirements are the *wicked* or *immoral* regimes. Their citizens have the same views as those of the virtuous regime; yet their desires do not serve the rational part in them but turn them away to pursue the lower ends pursued in ignorant regimes. (3) The regimes whose citizens have acquired false or corrupt opinions about these things—that is, opinions that claim to be about divine and natural beings and about true happiness but in fact are not—are the regimes that have been led astray, or the *erring* regimes. The similitudes presented to such citizens are, consequently, false and corrupt, and so also are the activities prescribed for them. The citizens of such regimes do not possess true knowledge or correct similitudes, and they, too, pursue the lower ends of the ignorant regimes. The regimes in error may have been founded as such. This is the case with the regimes

> whose supreme ruler was one who was under an illusion that he was receiving revelation without having done so, and with regard to which he had employed misrepresentations, deceptions, and delusions. (*Virtuous City*, 63.6–7; cf. *Political Regime*, 103.14–104.6)

But they may also have been originally virtuous regimes that had been changed through the introduction of false or corrupt views and practices.

All these types of regimes are opposed to the virtuous regime because they lack its guiding principle, which is true knowledge and virtue or the formation of character leading to activities conducive to true happiness. Instead, the character of the citizens is formed with a view to attaining one or more of the lower ends. These ends are given by Alfarabi as six, and each of the general types of regime mentioned above can be subdivided according to the end that dominates in it: (1) the regime of *necessity* (or the *indispensable* regime), in which the aim of the citizens is confined to the bare necessities of life; (2) the *vile* regime (oligarchy), in which the ultimate aim of the citizens is wealth and prosperity for their own sakes; (3) the *base* regime, the purpose of whose citizens is the enjoyment of sensory or imaginary pleasures; (4) the regime of *honor* (timocracy), whose citizens aim at being honored, praised, and glorified by others; (5) the regime of *domination* (tyranny), whose citizens aim at overpowering and subjecting others; and (6) the regime of *corporate association* (democracy), the main purpose of whose citizens is being free to do what they wish.

The Philosopher-King and the Prophet-Legislator

To combine divine and political science is to emphasize the political importance of sound beliefs about divine beings and about the principles of the world. We saw that both Islam and classical political philosophy are in agreement concerning this issue. Muslims believed that the primary justification of their existence as a distinct community was the revelation of the truth about divine things to Muhammad and that, had he not come to them with his message, they would have continued to live in misery and uncertainty about their well-being in this world and the next. It was also because of such considerations that Plato thought kings must become philosophers or philosophers kings. Once the quest for the best regime arrives at the necessity of combining divine and political science, it becomes necessary for the ruler to combine the craft of ruling with that of prophecy or philosophy. The ruler-prophet or the ruler-philosopher is the human being who offers the solution to the question of the realization of the best regime, and the functions of the ruler-prophet and of the ruler-philosopher appear in this respect to be identical.

Alfarabi begins his discussion of the supreme ruler by emphasizing the common function of the ruler-philosopher and the ruler-prophet as rulers who are the link between the divine beings above and the citizens who do not have direct access to knowledge of these beings. He is the teacher and guide "who makes known" to the citizens what happiness is, who "arouses in them the determination" to do the things necessary for attaining it, and "who does not need to be ruled by a human in anything at all" (*Political Regime*, 78.8–79.8). He must possess knowledge, not need any other human to guide him, have excellent comprehension of everything that must be done, be excellent in guiding all others in what he knows, have the ability to make others perform the functions for which they are fit, and have the ability to determine and define the work to be done by others and to direct such work toward happiness. These qualities evidently require the best natural endowments, but also the fullest development of the rational faculty. (According to Aristotelian psychology as Alfarabi presents it in his political works, the perfection of the rational faculty consists in its correspondence to, or contact with, the active intellect.) The supreme ruler must be a human being who actualizes his rational faculty or who is in contact with the active intellect.

> This human being is the true prince according to the ancients; he is the one of whom it ought to be said that he receives revelation. For a human being receives revelation only when he attains this rank—that is, when there is no longer an intermediary between him and the active intellect. . . . Now because the active intellect emanates from the being of the First Cause [God], it can for this reason be said that it is the First Cause that brings about the revelation to this human being through the mediation of the active intellect. The rule of this human being is the supreme rule; all other human rulerships are inferior to it and are derived from it. (*Political Regime*, 79.12–80.3)

This supreme ruler is the source of all power and knowledge in the regime, and it is through him that the citizens learn what they ought to know and to do. As God or the First Cause of the world directs everything else, and as everything else is directed toward Him, "the case ought to be the same in the virtuous city; in an orderly fashion, all of its parts ought to follow in their activities in the footsteps of the purpose of its supreme ruler" (*Virtuous City*, 57.1–3; cf. *Political Regime*, 83.11–84.7). He possesses unlimited powers and cannot be subjected to any human being or political regime or laws. He has the power to confirm or abrogate previous divine laws, to enact new ones, and "to change a law he had legislated at one time for another if he deems it better to do so" *(Political Regime*, 80.16). He alone has the power to order the classes of people in the regime and assign to them their ranks. And it is he who offers them what they need to know.

For most people, this knowledge has to take the form of an imaginative representation of the truth rather than a rational conception of it. This is because most people are not endowed with knowledge of, or cannot be trained to know, divine things in themselves but can only understand their imitations, which should be made to fit their power of understanding and their special conditions and experience as members of a particular regime. Religion contains such a set of imaginative representations. The divine law is legislated for a particular group of human beings. It is necessitated by the incapacity of most human beings to conceive things, especially the highest or divine things, rationally. Still, they need to know these things in some fashion. They need to believe in the imitations of divine beings, and of happiness and perfection, as presented to them by the founder of their regime. The founder must then not only present a rational or conceptual account of happiness and the divine principles to the few but also adequately represent or imitate these same things for the many. All the citizens are to accept and preserve that with which he entrusts them:

> the ones who follow after happiness as they cognize it and accept the [divine] principles as they cognize them are the *wise human beings;* and the ones in whose souls these things are found in the form of images, and who accept them and follow after them as such, are the *believers*. (*Political Regime*, 86.8–10; emphasis added)

Thus far, Alfarabi identifies the ruler-prophet and the ruler-philosopher. They are both supreme rulers absolutely, and both have absolute authority with regard to legislating beliefs and actions. Both acquire this authority by virtue of the perfection of their rational faculty, and both receive revelation from God through the agency of the active intellect. Wherein, then, does the ruler-prophet differ from the ruler-philosopher?

The first and primary qualification that the ruler of the virtuous regime must possess is a special kind of knowledge of divine and human things. Now, a human being possesses three faculties for knowledge—sensation, imagination, and reason (both theoretical and practical)—and these develop in him in that order. Imagination has three functions: (1) It acts as a reservoir of sensible impressions after the disappearance of the objects of sensation. (2) It combines sensible impressions to form a complex sensible image. (3) It produces *imitations*. It has the capacity to imitate all nonsensible things (human desires, temperaments, passions) through sensible impressions or certain combinations of them. When the rational faculty later develops and a human being begins to grasp the character, essence, or form of natural and divine beings, the faculty of imagination receives and imitates these rational forms also; that is, it *represents* them in the form of sensible impressions.

In this respect, imagination is subordinate to the rational faculty and depends on it for the "originals" that it imitates; it has no direct access to the essence of natural and divine beings. Further, the imitations that it fabricates are not all good copies: some may be truer and closer to the originals, others defective in some respects, and still others extremely false or misleading copies. Finally, only the rational faculty, which grasps the originals themselves, can judge the degree of the truth of these copies and of their likeness to the originals. The rational faculty is the only faculty that has access to the knowledge of divine or spiritual beings, and it must exercise strict control to ensure that the copies offered by the imaginative faculty are good or fair imitations. It may happen in rare cases that this imaginative faculty is so powerful and perfect that it overwhelms all the other faculties and proceeds directly to receive or form images of divine beings. This rare case is the case of prophecy:

> It is not impossible that a human being, when his imaginative power reaches utmost perfection, should receive in his waking hours from the active intellect . . . the *imitations* of separate [immaterial] intelligibles and all other noble [sacred] beings, and to view them. By virtue of the intelligibles he had received, he will thus have [the power of] prophecy about divine things. This, then, is the most perfect stage reached by the power of imagination and the most perfect stage at which a human being arrives by virtue of his imaginative power. (*Virtuous City*, 52.7–17; emphasis added)

The description of the nature of prophecy thus leads to the distinction between the faculty of imagination and the rational faculty. It explains the possibility of prophecy as the perfection of the faculty of imagination and that imagination can almost dispense with the rational faculty and receive the images of divine beings directly and without the latter's mediation. There are two powers by means of which a human being can communicate with the active intellect: his imagination and his rational faculty, or his intellect. When he communicates with it by means of his imagination, he is "a prophet who warns about what will happen and who informs about what is taking place now"; when he communicates with it by means of his rational faculty, he is "a wise human being, a philosopher, and has complete intelligence" (*Virtuous City,* 58.23–59.2).

It would appear then that the ruler-prophet and the ruler-philosopher both can be said to possess the qualification of knowledge required for being the supreme ruler of the virtuous city; or that two kinds of equally virtuous regimes are possible, one ruled by a prophet without philosophy and the other ruled by the philosopher without prophecy. Yet in his political writings Alfarabi does not even consider the possibility of a virtuous regime ruled by a prophet who does not possess a developed rational faculty. The distinction between prophecy and philosophy is a psychological distinction, and it is useful for understanding the nature of both prophecy and philosophy. But in discussing the quality of knowledge required by the supreme ruler, Alfarabi is explicit in demanding the perfection of both faculties: the supreme ruler is called, not a perfect prophet or a perfect philosopher, but a "perfect human being."

To begin with the philosopher, even his philosophy or the wisdom he is seeking remains incomplete so long as he does not possess perfect mastery in imitating the rational or theoretical knowledge in his possession in order to teach it to the young or to present it to the multitude. This lack becomes an essential defect when he is faced with the task of governing a city and educating it. His very quality as philosopher (i.e., as one who devotes himself to theoretical knowledge irrespective of its use in, or relation to, the city) disqualifies him as a ruler. He cannot be a founding *ruler*-philosopher without the power of imagination, of which the prophet is the most accomplished representative.

As to the prophet, although his imaginative power seems to make him particularly fit for ruling, the workings of his imagination do not enjoy the benefit of rational control: he lacks the constant check on the degree of truthfulness or verisimilitude of the imitations produced by his powerful imagination, a function that only the rational faculty can perform. The best ruler for the virtuous city must therefore be a ruler-philosopher-prophet. Alfarabi does not say whether Muhammad the prophet was also a philosopher, but he requires the combination of prophecy and philosophy, or the exercise of the imaginative and the rational powers, in the supreme ruler of the virtuous city. Philosophy, or wisdom, is indispensable for ruling a virtuous city:

> If it should happen at any time that wisdom has no share in ruling, and [the ruling authority] fulfilled all other conditions, the virtuous city remains without a prince, the ruler who takes care of the business of this city will not be a prince, and the city will be exposed to perdition. Thus if it does not happen that there should exist a wise human being to associate with him, then after a time the city will surely perish. (*Virtuous City*, 61.11–15)

Law and Living Wisdom

Wisdom, or philosophy, is an indispensable condition for the founding and survival of the virtuous city. Prophecy, on the other hand, is indispensable for founding a virtuous city but not for its survival. In enumerating the qualities of the supreme ruler or the founder of the virtuous city, Alfarabi stipulates the coincidence of excellent rational and prophetic faculties. This requirement is imposed by the composition of the virtuous city as a political community, that is, the fact that it must be made up of two broad groups: (1) the few who are philosophers or can be addressed through philosophy and who can be taught the theoretical sciences and hence the true character of divine and natural beings as they are; (2) the many who (because they lack the necessary natural endowments or have no time for sufficient training) are not philosophers, who live by opinion and persuasion, and for whom the ruler must imitate these beings by means of similitudes and symbols.

While the few can be made to grasp rationally the meaning of human happiness and perfection and the rational basis or justification of the virtuous activities that lead to a human being's ultimate end, the many are incapable of such understanding and have to be taught to perform these activities by persuasion and compulsion, that is, by explanations that can be understood by all the citizens regardless of their rational capacity and by prescribed rewards and punishments of an immediate tangible kind. The supreme ruler teaches the few in his capacity as philosopher, and he presents similitudes and prescribes rewards and punishments for the many in his capacity as prophet. To be believed and practiced by the many, these similitudes and prescriptions should be formulated by the prophet and accepted by the citizens as true, fixed, and permanent; that is, the citizens should expect definite rewards and punishments for belief and unbelief and for obedience and disobedience. The prophetic faculty culminates, then, in laying down laws concerning both the beliefs and the practices of the many; and the prophet who assumes this function becomes a prophet-legislator. The rational faculty, in contrast, culminates in teaching the theoretical sciences to the few. In his summary of Plato's *Laws,* Alfarabi also understood Plato to say that these virtuous few "have no need for fixed practices and laws at all; nevertheless they are very happy. Laws and fixed practices are needed only for those who are morally crooked" (*Plato's "Laws,"* 151.3–6).

It is only as viewed by the subjects that laws are fixed and are of unquestionable divine authority. We saw that the supreme ruler of the virtuous regime is the master and not the servant of the law. Not only is he not ruled by any human being, he is also not ruled by the law. He is the cause of the law, he creates it, and he abrogates and changes it as he sees fit. He possesses this authority because of his wisdom and his capacity to decide what is best for the common good under given conditions; and conditions can arise under which the changing of the law is not only salutary but indispensable for the survival of the virtuous regime. In so doing he must be extremely cautious not to disturb the faith of the citizens in their laws and should consider the adverse effect that change has on attachment to the law. He must make a careful appraisal of the advantage of changing the law as against the disadvantage of change as such. Thus he must possess, not only the authority to change laws whenever necessary, but also the craft of minimizing the danger of change to the well-being of the regime. But once he sees that changing the law is necessary and takes the proper precautions, there is no question as to his authority to change the law. Therefore, so long as he lives, the rational faculty rules supreme and laws are preserved or changed in the light of his judgment as philosopher.

It is this coincidence of philosophy and prophecy in the person of the ruler, or at least the coincidence of philosophy and rulership, that ensures the survival of the virtuous regime. As long as rulers who possess such qualities succeed one another without interruption, the same situation obtains.

> The successor will be the one who will decide about what was left undecided by his predecessor. And not this alone. He may change a great

deal of what his predecessor had legislated and make a different decision about it when he knows this to be best in his own time—not because his predecessor had committed a mistake, but because his predecessor decided upon it according to what was best in his own time, and the successor decides according to what is best for a later time. Were his predecessor to observe [the new conditions], he would have changed [his own law] also. (*Book of Religion*, 49.9–14)

The coincidence of philosophy and prophecy is extremely rare, and chance may not even favor the virtuous regime with the availability of a human being who possesses all the necessary natural endowments and whose training as a philosopher proves successful. Thus the question arises as to whether the virtuous city can survive in the absence of a human being with all the qualifications required of the prophet-philosopher-ruler or of the philosopher-ruler. Granting that the best possible arrangement demands the existence of such qualifications in one person who must rule, can the regime originated by the prophet-philosopher-ruler survive at all in his absence and in the absence of a philosopher-ruler as his successor? Alfarabi is willing in the *Virtuous City* to consider the possibility that this city can survive in the absence of both such rulers, but only if provisions are made for the presence of proper substitutes for prophetic legislation. These substitutes consist of (1) the body of laws and customs established by the "true princes" and (2) a combination of new qualities in the ruler that make him proficient in the "art of jurisprudence," that is, in knowledge of the laws and customs of his predecessors; willingness on his part to follow these laws and customs rather than change them; the capacity to apply them to new conditions by the deduction of new decisions from, or the discovery of new applications for, established laws and customs; and the capacity to meet every new situation (for which no specific decisions are available) through understanding the *intention* of previous legislators rather than by the legislation of new laws or by any formal change of old ones. So far as the law is concerned, this new ruler is a jurist-legislator rather than a prophet-legislator. He must, however, possess all other qualities, including wisdom, that enable him to discern and promote the common good of his regime at the particular period during which he rules.

In the event that no single human being should exist who possesses all these qualifications, then Alfarabi suggests a third possibility: a wise man and one other human being (who possesses the rest of the qualities, except wisdom) should rule jointly. Were even this to prove unobtainable, he suggests, finally, a joint rule of a number of human beings possessing these qualifications severally. This joint rule does not, however, affect the presence of the required qualifications but only their presence in the *same* human being. Thus the only qualification whose very presence may be dispensed with is prophecy. The substitutes for prophecy are the preservation of old laws and the capacity to discover new applications for old laws. To promote the common good and preserve the regime under new conditions as these emerge, neither the coincidence of philosophy and prophecy in the same human being nor the coincidence of wisdom and jurisprudence proves to be an indispensable condition. It is sufficient to have wisdom in the person of a philosopher who rules jointly with another human being or a group of human beings who possess, among other things, the capacity to put old laws to new uses. Unlike prophecy, wisdom cannot be dispensed with, and nothing can take its place. Unlike the absence of prophecy, the absence of wisdom is fatal to the existence of the virtuous regime. There is no substitute for living wisdom.

War and the Limitations of Law

In addition to philosophy and prophecy (or else proficiency in the art of jurisprudence), there is a third and indispensable qualification that must be present in the ruler of the virtuous regime or in one of the group who rule it jointly: daring and warlike virtue. This qualification is required for carrying out the ruler's responsibility as the supreme educator of all the citizens, that is, to form and improve their moral character. Since not all human beings can be convinced or aroused to perform virtuous activities by means of persuasive and passionate arguments, the method of persuasion or consent is not sufficient. As the father does with his children and the schoolteacher with the young, so the ruler has to use force and compulsion with those who, out of nature or habit, cannot be educated or persuaded to obey the law spontaneously. Hence the ruler needs to employ two groups of educators: a group that educates the citizens by persuasion and by means of arguments; and a warlike group to compel the lazy, the wicked, and the incorrigible to obey the laws by force. The supreme ruler, or rulers, should lead, direct, and supervise the activities of both groups. To command the second group, he or they should possess a daring nature and excel in the art of war.

The nature and the extent of the compulsion and force to be applied in a certain regime depend on the character of the citizens: the more virtuous they are, the less need there is to apply force. But there are cases where the ruler may have to conquer a whole city and force it to accept his virtuous or divine law, or where the use of force would considerably shorten the time required to establish his law when successful persuasion is too uncertain and its prospects too remote. Compulsion is legitimate inside the regime with regard to those citizens who are of intractable natures or bad habits and with respect to a whole city as a prelude to the establishment of a new divine law where it is lacking. Physical force, overpowering, or war is a "fundamental element" of the law and one of the basic preludes for establishing it. Alfarabi seems to favor not only defensive war but offensive war also; and he speaks of the war conducted by the ruler of the virtuous regime as a just war and of his warlike purpose as a virtuous purpose (*Plato's "Laws,"* 126.1–13).

Further, like Plato and Aristotle, Alfarabi considers the city the first or smallest unit that constitutes a political whole and in which a human being can attain his political perfection, but unlike them, he does not seem to consider the city also the largest possible unit in which a virtuous regime can be expected to flourish. Instead, he speaks of three perfect human associations: the largest in size is the association of all human beings in the entire inhabited world; the intermediate is the association of a nation in a portion of the inhabited world; and the smallest is the association of the inhabitants of a city in a portion of the land inhabited by a nation. If we combine his teaching about just or virtuous war and conquest with the idea of a perfect human association extending over the entire inhabited world, we can be led to the conclusion that Alfarabi deliberately modified the teachings of Plato and Aristotle on an important issue with the intention of supplying a rational justification for the Islamic concept of holy war whose aim was to propagate the divine law everywhere on earth; that he favored a war of civilization whereby a more advanced nation justifies the conquest of more backward nations; or that he preached the idea of a universal or a world state. These conclusions must now be examined in the light of Alfarabi's views on war and the character of the law.

He mentions two extreme views regarding war. The first is the view that to overpower and dominate others is the natural state of man and that war is therefore the only universally just course of conduct. The second is that the natural state of man is universal peace and that peaceful coexistence therefore is the only just course of conduct. This latter view can in turn have the corollary that only in defensive war, war forced upon one by the unnatural conduct of a warlike enemy, is there just cause for taking up arms. These are, according to him, the views of the inhabitants

of the "ignorant and erring cities" that are opposed to the virtuous regime (*Virtuous City,* 75.7–80.3). They give rise to two types of regimes:
"tyrannies" and "peace-loving regimes." The latter are not considered
sufficiently important; and their view, though mistaken, is evidently not
dangerous. At any rate, he does not list them as a main subdivision of
the regimes opposing the virtuous regime, which is partly due to the fact
that, unlike war, peace is not one of the main ends pursued by human
beings but a means to other ends, such as pleasure or gain.

War, conquest, the overpowering and enslaving of others, and tyranny
over them constitute, in contrast, one of the supreme ends pursued by
human beings. They give rise to the tyrannical regime in which human
beings associate with each other, practice warlike activities, frame their
laws, and order their regime with the main purpose of enslaving each
other or other regimes. They do not enslave and kill to attain other ends
but to satisfy a supreme end common to all of them, "the love of tyranny." Indeed, the bad regimes pursuing other ends—such as wealth,
honor, or pleasure—are in many cases transformed into tyrannies when
these other ends are attained. The satisfaction of these desires seems to
free the citizens of bad regimes to pursue the highest evil of ignorant
and erring regimes, that is, the view that tyranny is the good. War as an
end in itself is for Alfarabi the supreme vice that can have no place in the
regime whose end is the supreme virtue.

Having made use of the advantages of war and compulsion to establish his divine law and to suppress the wicked and the incorrigible, the
ruler of the virtuous regime must return to promote friendship among
the citizens and to the peaceful work of persuasion and free consent. To
persuade the majority of citizens, he has to produce similitudes of divine
and natural beings, and of virtue and happiness, that are adequate with
respect to their proximity to the original forms of these things but that
are also adequate with respect to those who are to be persuaded by them.
The similitudes should bear some relation to the nature, past experience,
and habits of the citizens. Unlike the business of war, peaceful persuasion
requires the legislator to make concessions to the character of the ruled,
the degree of their preparation for virtuous laws, differences among
them, and the extent to which the citizens can be improved. These are
prelegal conditions that he does not create but must presuppose and that
he cannot change except to a limited extent and then only gradually.

Further, the legislator cannot produce similitudes and utilize persuasive methods designed to meet the particular nature and habits of each
individual citizen; the law cannot treat each human being as a case by

himself. General beliefs and practices must be prescribed for all the citizens and must correspond to their distinctive character as a group. Now, what is adequate for one group and hence just with regard to them may be inadequate for another group and hence unjust with regard to them. To legislate for all human beings with respect to human nature or what they all have in common will mean being unjust to most, if not to all, human beings. Therefore, if it is the case that the inhabited world is divided into nations and cities, and this division is based not on arbitrary but on natural distinctions or distinctions that are somehow related to nature, such distinctions could form the limits within which general beliefs and practices that are both effective and just could be prescribed.

Alfarabi qualifies his statement about the three perfect associations (the city, the nation, and the association of all human beings in the entire inhabited world) with the observation that the association of all human beings in the entire inhabited world is divided into nations.

> Nations are distinguished from each other by two natural things—natural makeup and natural character—and by something that is composite (it is conventional but has a basis in natural things), namely, language. (*Political Regime*, 70.5–7)

These distinctions are the product of geographical differences among the various parts of the earth (temperature, foodstuffs, and so on) that in turn influence the temperament of their inhabitants. But although they constitute the nation as a natural unit, these natural national similarities are not a sufficient political bond for the sake of which the members of a nation should like each other or dislike other nations. The proper objects of like and dislike are the perfections or the virtues, and these are not given by nature but by the active intellect, by science, and by legislation. The nation is in turn divided into cities or city-states that are distinguished by their regimes and laws.

Only the city is likened by Alfarabi to the perfect living body. The organs of the living body do not simply cooperate toward a common end; they have different ranks, each of which is perfect when it performs its proper function (be that a subordinate or a superior one), and all of which are ruled by the most perfect organ. Applied to the nation and the association of all human beings in the entire inhabited world, this similitude would require the subordination of cities to each other, and of nations to each other, according to their degree of perfection. Yet Alfarabi never speaks of such subordination as being legitimate except within a single city; and the cities opposed to the virtuous city are not investigated with a view to being subordinated to a virtuous city but to being transformed into such a city. A virtuous nation is not a group of cities ruled by a virtuous or perfect city but the nation "*all* of whose cities *cooperate* regarding the things by which happiness is attained"; and the association of all human beings in the entire inhabited world is virtuous "only when the nations in it *cooperate* to achieve happiness" (*Virtuous City*, 54.8–10; emphasis added). The virtuous community of all human beings presupposes virtuous nations, and the virtuous nation in turn presupposes virtuous cities.

The consideration of the specific character and function of the prophetic faculty and of the divine law points to the conclusion that religion should be particularly sensitive to the limitations imposed by the natural and conventional differences among nations and cities. If a religion or divine law is not spurious, obscurantist, or fanatic, it does not promote but suppresses and transcends the ends pursued in ignorant regimes (including tyranny) and substitutes for them the end that can be pursued only through the belief in adequate or salutary similitudes of divine and natural beings and through commands and prohibitions that promote virtue and happiness among a particular group ready for its message. It must therefore abandon the end of the tyrannical regime whose aim is absolute and universal tyranny and restrict the use of force to the extent to which it is necessary to establish a new regime and suppress the wicked and the incorrigible inside the regime. Otherwise, it will be forced to legislate beliefs and practices that can be accepted and performed by all human beings, that is, to lower its standards to conform to the natural capacity of the overwhelming majority of human beings rather than uphold the ones that help a relatively good city or nation to achieve true virtue or happiness. The alternative aim of promoting virtue or happiness among the best or the elect in every city and nation is ruled out because this is the proper function not of religion but of philosophy. We recall Alfarabi's distinction between the functions of prophecy and philosophy in the virtuous regime. The few who are endowed with rare natures and are given proper training are offered, not similitudes, but theoretical knowledge of the divine and natural beings themselves and of virtue and happiness, while the beliefs and practices legislated in the divine law aim at the many.

Now, the natural and quasi-natural distinctions among cities and nations need not form a barrier against the transmission of theoretical knowledge. Such knowledge presupposes the presence of a tradition of theoretical inquiry and of rare individuals; but once these conditions are fulfilled, it can be freely transplanted from one city to another and from one nation to another. The universal community of the superior human beings of every city and nation or of the uncrowned kings of humanity is not a community of believers in a particular set of dogmas. It is the community of lovers of the one and true wisdom. By its very nature, according to Alfarabi, a religion cannot provide the basis for such a community.

Religion arises because of the incapacity of the many to understand the true character of beings and of human happiness. It remedies this situation by presenting them with similitudes that take into account the limitations of their understanding and their natural and conventional characteristics as a distinct group. Also, because the true principles of nature and true political principles are invariable, they are inflexible and cannot themselves be adjusted to the degree of understanding and the particular character of a distinctive political group. Similitudes, in contrast, may be adjusted for this purpose because they can be nearer to or more remote from reality. In addition, there can be a number of good similitudes of the same reality. These similitudes are all good or virtuous if they succeed in making the members of the particular political groups for which they are designed good or virtuous. "Consequently, there may be a number of virtuous nations and a number of virtuous cities whose religions are different" (*Political Regime,* 85.18–86.1; *Virtuous City,* 70.14–15). Alfarabi's approach to religion leads to a philosophic science of divine laws. By presenting divine laws, jurisprudence, and theology as parts of political science, he points to the possibility of a neutral discussion of all religions or "sects" and of the features common to them all.

Democracy and the Virtuous Regime

Of the six regimes opposed to the virtuous regime, the first and the last, that is, the regimes of necessity and democracy, occupy the privileged position of supplying the most solid and the best starting point for the establishment of the virtuous regime and for the rule of virtuous human beings. The regime of necessity (as the counterpart of the city of pigs in Plato's *Republic*) offers the opportunity for introducing a virtuous regime among citizens who are not as yet corrupted by the love of money or honor, by indulgence in pleasures, or by the desire for glory. But since all of these exist in democracy, it is not clear at first sight what contribution democracy could make to the virtuous regime.

Following Plato's description (*Republic,* bk. 8), Alfarabi sets down the first principle of democracy (i.e., of pure democracy, or of extreme democracy, as Aristotle calls it) as freedom, and he calls the democratic regime also the "free" regime. Freedom means the ability of everyone to pursue anything he desires and to be left alone to do anything he chooses in the pursuit of his desires. The second principle is equality, which means that no human being is superior to another in anything at all. These two principles define the basis of authority, the relation between the ruler and the ruled, and the attitude of the citizens to each other. Authority is justified only on the basis of the preservation and promotion of freedom and equality.

Whatever the accomplishments of the ruler, he rules only by the will of the citizens, however unaccomplished he or they may be: he must follow their wishes and cater to their whims. The citizens honor only those who lead them to freedom and to the achievement of whatever makes possible the enjoyment of their desires and those who preserve that freedom and make it possible for them to enjoy their different and conflicting desires and who defend them against external enemies. If such human beings can perform these functions and still remain themselves content with the bare necessities of life, then they are considered virtuous and are obeyed. The rest of the rulers are functionaries who perform services for which they receive adequate honors or financial remunerations; and the citizens who pay them for these services consider themselves, because of this, superior to these rulers, whom they support. Such also is the case of those whom the public lets rule either because it takes a fancy to them or because it wants to reward them for a service rendered by their ancestors. Despite these differences, a close investigation of the democratic regime shows that, ultimately, there are really no rulers and ruled; there is one supreme will, which is that of the citizens; and the rulers are instruments serving the desires and wishes of the citizens.

Unlike the other five regimes, there is no single or dominating end desired or wished for by the citizens of the democratic regime. They form innumerable groups, similar and dissimilar, with a variety of characters, interests, aims, and desires. So far as ends are concerned, democracy is a composite regime: various groups, aiming at the ends characterizing the other regimes, exist side by side and pursue different ways of life; they form a conglomeration in which the different parts are interwoven with each other; and they are free to fulfill their distinct aims independently or in cooperation with others.

Because the democratic regime makes possible, preserves, protects, and promotes every kind of desire, all kinds of human beings come to admire it and consider it as the happy way of life. They come to love democracy and to love to live in it. A great number migrate to it from different nations; and residents and foreigners meet, mix, and intermarry. The result is the greatest possible diversity of natural character, upbringing, education, and way of life; yet every type of human being is encouraged, or allowed, to achieve what he desires as far as his capacity admits. A fully developed democratic regime presents a colorful spectacle of infinite diversity and luxury.

But this means that of all the regimes opposed to the virtuous regime, the democratic regime contains the greatest amount and variety of good and evil things; and the more it expands and becomes perfect, the more goodness and evil it will contain. It will therefore also contain a number of the parts of the virtuous city. Alfarabi mentions in particular the possibility of the rise of virtuous human beings and of the presence of wise human beings, rhetoricians, and poets (i.e., human beings who deal with demonstrative science, persuasion, and imitation) in all kinds of things. If the regime of necessity contributes citizens uncorrupted by unessential desires and pleasure, the democratic regime, most of whose citizens are corrupted by luxury, offers the highly developed sciences and arts essential for the establishment of the virtuous regime. And in the absence of the virtuous regime, in which these sciences and arts have the best opportunity to develop in the right direction, the democratic regime is the only regime that provides ample opportunity for their development and allows the philosopher to pursue his desire with relative freedom.

Prophecy and Revelation

The followers of the revealed religions are for the most part pious believers for whom religion consists of doctrines they hold to and try to understand as best they can and practices they perform to the best of their ability. Those who aspire to be theologians and philosophers find two main approaches in the traditions they study. First, one approach sees prophecy and revelation as contact between the highest form of human intelligence and a higher intelligence above and beyond it. This is the view of the major Muslim philosophers up to and including Averroes. The second sees prophecy and revelation as contact between a human being and something beyond all intelligence and transcending all intelligibility. This is the view of those who followed the Neoplatonic tradition, and it included not only philosophers but theologians and mystics as well. The difference between the two views corresponds to the technical distinction made by Scholastic theologians between the natural and the supernatural and to Maimonides' distinction between the second and first "opinions concerning prophecy" (*Guide*, II.32).

The second approach was known to Alfarabi through the works of Plotinian Neoplatonists and Christian and Muslim theologians; and he reports some of their arguments (*Enumeration of the Sciences*, 108.10–110.14). Prophecy and revelation, so the argument went, are beyond human comprehension: they are suprarational. What is received on the authority of divine revelation surpasses human intellect and its examination; it contains divine secrets that human intellect is too weak to apprehend. Through revelation, religion provides certain kinds of knowledge that human intellect cannot attain. Human intellect may even reject them. But the more our intellect rejects them, the more useful and valid they must be. They may seem objectionable or absurd to our human mind, but they are correct in the divine mind and for those endowed

147

with divine knowledge. Even the perfect human being—the one who is perfect in humanity—is to those who possess a divine mind as a child is to the perfect man. For this theological position, miracles and the testimony of truthful witnesses are enough to prove that the human being who receives the revelation is truthful and could not have lied: therefore everything he says should be accepted without examination.

The rest of the theologians and the philosophic tradition initiated by Alfarabi, on the other hand, recognized the transhuman character of prophecy and revelation but held that both are analyzable by human intelligence: students of prophecy and revelation can grasp how prophecy and revelation take place although they cannot generate this on their own. The source of prophecy and revelation is a higher, superhuman intelligence, but it is an intelligence nevertheless. The laws promulgated in the revelation are rational *nomoi*.

The difference between the two approaches must have reminded Alfarabi, as a student of the history of philosophy, of what was perhaps the central question throughout the history of ancient metaphysics, namely, whether the ultimate ground of being is an intelligence or something above and beyond intelligence to which intelligence is subordinate. The former had been the view of Aristotle and Plato as interpreted by certain Platonists after Aristotle, while the latter was—in its clearest and most radical form—the point of view of Plotinian Neoplatonism. Unlike his immediate predecessors and most of his contemporaries among the students of ancient philosophy, Alfarabi adopted what appears as a novel harmonization of the views of Plato and Aristotle. His Aristotelian Godhead is modified in Platonic ways, embedding in it the ideas—including the ideas of morality and the arts—as intelligibles and attributing to certain of its manifestations demiurgic characteristics.

The Godhead he presents in his political writings is clearly not the Plotinian One. For he presents the ultimate ground of being, the First, simply, as the supreme, superhuman intelligence. The pursuit of the ultimate ground of being became central also for both theology and philosophy within Islam, and it made all the difference which side of the fence one chose to sit on. In the case of theology, the choice of the Plotinian One accommodated all supernatural demands, events, and miracles. It made life easier for mystics and for philosophers who could give no rational account of the seemingly nonrational or irrational phenomena pervading religion, the acts of its founders, and the beliefs and practices of the community. When we hear about conflicts among Muslim thinkers and schools of thought, we must remind ourselves that the most significant conflicts are to be understood in terms of this fundamental difference of approach to the nature of the Godhead.

As we try to get closer to Alfarabi's views on religion in general and on prophecy and revelation in particular, we are faced with a puzzling variety in his works on these subjects. That variety, in turn, has led Muslim philosophers and modern scholars to a variety of interpretations. The only thing on which they all seem to agree is that these works contain different and sometimes inconsistent positions, as well as numerous doctrines for which no antecedents can be discovered in Greek or Islamic philosophy. This includes his general theories of cognition, prophecy, and revelation. It would be tedious to discuss the various hypotheses meant to account for the differences and inconsistencies, such as the possibility that he was copying different Greek originals or reading different texts and authors at different times, the degree to which he wished to remain faithful to Aristotle or to show himself as partisan of one Muslim sect or another, the change in his attachment from Neoplatonism to Aristotelianism, or the degree to which he wished to dissimulate his veritable beliefs. Instead, I will confine myself to the following observations.

First—setting aside his commentaries on Aristotle's logical works and his technical works on music—Alfarabi's political-religious works present us with a situation similar to the one presented by the Platonic dialogues: we cannot easily identify the views in any of them as those of Alfarabi himself. Second, in many of these works he says quite a bit about religion but surprisingly little about prophecy and revelation, implying thereby that religion need not necessarily be revealed or prophetic. It is therefore important to identify what characterizes a prophetic and revealed religion and to distinguish it from a religion that is neither revealed nor prophetic. Third, since Alfarabi does not use revelation and prophecy synonymously, it is also important to ask about the difference between them. Finally, given the importance and difficulty of the task, we should not be surprised to find that Alfarabi goes about his investigation of prophecy and revelation with great caution and measured steps, and it is therefore important not to be too hasty in declaring any of these steps as his final position.

So I will proceed as follows. I will assume that any work that deals with religion belongs to the category of what Alfarabi calls "public philosophy." I will also assume that, as a student of the ancients, Alfarabi saw revelation and prophecy as historical phenomena, was interested in ascertaining how the new religions differed from what the ancients believed was the *best* religion, and was concerned with what needed to be done now that revelations and prophets had appeared and left the scene. I will therefore ask the following questions: (1) What was Alfarabi's account of religion, and especially the best religion, according to the ancients? (2) What, for Alfarabi, is prophecy and what is revelation, and what are their respective roles in founding the revealed religions? (3) What does Alfarabi take to be the role of the philosopher as a member of a religious community in the postprophetic period?

Human Religions

The first step in appreciating the virtues of prophecy and revelation is to consider the claims of the revealed religions and their founders to absolute superiority over all other religions and founders, including the religion envisaged by the wise philosophers of antiquity. At first sight, it would seem that a philosopher like Alfarabi could have learned very little about religion from the great philosophers of antiquity, especially when one considers Plato's *Euthyphro* and *Phaedrus* and Aristotle's *De divinatione per somnum,* where those authors appear skeptical and suspicious of religious phenomena. Still, not being a literalist, he was able to see a great deal in their writings, from which he constructed an account of the development of human society, the creation and use of human speech, and the development of the practical and intellectual arts (*Book of Letters,* pt. 2). Human religion, since it consists of beliefs and practices prescribed by a human lawgiver, can be founded at any point in the course of this development; but its excellence will depend on how advanced human thought and experience happen to be at that point. Human religion is also caught up in the cyclical movement of human history, it is entangled in the movements of cultural goods across national borders, and it is subject to being plagiarized by would-be founders in search of fame and glory. The best human religion, therefore, is a religion founded at the highest point in the development of the practical and intellectual arts by a human being who has attained the highest theoretical and practical knowledge and who is willing or can be persuaded to embody what he knows in concrete civic beliefs and practices. According to Alfarabi, this point was reached in the past at the time of Plato and Aristotle, when the perfection of knowledge could have been followed by the institution of the best human religion. It was not their fault that no one was willing to listen to them.

So the founding of the best human religion is problematic because the many refuse to allow the best philosophers to rule. But there are also the conflicts arising between philosophy and less perfect human religions. For example, a religion may have been established at a point earlier than the full development of the intellectual arts and thus reflects a more primitive view of reality than the one represented by philosophy after its full development. A religion may have been founded in a nation at an early stage of its development and philosophy then imported from abroad. A religion could have been borrowed and philosophy then imported. Or a lawgiver might be afraid that his views and actions would be subjected to inquiry by the wise. The grounds for conflict between religion and philosophy are unfortunately quite numerous, and there are alternative modes or situations. But they all result either from the religion having been founded upon incomplete knowledge or from the followers of the religion having forgotten the philosophic origin of their religion. The best human religion ought to exemplify and imitate the most perfect philosophic knowledge.

As we turn to what Alfarabi says about revealed religion, it is well to remember that he does not pretend to have any special kind of knowledge of the revelation provided by faith. His philosophy of religion is only human wisdom, an effort to puzzle out divine things and events that had changed the face of the earth and introduced human beings to radically new ways of thinking and acting, resulting in new kinds of regimes founded by lawgivers receiving their information directly from God or His divine agents and possessing powers and experiencing preparations different from those deemed necessary or useful for pagan lawgivers. The question for philosophy was how to make this phenomenon intelligible; or, to use a term dear to Muslim theologians when arguing the question of prophecy, how to show that this phenomenon is at all possible.

Toward the end of the work entitled *Selected Aphorisms* (aphorism 94) and devoted largely to the views of Plato and Aristotle, and in a passage that begins as a direct quotation from the *Attainment of Happiness* (secs. 11–19, 9.17–15.15), the introduction to his *Philosophy of Plato and Aristotle*, Alfarabi raises the question of revelation. It is a bewildering passage that seems to raise a bewildering question. It begins by speaking of the uses of theoretical philosophy in the practical part of philosophy and asserts that theoretical philosophy (which includes knowledge of virtue and vice and the end of man and his perfection) is indispensable for practice. One needs to begin with it, complete it, and then turn to the practical part and do it.

All this account of human religion and philosophy is well and good, but what about revelation? What about the one who is given the practical part by revelation? His first reaction is to say that this is "another way," perhaps in reference to its being divine in contrast to the human way described so far. To explain the difference, Alfarabi compares the knowledge possessed by the natural scientist with the knowledge possessed by the seer or soothsayer: the natural scientist knows the nature of the possible but cannot predict future events; while the soothsayer, even though he may lack knowledge of the nature of the possible, can predict future events. However, Alfarabi does not leave it at saying that the one has theoretical knowledge while the other can do things like predicting the future. For he is interested especially in the one who has both; that is, he continues to be interested in the Platonic question of the relation between theoretical knowledge and practical knowledge or in the notion of what he calls complete *(tamm)* practical judgment *(ta'aqqul, phronēsis)*.[1]

One notices that revelation here is (1) a substitute for the practical part of philosophy. The soothsayer, too, is presented here as having a practical function rather than dealing with intelligibles as he will be presented in the final account of prophecy in the *Virtuous City*. (2) In the case of revelation, the practical part is given—nothing is said about its source. The main advantage of revelation over practical knowledge is that, for the most part, practical knowledge is problematical: one may come to know the general rules or the first principles of morality and the arts and develop practical judgment through long experience in practical matters and yet find it hard to hit on the right means to the right end. Furthermore, even when one thinks one has done the right thing, one lacks absolute certainty about it. Revelation could provide the true first principles of action as well as the power to choose the right means. (3) Revelation comes to light as a substitute for practical judgment, for we are told that by means of it one is directed to determine particular things that ought to be preferred or avoided. One may even say that revelation is a form of practical judgment, the ability to hit the mark swiftly and without deliberation—"revelation" in Arabic is said to mean "quickness" or "swiftness."[2] Further, (4) revelation is *political* wisdom, since it is said to provide the ability to determine the actions of the citizens of a whole city or many cities. This, too, is a traditional understanding of revelation:

1. See *Selected Aphorisms,* aphorisms 42 (58.8), 51 (61.8), and 58 (66.4); also *Virtuous City,* 244.12 Walzer. Alfarabi speaks of "Aristotle's view" of practical judgment in *Selected Aphorisms,* aphorism 85 (89.12–15), but there is no reference to "complete" practical judgment in that context.

2. See the references under *w.ḥ.y.* in Lane, *Arabic-English Lexicon,* 3050.

revelation *(waḥy)* has to do with the whole community, unlike inspiration *(ilhām)*, which has to do with the individual saint or mystic. (5) Finally, revelation here is a gift that may be given indifferently to a person who is fully innocent of theoretical knowledge or who has partial theoretical knowledge or who has complete theoretical knowledge.

Next, in the work entitled the *Book of Religion* (sec. 1), Alfarabi considers a new case, that of the founder of a religion who combines the royal art—which includes full theoretical and practical knowledge—and revelation from God. This is obviously an attempt to graft revelation (whose source is now specified as the God of a revealed religion) onto the Platonic notion of the philosopher-king. Revelation again has to do with determination. We are still not told how this revelation takes place or how a human being acquires the power to determine things through revelation; for this we are referred to theoretical science. Yet the *Book of Religion* provides a number of new elements. (1) It offers an account of revelation that is not contrasted to philosophy as another way but joined to philosophy in the person of the philosopher-king who is in possession of the royal art. Prophets are mentioned later on along with supreme rulers and kings, indicating that being a prophet is one aspect or qualification of the founder and supreme ruler. (2) Revelation provides beliefs as well as practices, not practices alone as in *Selected Aphorisms*. (3) Revelation can give, not only practical judgment or the power to determine beliefs and practices, but the particular determinations, the beliefs and practices themselves, ready-made as it were.

Despite these elements, the *Book of Religion* remains largely within the orbit of the earlier view of human religion, as can be seen from the continued presence of the notion that religion exemplifies and imitates philosophy. The most important question that remains unanswered is perhaps how to make room for the revelation of genuine theoretical knowledge, in fact the revelation of a theoretical knowledge that is above and beyond what is attainable by unaided reason (if possible, without the normal training and learning process). For it is the completeness and certainty of beliefs about theoretical matters, divine and human, that appear to distinguish the revealed religions and account for their size, continuity, and success.

The Active Intellect and the Human Imagination

To account for revelation as the acquisition of the highest knowledge of all things, Alfarabi had to develop a theory of knowledge, starting with Aristotle's account of the process and types of intellection in the *De an-*

ima but modifying it in important respects. Since we do not possess his commentary on the *De anima*, we must be satisfied with the brief account in the *Epistle on the Intellect* (17ff.). The crucial element in this theory is the way he understands the role of what, since Alexander, had come to be known as the "acquired" intellect. For Alfarabi, this is the highest power of the human intellect. It begins to function after the potential intellect has become fully, or almost fully, actualized, that is, after the mind has detached or abstracted all or almost all the forms of material things, which are now its own intelligible forms. At this point the mind begins to engage in self-knowledge in which it has no need of anything outside itself, by scanning, as it were, these intelligible forms and seeing them as a whole, understanding their relationships and hierarchic order, and bringing them together into the unity they lacked when they were being individually and incrementally acquired. Once the actual mind understands the intelligibles in this fashion, it transforms itself into what was called the "acquired" intellect.

The term "acquired" had originally meant received from outside and identified with the divine mind, which was understood to be an eternal, separate, and always actual intellect in which all the forms reside in an indivisible unity—in sum, an active intellect. Alfarabi's acquired intellect is neither received from outside in this sense nor identical with the divine mind. It is rather the upper limit of human intellection and the borderline between it and the separate divine mind. (Alfarabi never admits that the two can be united. This would of course set him apart from such contemporary mystical figures as al-Ḥallāj. But it seems also to set him apart from the philosophic tradition that was to develop in Andalusia and that saw in such a unity the only path to immortality—and therefore accused Alfarabi of denying the possibility of immortality.) But they are, as he puts it, of the same kind and they closely resemble one another. The acquired intellect functions in the same way as the divine mind: both know all, or almost all, things by means of self-knowledge.

More important, however, is the next step. The acquired intellect—having become used to scanning actual intelligibles that are separate from matter, or having become used to knowing separated intelligibles in their proper order, hierarchy, and unity; and placed as it is on the borderline between material and immaterial beings—can make "contact" with the divine mind and get to know it directly and without effort, because the intelligibles in the divine mind are already separate from matter, ready to be known. This contact will lead to what will be described later as a kind of incarnation, not unity, which leaves open the question of the kind and degree of knowledge and powers that a person receives from the divine mind. For the role of the divine mind in this work is not merely that of mediating between God and man but also that of acting as the vicar of God in creating things here below by providing the forms to all natural beings when their matter is readied by the movement of the heavenly bodies. It is not clear to what extent Alfarabi allows the human mind to receive the demiurgic powers of the divine mind. But, as one can well see, the contact between the human mind and the divine mind opens many possibilities for a novel theory of prophecy and revelation.

A first attempt to combine the account of religion in the *Book of Religion* and the theory of knowledge expounded in the *Epistle on the Intellect* is made in the *Political Regime,* one of Alfarabi's two comprehensive political writings. The crucial passage in this work repeats the qualifications of the founder and supreme ruler listed in the accounts of human religion, but with the significant addition that, after coming to possess the most powerful and superior nature, one becomes a supreme ruler as described by the ancients "only . . . if his soul makes contact with the active intellect" (*Political Regime,* 79.8–9), which means only after his mind reaches the level of the acquired intellect, for it is through the realization of the acquired intellect that contact with the active intellect or divine mind takes place.

Alfarabi here reverses the meaning of both the ancient philosophic and the modern revealed traditions. The ancients' view of the true king (the philosopher-king) is now modified to refer to the human being who realizes the acquired intellect and makes contact with the active intellect or divine mind: "this human being is the true king according to the ancients" (*Political Regime,* 79.12). Similarly, the view of the moderns is now reversed so that this human being who achieves contact with the active intellect or divine mind becomes the one "of whom it ought to be said that he receives revelation. For, only a human being who reaches the stage at which there is no intermediary between him and the active intellect can receive revelation" (*Political Regime,* 79.12–14). This is what the moderns mean by revelation as the acquisition of knowledge from a divine source. The fact that the moderns say that revelation is from the First Cause does not present a serious problem, for the active intellect or divine mind proceeds from the First Cause: "for this reason one can say that it is the First Cause that reveals to this human being through the mediation of the active intellect" (*Political Regime,* 80.1–3). At the beginning of this work, Alfarabi says that the active intellect ought to be identified with the Trusted Spirit and the Holy Spirit, traditional names for the agent of revelation (*Political Regime*, 32.11).

A certain ambiguity regarding the meaning of revelation persists, however. Since the mediating human power in the contact with the active intellect or the divine mind is the acquired intellect, and this is apparently a theoretical intellect, it would seem that revelation means the reception of the theoretical intelligibles or forms. Yet the contact itself is not called revelation but is presented as a necessary precondition for revelation, which seems to be yet an additional thing that follows the contact, an overflow from the active intellect or divine mind, through which a human being acquires the "power with which one can understand how to define things and actions and direct them toward happiness" (*Political Regime*, 79.15–17). Thus revelation is the gift of the power of practical judgment, with which the receiver himself determines the beliefs and practices of the religious community. So we are still close to the position represented by the *Book of Religion*, where the founding of religion requires the royal art—the true king according to the ancients—along with revelation. Alfarabi seems to be particularly interested in developing the model of revelation received by someone who is in possession of complete theoretical knowledge. Nothing is said about revelation as providing the beliefs and practices already determined or how the two types of revelation can be combined in the same person.

Virtuous City 1

It has been traditionally assumed that Alfarabi's views on prophecy and revelation, in fact every aspect of his philosophy, can be found in the book entitled the *Virtuous City*. Alfarabi himself refers the reader to his works on theoretical science in general and on psychology in particular—his commentary on the *De anima*—for the explanation of what revelation is and how it takes place (*Book of Religion*, 44.12–13; *Political Regime*, 79.11). But since these works have not survived, one has been quick to turn to the *Virtuous City* for an account of Alfarabi's theoretical science and psychology as well. It is true that the account of prophecy and revelation in the *Virtuous City*, brief as it is, remains the fullest account we now possess about these questions. Yet almost everything stated there remains puzzling and somewhat problematic due to the manner in which the author defines the book's subject matter in the title, *The Principles of the Opinions of the Inhabitants of the Virtuous City*, an indication that this is a work on political science or political philosophy and that it deals with a particular aspect of this discipline: it is meant to suggest the principles useful to a future lawgiver when determining the beliefs the citizens of his city must hold (keeping in mind that "city" in this context means the regime and religion). In fact, there is a passage (*Virtuous City*, 276–78 Walzer) in which Alfarabi says that the citizens of the virtuous city should be made to believe in the opinions expounded earlier in the book.

But the ambiguous location of the doctrines expounded in this book—the fact that they fit somewhere between theoretical and practical knowledge, on the one hand, and the proposed beliefs to be held by the citizens of a future city or cities, on the other—does not prevent us from observing that, in comparison with the earlier philosophic and theological tradition, or even with Alfarabi's other works, the *Virtuous City* contains a number of novel doctrines. Elements of, or preparations for, these doctrines can be attested in the earlier philosophic tradition and in Alfarabi's other works, but the doctrines themselves are not found elsewhere in the manner developed and presented here. I suggest that perhaps the main reason Alfarabi is not always hesitant or bewildered when presenting these novel doctrines is that the purpose of the book does not allow for much hesitation or bewilderment: the citizens of the future virtuous city will need clear and precise instructions. This may account also for the fact that Alfarabi presents no philosophic arguments for the principles expounded in this book.

I shall have to forgo speaking here of the novel doctrines about the divine attributes; the number and order of the cosmic intelligences; the use made of the light, illumination, and overflow metaphors; and the relation between the divine mind, the heavenly bodies, and the sublunary world—important as these are for the belief structure proposed for the citizens of the virtuous city. Instead, I invite you to consider with me the human side of things. And since Alfarabi has been accused of thinking that prophecy has to do with the power of imagination, let us begin here.

The human power of imagination, *phantasia,* was traditionally conceived as a "bodily" faculty in the sense that it preserves, combines and separates, and imitates the data acquired by the senses. The relatively extensive and unusual account of the imagination in the *Virtuous City* presents it as a power that is continuous and communicates with the powers of sense perception, on the one hand, and of reason, on the other. It provides the link that unifies the process of human cognition. And it plays an active, creative role as a mediator. It receives information from either reason or the senses, transforms it, and transmits it to, or prepares it for, the other power. Its first activity in this regard is preparing the way for reason to grasp the first principles of knowledge provided by the active intellect or divine mind.

The doctrine that in order to explain the actualization of human reason one must posit a divine mind that is incorporeal, eternal, and one is at least as old as Aristotle's *De anima* and has roots in the Platonic forms. So is the view that the divine mind, being pure intelligence, cannot act upon or contact the imagination, at least not directly. It can only directly contact and act upon reason; but since reason is continuous with the imagination, the lightlike illumination provided by the divine mind enables reason to grasp the intelligible ideas through scanning the sense perceptions preserved in the imagination. And the first activity of reason in this regard is the grasp of the primary intelligibles, the first principles of reason common to all human beings and used by them to obtain further knowledge.

Were these first principles confined to the first principles of theoretical knowledge, we would have had no reason to be concerned with them here. But Alfarabi states that there are *three* groups of such first principles: those of theoretical knowledge, those of morality—the first principles of the noble and the base—and those of the practical arts. This is significant in itself and also because elsewhere Alfarabi follows the traditional Aristotelian view that the first principles of morality and the arts—which are the major premises on the basis of which practical judgment determines what is noble and base, useful and harmful, in particular instances—can only be acquired by human beings through experience in practical affairs over a long period of time and that they are not certain but generally held opinions, *endoxa* or *mashhūrāt* (see *Attainment of Happiness,* secs. 20–21, 15.16–16.18). Here, in contrast, the first principles of morality and the arts are presented as having the same source, being grasped at the same time and in the same way, and leading to conclusions that have the same status as the conclusions of theoretical knowledge. This radical departure from the Aristotelian tradition and from what Alfarabi himself asserts elsewhere is apparently meant to facilitate the conclusion that there is such a thing as a natural law or law of reason in morality and the practical arts and that the conclusions drawn from such a law regarding what one ought to do or avoid are just as certain as the conclusions of theoretical knowledge. It is also a return to Platonism: to the "idea" of the good and the products of the arts—of the "bed," for example—placed in the divine mind and given through its light or illumination.

Virtuous City 2

When we next meet the imagination, we find it connected with both powers of reason: the theoretical, whose function it is to know the intelligibles that are not such as to be done, and the practical, whose function it is to know the particulars to be done now or in the future. Practical reason is not required here to know the first principles of morality and the arts; these are now supposed to be known by all to begin with, perhaps through some form of Platonic "recollection." Furthermore, the imagination is connected somehow with the divine mind. I say "somehow" in order to point out the problematic character of this connection. Given the ambiguity of the relation between the divine mind and practical reason and the fact that the activity of the divine mind centers on theoretical reason exclusively in the *Epistle on the Intellect,* it is not surprising to see Alfarabi say that the illumination obtained by reason from the divine mind "may" overflow to the power of imagination, without making it quite clear whether the overflow is from the divine mind or from reason or from the illumination itself. And he concludes that in this fashion the divine mind "acts in some way" upon the imagination, providing it sometimes with the intelligibles that properly belong to theoretical reason and sometimes with the particulars that properly belong to practical reason—a statement that is particularly difficult to understand when we remember that even in the case of reason the divine mind provides only the illumination through which reason grasps the intelligibles, not the intelligibles themselves.

In any case, being a power with a corporeal base, the imagination cannot receive the intelligibles as such; it can only receive the intelligibles by imitating them by means of the sensible things it has stored, combined and separated, or imitated already. It can receive the practical, particular, sensible things in either of two ways: representing them as such or imitating them by means of other sensible things. These particular, sensible things, whether they exist now or will exist in the future, are the things that practical reason normally arrives at by deliberation and practical judgment. The imagination, in contrast, grasps them immediately, without having to discover them through deliberation or the use of practical judgment. In this manner the divine mind is made to provide the imagination with the intelligibles, which are the conclusions of theoretical knowledge, as well as with the particular, sensible things, which are the minor premises of the practical syllogism, all this while theoretical and practical reason are somewhat inactive. The functions of theoretical and practical reason are performed by the imagination. True dreams and true waking visions substitute for the activity of practical reason, and divinations concerning things divine substitute for the activity of theoretical reason. The degree and rank of what is thus received depend on the power of a healthy imagination. The most perfect imagination enables a human being to engage in prophesying about present or future particular things as such or through the use of their imitations, or prophesying about divine things through the use of their imitations. This is as far as the imagination goes and the highest rank a human being achieves through the use of his imagination.

The most attractive aspect of Alfarabi's discussion of the imagination is the vast area of activity and creativity assigned to this power, the way it is made to take over almost completely the role of theoretical and practical reason, and the seriousness with which its poetic function is considered and expounded. The discussion covers much of what one would normally think of as the realm of religious experience. The imagination is represented as a likely candidate to preempt the functions of theoretical and practical reason and to perform something like their functions without the need to undergo the labors and uncertainties involved in the pursuit of theoretical knowledge and the even greater uncertainties involved in deliberating and making practical judgments about important practical matters. The imagination makes use of a possibility in which the principles as well as the conclusions of both theoretical and practical knowledge appear to be given by a divine source. It may not have been easy for Alfarabi to find many philosophic arguments to justify the divine mind as the source of all this knowledge, especially since the divine mind does not create the sublunary world in this book and in principle ought to have possessed only the intelligibles and confined its role to giving them to theoretical reason. God's knowledge of particulars had been one of the most difficult problems for philosophy to handle, and transferring the difficulty from God to the divine mind does nothing to make it easier to resolve.

However this may be, it is important to notice that so far nothing has been said about revelation. On first view, it would seem that we are dealing with some of the types of revelation discussed earlier, especially revelation as providing particular determinations, which would seem to require the functioning of the imagination. But, in fact, not even prophesying, the highest activity of a perfect imagination, is identified as revelation. It might also seem that the human being who prophesies ought to have been considered the lawgiver and founder of a religious community based on revelation. Yet nothing is said in this context about human association, the city, or religion. Everything discussed so far seems to be pre- or subpolitical. And it seems that the discussion of things political will require us to leave this region in which the imagination reigns supreme.

Revelation

Higher and far beyond the perfection of the imagination and the perfection a human being achieves in virtue of his imagination is human perfection simply, the highest good and ultimate happiness, which becomes available only in the city and through the activity of founding a virtuous city ordered after the pattern of God's governance of the universe. This end cannot be achieved nor this function performed by any chance person, for they require appropriate natural gifts and effort and training. Alfarabi is willing to list the required natural gifts, but he offers only a summary account of the effort and training required, giving the impression that perhaps they need not be all that time-consuming or strenuous. The perfection of the imagination and its ability to receive or else imitate particular, sensible things in dream or in waking, or to imitate the intelligibles, is now relegated to a natural requirement, one of the requirements one needs to be born with or obtain early in one's career; and nothing is said about the need for effort and training in this connection. The emphasis now is on the perfection of the mind, offering a brief summary of the scheme presented in the *Epistle on the Intellect*.[3] However, the actual intellect now must know "all" the intelligibles–it is apparently no longer sufficient to know "all or most" of the intelligibles, as was the case in the earlier and more technical account—and Alfarabi uses the analogy of the relation between matter and form to explain the relation of the lower stages of intellection to the higher; hence instead of mere "contact" between the acquired intellect and the divine mind, the divine mind becomes, as it were, the form of the acquired intellect.[4]

---

3. Cf. *Epistle on the Intellect*, 12ff., with *Political Regime*, 32ff., for the account of the intellect in act, the intellect in potency, and the passive intellect; the matter-form relationship among divine intelligences is found in *Epistle on the Intellect*.

4. *Virtuous City*, 240.10–242.9 Walzer. The stages are: bits of knowledge, self-conscious and self-knowing mind, and then contact. Consider the use of the terms "passive" and "in potentiality" in *Epistle on the Intellect*, *Political Regime*, and *Virtuous City*.

Taking the entire structure "as a single thing," Alfarabi permits himself to say that the person who achieves this rank will be "the human being in whom the divine mind incarnates itself." If the incarnation takes place in both the theoretical and the practical powers of reason, and then in the imagination, this will be the human being who receives revelation: the overflow is from the divine mind as God's agent to the acquired intellect, to the passive intellect, and to the imagination. The overflow thus extends to the imagination as well, and since the imagination is "continuous" with sense perception, Alfarabi is able to conclude that this human being's soul is united, "as it were," with the divine mind. Through the overflow of the divine mind to reason he will be "wise, a philosopher, and in possession of complete practical judgment"; while, through the overflow to the imagination, he will be a "prophet, warning about future events and telling about particular things existing in the present."[5]

These oracular statements are not easy to interpret. Yet a few things seem to be clear. Although Alfarabi is not willing to enter into detail on how revelation or prophecy takes place, he asserts that it is not prophecy (defined as the overflow of the divine mind to the imagination) but revelation (defined as the overflow of the divine mind to reason) that is the vehicle for the achievement of a human being's highest perfection and for the excellence of the city he founds and rules. With the divine mind having been incarnated in him, he cannot possibly lack any kind of knowledge, for the incarnation provides him with ultimate knowledge of theoretical things far superior to, and more complete and certain than, any theoretical knowledge acquired by unaided human reason. It is revelation also, rather than prophecy, that provides certain knowledge about all practical things, which would take the philosopher a long time to learn from experience and then without necessarily knowing them with certainty. Finally, revelation provides practical judgment that is fully informed by the most comprehensive and certain theoretical knowledge, free of the vagaries that may attend long experience and training when a human being tries to perfect this power on his own.

The Political Dimension

The meaning of revelation in Alfarabi's political writings has now shifted its position from having been an appendage to the philosophic perfection

5. See *Virtuous City*, 244.3–14 Walzer. Readers of Walzer's English translation should not be confused by his translation of "in possession of complete practical judgment" *(muta'aqqilan 'alā al-tamām)* as "accomplished thinker" in *Virtuous City*, 245 Walzer, or by his

and the kingly art and from having to do exclusively with practical matters to being first and foremost the gift of wisdom, whose true meaning is stated by Alfarabi to be consummate knowledge of the most exalted beings and of the distant causes of all the beings below them, including the end of human beings and what constitutes their true happiness.[6] But philosophy, the love and pursuit of wisdom, is nonetheless present. Like wisdom and complete practical judgment, it, too, is a divine gift. Revelation includes prophecy as a second component—not prophecy in the earlier sense, dominating the soul through the power of the imagination, but prophecy as subordinate to fully actualized theoretical and practical reason and complete practical judgment, from which it receives the overflow, which it serves, but with which it does not compete. The exclusive role of prophecy now is to perform such functions as cannot be performed by reason: foretelling future events and doing other kinds of miraculous things for those who may require validating the revelation beyond its own content. It no longer has to do with the intelligibles or with representations of divine things, which can now be controlled by theoretical and practical reason and practical judgment, while the power of the imagination functions under their direct control.

This prophet is not an apolitical seer crying in the wilderness. He is, rather, part of a collective leadership, one that works in cooperation with the rational powers of the soul. In addition, such things as foretelling future events are not particularly a significant function of the person who receives revelation. He is being prepared for higher tasks, to be the model for all other human beings, to found a new religion if necessary, or else to act as the supreme ruler of a virtuous city or nation, if not of the entire *oikoumenē*. More to the point would be such abilities as representing what he knows in speech, guiding others to happiness and the things that lead to it, and leading his city or nation in war.

It is therefore not surprising that, when Alfarabi considers how rare

---

habit of translating "wise" and "wisdom" (*ḥakīm* and *ḥikma*) as "philosopher" and "philosophy" in the remaining parts of the work.

6. "Wisdom" as a faculty and as one of the qualifications of the supreme ruler is defined in *Selected Aphorisms*, aphorisms 37, 52 (practical judgment would be the same as wisdom if humans were the most excellent things in the world and the most excellent things that are), 53 (on the relation between wisdom and practical judgment), and 58 (wisdom as a component of the ruling craft). Like Aristotle (*Nicomachean Ethics*, 6.7.1141a9–11), Alfarabi states (aphorism 37 [54.8–9]) that wisdom is used to denote also those who are the most perfect masters of their art; but Alfarabi calls this a figurative, rather than a true, meaning of wisdom. It is to be noted that the term "philosophy" does not appear in *Selected Aphorisms* until aphorism 94.

it is to achieve the required nature and nurture for this kind of human being, how extremely difficult it is to find someone with all the natural gifts and the appropriate training, even were the existence of a virtuous city to be assumed—that is, the best possible place for recognizing and training such an individual—he is willing to dispense with the requirement that the one who receives revelation should also be a prophet, even in the more restricted sense assigned to prophecy under revelation.[7] Thus revelation need not go beyond making its recipient wise, a philosopher, and in possession of complete practical judgment; this will not disqualify the person from being the supreme ruler of the virtuous city, having the same rank as the original founder, and continuing the founder's role as a living lawgiver (*Virtuous City*, 248.15–250.4 Walzer).

Now, dispensing with prophecy but not with revelation as a requirement for the supreme ruler and lawgiver may seem a final attempt on the part of Alfarabi to debunk prophecy, after having first banished it to the pre- and extrapolitical realm and then limited its function in favor of revelation to the powers of reason. He is, of course, careful to dispense with prophecy completely only in the case of the successor of the founder of the religion and the virtuous city. Further, the de-emphasis on prophecy in the postprophetic period was a legitimate and indeed necessary exercise in Islamic thought. In addition, Alfarabi exploits here a resource that is very much part of the Islamic tradition concerning revelation and prophecy, which is expressed through the distinction between a "messenger" *(rasūl)* of God and a "prophet" *(nabī)*, and also between "prophecy" *(nubuwwa)* and "prophesying" *(nubū'a)*. Messengers are sent by God, each to his own nation, with a divine message to inform the people about divine things and guide them to the right path, and to act as lawgivers and founders of new religions or as reformers of older ones. It is not necessary that a messenger also be a prophet in the particular sense of prophesying, although in a more general sense the expression "prophet" may be used for any messenger. The Quran mentions numerous prophets who were not lawgivers or founders of religions or supreme rulers of their communities and who in fact lived apart from the political order and even tried to subvert it. Finally, it is well to remember that, although the founder of the Islamic community was certainly a prophet as well as a messenger, the Islamic revelation dealt largely with the founding of a religion and with the establishment of a moral and political order; proph-

---

7. See *Virtuous City*, 250.3–4 Walzer. Alfarabi mentions, in particular, foretelling future events through the imaginative faculty. This was the central function of prophecy in *Virtuous City*, 244.13 Walzer.

ecy played a relatively minor role in all this, especially after the initial Meccan period.

I say all this to show that, both as a student of the revealed religions and as a member of a religious community founded by a revelation and a prophet, Alfarabi is not saying anything about prophecy that is particularly offensive. The fact that he attributes prophecy to the imaginative faculty in particular does not mean that he disbelieved in prophecy, as the Andalusian philosopher Ibn Ṭufayl (*Ḥayy ibn Yaqẓān,* 14.7–8) would like us to believe. If by "believing" in prophecy is meant believing that the phenomenon is genuine and its source is divine, Alfarabi was very much a believer, not only in prophecy but in true dreams, waking visions, and divinations as well. He does not say a single word about any of these phenomena being possibly false or fake, when he could very well have done so. What seems to be true is that, although Alfarabi recognized the enormous power and use of the imagination in the practical human sphere, not only in the founding of religions but in every aspect of political life, he was distrustful of its functioning in isolation and without the control of reason. This is especially true in the case of religion and politics, by nature spheres in which the passions seem to dominate. Also, he saw that the continuous conflict between philosophy and certain followers or representatives of the revealed religions and their popular followings was due in large measure to the works of the imagination (the images or similitudes) losing their mooring and rebelling against their source in reason and divine intelligence, or due to the fact that those believing in them had forgotten that they are images, similitudes, or symbols of a higher truth.

Alfarabi is therefore ambivalent regarding the work of the imagination: he suspects and denigrates it when working by itself or with little rational control, yet recognizes its necessity and great utility for social life. And the control in question cannot cease with the termination of the original revelation in which the religion and the political regime are founded. The founder is able to depict in correct images what he receives through the illumination of a divine mind. Because the divine mind's light informs and controls its perfect imagination, it is able to grasp what is given to it with the most perfect image possible. The problem arises because images are necessarily particular and corporeal, which is true of both the images depicting theoretical things and those depicting practical things. They are also meant to be right, perfect, or adequate for the particular time and place and people for whom they are projected. But times change, religions expand, and followers with new and different traditions, languages, habits, and experiences enter the fold for whom the older images need to be interpreted or reinterpreted. And they need to be interpreted correctly, that is, turned back to their source. This is why the philosopher who wishes to interpret the images correctly needs to be concerned with the nature of images as well as with the truth.

Novel Doctrine

Let me now make a few remarks on the last major novel doctrine in the *Virtuous City*, which relates to the question of the qualifications of those who succeed the founder of the revealed religion. The best case is, of course, that the religious community be led by a succession of rulers who possess the very same qualifications as the founder. We have also just seen that the absence of prophecy does not disqualify a person who possesses all the other qualifications from assuming the same title and assuming the role of a living lawgiver. He, too, is a ruler who is at liberty to change the laws of his predecessors concerning the beliefs to be held by the community and the actions to be practiced at will, but always according to his wisdom, philosophic inquiry, and practical judgment as to what is appropriate in the here and now. For the founder, too, would have changed these laws had he lived to observe the new conditions.

Should a time come, however, in which no person of equal rank is found, then the second-best arrangement is to have successors of a lower rank who will not be living lawgivers in the sense just indicated but who will possess a new set of qualifications that enable them to understand, preserve, and interpret the laws laid down by the founding fathers and true lawgivers. In essence, these qualifications make of them superior judges and jurists able to consider the intentions of the lawgivers, the changes that have taken place since the departure of the lawgivers, and the conditions obtaining in the here and now, and to meet the need of the times by exerting themselves to reach legal opinions that promote the welfare of the city (*Book of Religion*, secs. 9–10). This second-best arrangement had been considered by Alfarabi on two earlier occasions. But in both cases he had concluded that it would be sufficient if the ruler in this case were a jurist-king rather than a philosopher-king—that is, a king who rules according to the law rather than a king who makes the law. Such a doctrine corresponds to the notion that the learned jurists are the true successors of the Prophet in the Islamic community or that kings should rule jointly with them.

It is therefore quite surprising to find Alfarabi insisting in the *Virtuous City* that this second-best arrangement requires the presence of wisdom also as one of the qualifications of the ruler, so that he would have to be a wise human being, a jurist, and a king. He is willing to consider the possibility that the qualifications in question may not be present in a single individual, and he has no objection to a collective leadership in which each individual possesses one or more of those qualifications, provided the group can work and rule together. Under any circumstances, however, wisdom must be present. Should a time come in which wisdom were absent, then, even though all the other qualifications were present, the virtuous city would remain without a king, the ruler of the city could not be called king, and the city would be in danger of perdition. The only hope for its survival is that by chance a wise man would be found and included in the ruling body; otherwise the city is sure to perish.

Wisdom in this context cannot mean the wisdom spoken of in the account of revelation, for revelation has ceased with the disappearance of the supreme rulers and living lawgivers; and philosophy, the love and pursuit of wisdom, is no longer present as a necessary component of the ruling craft. In the *Book of Religion* (secs. 9–10), Alfarabi has already explained that the principles of jurisprudence are to be found in theoretical and practical philosophy and that jurisprudence is therefore subordinate to philosophy in the way that a discipline that deals with particulars or examples is subordinate to a discipline that deals with the universals of those particulars. But he leaves it at that. As in the *Virtuous City*, he does not insist on philosophy having a share in ruling for the virtuous city to survive. It can survive in the absence of the philosopher, provided the ruling craft includes what he calls "knowledge of the universals of this [political] art" along with practical judgment. In the absence of the philosopher, knowledge of the universals of political science or political philosophy remains a necessary component of the ruling craft; otherwise the ruling craft is called ignorant rather than virtuous (*Book of Religion*, sec. 18, 60.6, 14, and 21). Thus, in the absence of the philosopher-king or the philosopher-prophet-king, a combination of jurisprudence, practical judgment, and political knowledge seems to be sufficient.

Why, then, the insistence in the *Virtuous City* on the presence of wisdom as a necessary component of the ruling craft? It is not easy to figure out what may have brought this change about. Yet, in some respect, it follows from the manner in which Alfarabi presented prophecy and revelation as the central theme of the *Virtuous City*.

What appears as political radicalism reflects a radicalism latent in the revealed religions, which insist on the primacy of wisdom about the whole and knowledge of divine things and distant causes in determining the ultimate fate or happiness of human beings and in defining the character of the religious community. We should never forget that the revealed religions were not meant to promote a regime meant for gentlemen ruling and being ruled in turn. They raised the sights of their followers too high to remain satisfied with a moderate regime, intermediate between the best and the worst, the virtuous and the ignorant. And Alfarabi the Platonist is willing to bask in this kind of radicalism.[8] The city will have to be based on consummate knowledge of remote causes or it will be judged as based on ignorance; the citizens must attain ultimate felicity lest they disintegrate into nothing or suffer in the hereafter (*Virtuous City,* 270.6ff. Walzer).

The absence of revelation and of the philosopher means that knowledge about the whole is no longer being received or pursued in the city. What wisdom can mean in such circumstances is hard to imagine. Or did Alfarabi mean by wisdom as a component of the ruling craft in the *Virtuous City* something other than divine wisdom or consummate knowledge of divine and human things, perhaps something like political wisdom or art (see *Selected Aphorisms,* aphorisms 4 [25.6, 10, and 12] and 21 [39.14]), in which case he was using the term in a figurative sense after all? However this may be, rulers who lack this component of the ruling craft may be able to rule for a while without it and interpret the law as jurists do and get away with it, especially in times of relative peace and stability. But they will not be able to preserve the community from rapid disintegration, revolutionary change, and messianic hopes for a new order. Only a philosophic refraction of the revelation can keep the otherwise unmitigated religiously fueled perfectionism from devouring itself.

Concluding Remarks

Prophecy and revelation have always been a source of wonder and amazement for all those who have observed and believed in them, as well as for most of those who have studied them. The historically revealed religions were seen by their followers as ushering in a new era, and they have indeed proved to be the most significant events in the history of our part of the world and, more recently, in world history. We conduct our lives

---

8. It would be worth developing this entire question in its own right. Do the monotheistic revealed religions have any room for the gentleman? What is the peculiar Farabian synthesis—if one can call it that—of the Platonic radicalism whose perfectionism is expressed by the city in speech, and of a Quranic radicalism whose perfectionism is expressed in a city to be constructed by the faithful here on earth?

and think about things in an environment permeated with these religions. We tend to argue about different interpretations of their meaning and intention—about fundamentalism and liberal theology, as well as various ethical and political implications. We are not always aware of the broad historical impact of these religions, nor do we always bear in mind the characteristic features of the new era as opposed to pagan times. Yet early followers of the revealed religions saw the transition from pagan times as the crucial event in human history: a transition from hope to realization, from the ideal rulers and cities projected in speech by the wise men of antiquity to actual divinely sent messengers and divinely ordered human communities. And today, whether we are the children of the Enlightenment, nineteenth-century romanticism, twentieth-century science, or the more recent fundamentalist movements in the revealed religions, whether we are conservative or liberal in our theology, we all base our views on some understanding of the nature of prophecy and revelation and the characteristic features of the communities established by them. The dominance of ideologies in the last half-century or so, the questions constantly raised by the developments in science and technology, the spread of belief in the imminent end of the world—all point to the need to take a fresh look at the origin of the revealed religions, their place in history, and their social and political role.

   An important aspect of Alfarabi's originality is that he seizes upon the social and political framework of the revealed religions as a new kind of *politeia* or *res-publica* and tries to understand the new kind of founder and lawgiver and the community he founded in terms of classical political philosophy, while constantly inquiring about what is new and how the new differs from the old. Major philosophers—among them Avicenna, Maimonides, and Roger Bacon—have turned to him when radical and revolutionary changes in their societies required a fresh understanding of the intentions of their respective revealed religions. He helped them recover the original theological-political intention of the revealed religions and the characteristic features and aims of the revealed religious regimes as compared with pagan regimes. For this purpose, he developed a philosophy of religion that looks at the new religious phenomena and the human link between the divine and the religious community with the same sense of wonder that had led Greek philosophers to look at nature. This was a delicate, hazardous, and difficult undertaking, perhaps the greatest challenge that faced philosophy since it came into contact with the new religions. It was, to begin with, an act of piety and justice on the part of a philosopher who tried to meet an urgent need of his own religious community. But it was also the kind of challenge philosophers were happy to meet. "The discussion of these matters," says Averroes in his commentary on Aristotle's *Parva naturalia* (75.5–7), "even though it is extremely difficult to conduct on the level of human understanding, must nevertheless reach the farthest limit the nature of human understanding permits; for this, and nothing else, is the very essence of happiness."

PART THREE

On the Philosophy of Plato and Aristotle

EIGHT

The Attainment of Happiness

The *Attainment of Happiness* does not begin with an explanation of what happiness is or a description of the way to it. Instead, it enumerates four *human* things (theoretical virtues, deliberative virtues, moral virtues, and practical arts) whose presence in political communities (nations or cities) indicates that happiness is present and that the citizens are already in possession of it (sec. 1, 2.2–5). The presence of these four human things seems to be the condition whose fulfillment will produce two kinds of happiness: the worldly happiness of this present life and the supreme or ultimate happiness of the life beyond, the life to come. The opening sentence declares all this abruptly, without justifying it or promising to do so in the sequel; apart from the sequence in which these four human things are enumerated, and naming the first three "virtues" and the last "arts," it offers no clue as to their order of rank or how they are related. It is followed immediately by an exposition of the first class of virtues, the theoretical. The reader is thus led to expect four consecutive expositions, treating the four human things in the order in which they have just been enumerated. He will pursue the discussion with the hope of learning what these four human things are in order to judge whether the political communities he sees around him possess them.

The distinction between the happiness of this life and the happiness of the life to come may not be the exclusive property of religious communities or revealed religions. Yet the Arabic expressions employed by Alfarabi are standard Islamic—even Quranic—terms. It is possible that he means to give them a meaning or a content different from their generally accepted meaning or content. But he does not do so explicitly, here or in what follows. Indeed, he does not mention "worldly happiness" or "this present life" anywhere else in the trilogy. One can explain this by suggesting that Alfarabi's main interest lies in the attainment of the highest happiness, the happiness of the world to come; as a true Muslim, he was entitled to consider worldly happiness unimportant, secondary, or instrumental. But this makes all the more urgent the question whether the possession of the four human things is a sufficient condition for the attainment of this happiness, and whether one can hope to attain it by unaided effort. The "philosopher of the Muslims" (as Alfarabi was called) could not simply have overlooked what most Muslims believed to be the primary condition for attaining ultimate happiness, which is the presence in nations of certain divine favors, a condition realized, not by human, but by divine choice: knowledge of divine things, divine providence, divine moral virtues, and divine arts—divine revelation, the legislation of divine laws, and the example of a prophet.

Alfarabi begins, however, with a discussion of theoretical virtues and a recapitulation of the elements of Aristotle's theory of scientific knowledge: its ultimate purpose; its division into the preexistent and acquired; the division of the acquired into what is acquired through investigation, inference, instruction, and study; the distinction between problems and conclusions; and the description of the latter as conviction that may constitute either opinion or science. Concern with nations and cities and with men as citizens is set aside; knowledge of the things that are is spoken of as preexisting in, and pursued or acquired by, man as an individual.

The distinction between opinion and science raises the question of the different ways or methods leading to knowledge; and although Alfarabi's immediate purpose is to describe knowledge that is certain, the description of the method that leads to certainty requires that it be differentiated from methods that do not lead to certainty and, consequently, to a description of the kinds and arrangements of premises characteristic of each one of these methods. Like the knowledge of which Alfarabi has spoken, these methods are not the special property of any nation or city. They are the methods through which man as man arrives at different sorts of convictions.

Yet Alfarabi does not proceed to describe the method that leads to certainty but diverges to what appears to be a plea for the need to understand the *differences* among these methods, for the necessity of knowing with certainty the characteristic features of each, and for the view that such knowledge is a prerequisite to the investigation of the things that are and to distinguishing conclusions that are certain from those that are not (secs. 3–4, 3.3–4.15). Throughout this passage—that is, until he resumes the description of the method that leads to certainty (secs. 5ff., 4.16ff.)—Alfarabi speaks exclusively of *us* rather than of man in general.

The topic as such does not indicate that he means by us anything more than "human beings": for lack of clarity about the specific differences among the methods is a general human predicament. It is only when he refers to the investigators and speculative thinkers "whom we observe" (3.16) that the reader is compelled to consider the possibility that he may be in the presence of something more than stylistic variation.

Alfarabi usually takes advantage of the construction of the Arabic verbal sentence to leave the subject or the actor implied or hidden in the verb.[1] But in four distinct passages, to which I shall refer, Alfarabi makes certain that no ambiguity remains regarding the fact that he is now speaking in the first person plural or in the second person singular. These passages are not evenly distributed. The longest occurs near the beginning (secs. 3–4, 3.4–4.15). They become less frequent and shorter as one advances toward the center (sec. 32, 25.11–12). Thereafter, they disappear completely, except for a single sentence that occurs toward the end (sec. 58, 43.19–44.2). The last passage is the author's colophon (sec. 63, 47.3–10).

Interlude

The interlude in question is divided into two sections (secs. 3–4), each in turn divisible into two parts.[2] The first section begins with the assertion (in the passive voice) that what is sought in every question is "the certain truth" (3.3–4), yet Alfarabi proceeds immediately to assert also that we do not attain certainty in most cases. What actually happens in such cases is (1) we attain certainty about part of the question and "belief" in the rest; (2) we "imagine" something about it; (3) we stray from it and still "believe" that we have grasped it; or (4) we are perplexed about it.

In the second part of this section (3.8–16), Alfarabi offers to explain the cause of this state of affairs. We must be following a variety of methods; and since we seem to consider these conclusions satisfactory and in one case (3), at least, we are satisfied with a belief that is not true, we must be unaware that these methods are different or where the differences among them lie; indeed, we must believe that there is only one

---

1. This gives rise to serious problems when an editor or translator is forced to specify the implied noun or pronoun in question. The manuscripts differ in the extent to which they supply the necessary diacritical points and are not reliable in the vowel signs they provide. To supply these means to decide upon the gender, number, person, and tense of the verb; not infrequently, all this may have to be decided on the basis of what might be called circumstantial evidence.

2. For these references, see the English translation cited in References.

method and that it is the one we happen to follow. Alfarabi repeats this
through an example in which he indicates that we may have to follow
different methods for different questions: for one problem, for example,
a method that leads to certainty, and for another a method that leads to
an image of the truth or a method that leads to belief about it. Here
again, being unaware of the differences among these three methods, we
hold that there is only a single method.

Now, since according to Alfarabi what is sought is the certain truth,
the fact that we believe that there is only one method implies that we
believe this single method to be the method that leads to the certain
truth; and the fact that we are unaware of the varieties of methods implies
that we are unaware of the varieties of conviction or of the different states
of the soul that correspond to them. We are unaware of the difference
between truth, belief, and image; and we are unaware of the difference
between certainty, persuasion, imagination, straying away or being lost,
and perplexity. Alfarabi's example does not deal with the last two states
of the soul. He is more particularly interested in the fact that we are unaware of the difference between imagination-representation and per-
suasion-belief, on the one hand, and certainty-truth, on the other. He
concludes this section by emphasizing again that this is how we find the
matter to stand *with us* in most cases and specifying that this is how the
matter stands with the overwhelming majority of those who investigate
speculative matters whom *we* observe around us.

Who are *we*? Although all the terms that Alfarabi employs and the
methods he mentions in this section have their technical meanings in the
art of logic, the need for a technical knowledge of these matters or even
of the fact that they are the object of a special art is not presupposed in
this section; on the contrary, we only become aware of the need for such
technical knowledge when we consider the consequences of its absence.
We may therefore call Alfarabi's use of these terms pretechnical.

All the terms used by him, whether referring to the methods or their
conclusions, are also Quranic terms. The most notable among them are
"the certain truth" *(al-ḥaqq al-yaqīn)* and "going astray" or "being lost"
(ḍalāl), which describe the Islamic revelation and ignorance of it, respectively. Yet Alfarabi does not draw the distinction between those of *us* who
are Muslims and those of *us* Muslims who have observed the condition
prevalent among us. Also, the awareness of the cause of the prevalent
confusion (the variety of methods) does not result from possessing a
non-Islamic or foreign science but rather from observing the existence
of various kinds of convictions among us. Alfarabi speaks here as a Mus-

lim; he tacitly identifies himself with those Muslims who, observing the prevalence of confusion among their coreligionists, are concerned with its cause and remedy. In this respect, the *Attainment of Happiness* is an exoteric work.

The second section begins with a request to the party to whom the work is addressed (sec. 4, 3.17–4.10). It is not the nations and the cities or man in general or *you* in the plural. The addressee is referred to in the second person singular and asked in the imperative form to consider the condition prevalent among us and its cause and to reach the evident conclusion that—unlike the rest of us who are investigating questions and arriving at hybrid convictions—*we* cannot escape the need to abandon their ways and to realize three things that they do not realize: (1) that all these methods are technical, that is, not natural to us or revealed and established by authority; (2) that we need a science by means of which we can discern the specific differences among these methods; and (3) that our natural aptitude for science is not sufficient for discerning these differences. Therefore, in addition to natural aptitude, we need a special art to develop this aptitude and give us an account of the differences in question. Through this art "we become certain" about those premises and their arrangements that lead to certainty-truth, being lost-perplexity, belief-persuasion, and imagination-representation.

In the second part of this section (4.11–15), Alfarabi repeats that only after acquiring this knowledge should we take further steps. In the repetition, he substitutes the "science of beings" for the "investigation of problems" mentioned at the beginning of the section. Also, both there and in the entire preceding section he was entirely silent about instruction and study, about "what *we* had learned from others" and "what *we* ourselves teach others." But now we are ready to look for the "science of beings" in all these ways. For now we know what manner of thing each of them is; we possess the power to distinguish the various sorts of conclusions we reach and the various sorts of convictions we achieve. Finally, we can *test* what we have learned from others and what we ourselves teach others.

Only on rare occasions does Alfarabi identify his addressee or direct our attention to him. But once he is introduced, we have to learn all we can about him and keep him in view. For it is to him that Alfarabi speaks directly and not to us: we are only the audience of the dialogue. When Alfarabi speaks of *us*, he is speaking of himself and of his addressee; he means *I* and *thou* or a larger group to which *I* and *thou* belong but which is still delimited: *we*; *we* Muslims; *we* who have observed the condition prevalent among *us* Muslims regarding the methods; *we* who cannot escape realizing that these methods are technical or the product of art, who need a science by means of which to designate their specific differences, and who possess natural aptitude for science and need to develop it through an art that makes it possible to ascertain the character of the premises and the arrangement proper to each method; *we* who set out to seek the science of the things that are only *after* acquiring this prerequisite knowledge; *we* who claim to know how to investigate and teach and learn only *after* proficiency in logic; *we* who have the power to test the truth of what we discover, of what others teach us, and of what we teach others, and who can distinguish between truth, beliefs, and representations.

There is, of course, a difference between the *I* and the *thou* of these *we*'s. On the very rare occasions when Alfarabi speaks of himself in the first person singular, he says *I mean:* that is, he proceeds to explain a statement whose meaning is clear to himself but not to the addressee. And whenever he speaks directly to his addressee, he commands him to do something or indicates the way in which the addressee can reach a certain conclusion. The addressee does not yet belong to the more restricted *we* to which Alfarabi belongs; he is being led by the hand. At this stage, for instance, he is required to train himself in the art of logic so as to qualify for stepping up from membership in *us,* the Muslims who are observing the methodological confusion we are in, to membership in *us,* the logicians who have overcome that confusion and who possess the proper equipment to acquire knowledge of the things that are.

If the reader now follows the discussion of logic and the sciences of the things that are (mathematics, physics, divine science, and human or political science) with this last distinction in mind,[3] he will notice that in every instance where Alfarabi interrupts the progress of the anonymous "investigator" (8.16ff.) to speak of us, the topic is the same: the distinction between things as they are known to us and things as they are known by nature. Alfarabi develops the logical implications of this distinction (the classical statement about it occurs in the opening chapter of Aristotle's *Physics*) immediately after concluding the passage just analyzed. From this discussion it becomes clear that *certain truth* and the *way* to it are equivocal terms and that to begin with primary cognitions is the necessary but not sufficient condition for achieving the ultimate aim of theoretical science. This is brought out by the distinction between the "prin-

3. See secs. 5–20, 4.16–16.15.

ciples of instruction" and the "principles of being," a distinction that goes beyond the formal differentiation of the various logical methods.[4]

Thus *our* scientific method is distinguished by our recognition that the principles of instruction we employ may be different from the principles of being. (In the case of one being, the ultimate principle or God, we possess only the principles of *our* knowledge of it.) We persist in progressing through the effects known to us toward the causes or the principles that we do not know; only when we come to know these principles on the basis of what is clear to us do we proceed to explain the effects of these principles that are hidden from us. In mathematics, these problems do not arise. The principles of instruction are identical with the principles of being, and mathematical proofs (as Alfarabi emphasizes through the interjection *I mean* [sec. 11, 9.19]) are purely formal. It is in this sense that the inquiry into numbers and magnitudes is "easier" and least susceptible to "perplexity and confusion," and hence less likely to give rise to differences of opinion regarding the character of its method and the certainty of its proof. Alfarabi does not speak of *us* anywhere in connection with the mathematical sciences. In natural science, in contrast, the principles of instruction are for the most part different from and subordinate to the principles of being; here Alfarabi refers again to those of us who ascend from the principles of instruction to the principles of being and then descend to explain the things that originate from the principles of being, which were originally unknown to us.

It is curious, however, that when Alfarabi proceeds to describe the progress of the investigator through the part of natural science that deals with man, his perfection, and sociability, through divine science, and through human or political science, he does not refer to *us* again; the "investigator" is now mentioned more frequently; and instead of being given "demonstrations," we are told that the conclusions of these matters "become evident *to him*." For the time being, I restrict myself to the following observations. Alfarabi's last reference to *us* occurs at the end of the science of nature in the strict sense—that is, the investigation of bodies and things corporeal. The investigation of the principles of being

4. In his *Short Commentary on the Posterior Analytics* (MS Ḥamīdiyya, 812, fol. 67r), Alfarabi explains this distinction by the following example. We observe a gradual increase in the light of the moon as it turns from crescent to full moon. From this we infer that the moon is spherical. The increase in the light of the moon is the cause of our knowledge that the moon is spherical. Yet it is the spherical shape of the moon that is the cause of the gradual increase in its light. This is what Alfarabi means by saying that the principles of instruction are the causes of our knowledge of the principles of being, and yet the principles of being are the causes of the existence of whatever we happen to employ as principles of instruction.

of the heavenly bodies and of the human intellect leads to the recognition that these principles "are not natures or natural beings . . . nor bodies nor in bodies" (sec. 16, 12.16–17).

The investigation of metaphysical or divine beings begins with principles of instruction, then the investigator recognizes that none of these beings possesses a material cause, and his investigation of their other three causes leads him finally to a Being that has no cause or principle of being at all. Hence the ultimate aim of divine science, which is the knowledge of this Being, is confined to the knowledge *that* this Being exists and does not include any knowledge of the principles of its being. As for the investigation of man, it too leads to the recognition that "natural principles" are insufficient. As it considers soul and intellect, it recognizes that their principles consist of certain "ends" and of the "last perfection" of man, which, again, do not act as natural causes but are objectives for which man has to work by making use of certain rational principles that are in him.

Having learned about this perfection, the investigator now knows the end of human deliberation, moral acts, and practical arts, and this knowledge enables him to distinguish those of them that serve man's perfection from the ones that do not, or that obstruct man's perfection. Unlike the investigation of bodies or corporeal things, the theoretical investigation of man leads to knowledge, not of the causes or the grounds of an existing thing, but only of the "perfection which [man] should achieve." Whereas in things that are strictly natural the investigation starting from the principles of instruction can lead to certainty regarding their existence and all the grounds of their existence, in divine science the principles of instruction make it evident "to the investigator" merely *that* an ultimate principle exists and *that* it must be perfect without qualification, and in human or political science the principles of instruction lead him to see the *what* and *how* of man's perfection or end—that is, the *that* of such a perfection remains a problem.

At the end of his description of theoretical science, Alfarabi turns once again to the addressee and speaks to him as follows: "This, then, is theoretical perfection. As *you see*, it comprises knowledge of the four kinds of things through which the citizens of cities and nations attain the utmost happiness" (sec. 18, 16.15–27; emphasis added). "To see" (*ra'ā*) is the verb from which the technical term "opinion" (*ra'y*) is derived and in turn gives its signification back to the verb, which thus means also "to opine" or "to form an opinion." Alfarabi does not expect his interlocutor, who not long ago had to be asked to reflect on the confusion of methods among *us,* to have had an opportunity to attain "the certain truth" or "knowledge" about theoretical perfection. But he does expect him to be able now to form a likely view or opinion about what theoretical perfection comprises or about the kind of knowledge it is.

His ability to form such an opinion presupposes the ability to see the necessity of discerning the character of the various methods, learning the method that leads to the certain truth, and joining those of *us* who are logicians. But it presupposes also that he had an opportunity to observe how *we logicians* proceed in attaining knowledge of the things that are in the way they really are, and especially how *our* method ascertains the *that* and *why* of natural beings. This means that our associate has had an opportunity to observe how *we physicists* apply the method that leads to certainty first and foremost in the study of nature and natural beings, including man; how we refuse to discourse about things that do not form part of the natural world in which we live until the investigation of the principles of the things we know *forces* us to inquire into things that are "not nature or natural"; and how we proceed then to investigate divine things on the basis provided by the knowledge of nature and natural beings, admit only what becomes evident through this investigation, and refuse to accept as certain that which we have not been able to ascertain. Alfarabi is not instructing the addressee in the theoretical sciences; he leads him through them to show how they operate and helps him form a conviction that theoretical perfection consists of what can be known in and through these theoretical sciences alone.

Since we have no way of measuring the addressee's reaction apart from Alfarabi's speech, we can only express our amazement at the implications of the question that follows; for the mere fact that it is asked indicates the measure to which Alfarabi's enterprise has been successful: "Are you, then, of the opinion [do you suppose, is it possible] that these theoretical sciences have also supplied what can make these four [bases of happiness] actually exist in nations and cities?" (sec. 22, 16.19–17.1). The addressee does not seem to object to the definition of theoretical perfection or the claim that it is knowledge of all the things required for the attainment of happiness. On the contrary, he is ready to be asked the question—and the two interlocutors are ready to consider the problem—whether theoretical perfection by itself comprises everything needed for the attainment of happiness; whether it supplies, in addition to knowledge, whatever is needed to bring everything that leads to the attainment of happiness into actual existence among citizens and in political communities.

Before undertaking to describe the method of certainty and the different theoretical sciences, Alfarabi chose to draw the addressee's attention to *us* Muslims and the confusion of methods prevalent among *us*. Now, with more important issues at stake—what constitutes perfection and ultimate happiness, and how they are realized—he is oblivious to what *we* Muslims believe them to be or how *we* believe they should be realized. It is possible to explain Alfarabi's silence in part as follows. Because *we* do not differentiate the methods from each other, *we* cannot distinguish certainty from persuasion or imagination and cannot judge which is knowledge of the truth and which is an opinion about it or an image of it. Therefore, only *we* Muslims who are also logicians and physicists know what science is and can determine what "theoretical perfection" consists of. Since the theoretical knowledge that concerns man includes knowledge of his perfection and happiness, *we* alone are competent to judge what these, too, consist of. Yet even *we* do not know, at least not prior to examination, whether theoretical perfection is sufficient for the attainment of happiness or whether something else is needed.

Before exploring Alfarabi's understanding of religion, it would be premature to question the implicit claim made here for *us* logicians and physicists. Those of *us* who are Muslims without being logicians or physicists would certainly dispute that claim and suggest that the best knowledge of man's happiness, especially his "ultimate" happiness, is what is presented in the divine law, and that the divine law also shows the way to achieve this happiness. We shall see that Alfarabi does not dispute this suggestion but acknowledges everything it claims. However, since even *we* logicians and physicists are willing to consider the question whether theoretical perfection is sufficient for the attainment of happiness, a superficial examination does not make clear why Alfarabi does not indicate how this question appears to *us* Muslims. Furthermore, by asserting that knowledge of man's perfection and happiness can be acquired through unaided reason, Alfarabi the logician and physicist does not cease to belong to *us* Muslims; otherwise, the Quranic injunction that *we* ought to investigate the heavens and all existing things (7, 185) would have been in vain. The question is thus relevant to *us* Muslims; yet, to be relevant to *us*, it has to be formulated as follows: does this theoretical perfection supply everything needed for the attainment of ultimate happiness?

Should the answer to this question be in the affirmative, it will inevitably lead us to wonder about the use of religion and the divine law, apart, that is, from urging us to acquire this theoretical perfection. If, on the other hand, theoretical perfection supplies only knowledge of ultimate happiness and what leads to it, there will still be need for something else that brings what is known theoretically into actual existence, and this can be the function of religion and the divine law. This latter position, which implies that the function of religion and the divine law is to bring into actual existence what man's unaided reason comes to know in theoretical science, is said by some to have been taken by the Muslim philosophers, including Alfarabi. It is therefore all the more surprising that in this context Alfarabi refuses to take a stand on the issue of religion and that his interlocutor also finds no difficulty in accepting Alfarabi's answer, which is this: theoretical perfection is not sufficient for actualizing happiness in cities and nations; what is needed additionally, however, is not religion and divine law but something like prudence.

The interlocutor seems to show an unexpected readiness in accepting this answer. Yet it is possible that we have underestimated him from the outset. Alfarabi hints at this possibility by reminding his interlocutor of the opening sentence, which asserted that every kind of happiness can be attained by citizens of cities and by nations, provided they come to possess the four human things enumerated there, and that he, the interlocutor, had already accepted that assertion. The question now is whether knowledge of what these four things are is the same as their possession by, or realization among, the citizens and political communities. To answer this question negatively is to affirm Alfarabi's original statement—that is, that the attainment of happiness presupposes the possession of all the four accomplishments, not theoretical virtue alone; and the present discussion proceeds to show why, besides theoretical virtue, we need the deliberative virtue, or the virtue of prudence. The problem that is of immediate interest to the interlocutor is not whether we need divine assistance in addition to the four human accomplishments but whether we need any other human virtue and art besides theoretical virtue and its perfection; and the fact that Alfarabi devotes almost half of the *Attainment of Happiness* to convince him that such a need exists is indicative of the importance of this problem as well as of the interlocutor's defective knowledge of practical matters.

The Investigator and the Prince

In contrast to parts 1 and 4, in each of which Alfarabi speaks twice directly to his addressee, parts 2 and 3 (which attempt to find a solution to the problem just mentioned) contain no direct reference to the addressee.[5] Moreover, we find only two cursory references to *us* in part 2 and none in part 3. The reason Alfarabi could refer to *us* on numerous occasions in part 1 (at the end of which he was also able to say with confidence that the addressee could form his own opinion about the presentation that had preceded and that this opinion agreed with his own) no longer seems valid. This change corresponds to a change in the main theme.

The theme of part 1 was theoretical virtue; its hero was the "investigator," whose aim is to make intelligible with certainty the things that are; logic and the investigation of nature held the central position. The theme of parts 2 and 3 is the realization of the four human things in cities and nations. Part 2 attempts to show that this requires not only theoretical perfection but also the highest deliberative virtue, the highest moral virtue, and the highest practical art; and that all four should be acquired by a human being equipped for them by nature. Its hero is not the investigator of the theoretical sciences as such but someone who possesses the will and decides to bring the four human things required for the attainment of happiness into actual existence in cities and nations. Therefore, he needs another faculty besides the theoretical and should acquire the political virtue and all the other qualifications of the prince.

Alfarabi's arguments are still directed to the addressee, to the logician and physicist. Nevertheless, at the beginning of part 2, Alfarabi indicates that the matters under discussion do not fall within the domain of physics; they emerge only when one sees the distinctions between them and natural beings. Particular natural beings are actualized and given their attributes by nature, while it is by the activity of the will that virtues and arts are realized. Alfarabi uses natural beings to explain and make evident to his addressee some of the problems involved in realizing things that depend on the will and to explain that the latter fall in a class by themselves.

Alfarabi's difficulty in guiding his addressee in the direction that he intends can perhaps be seen best from the particular manner in which he formulates the two phrases in which he refers to *us* in this part. Temperance and wealth, like man, are intelligible notions; but unlike the notion man, they are not natural but voluntary. Therefore, "*if we decide* to bring them into actual existence, we have to know how their attributes vary in

5. I follow here the fourfold division of the text into "parts" as in the translation cited above.

time, place, and so forth (sec. 24, 19.5ff.; emphasis added). Again, the most authoritative or the highest art is that which precedes all other arts; "*if we decide* to perform its functions" (sec. 32, 25.16ff.; emphasis added), we will have to make use of the functions of all the other arts.

In the case of natural beings, it is sufficient to know the intelligible notions, for nature itself brings the particular natural beings into existence and supplies them with the required attributes. But in the case of voluntary notions, the knower himself performs this function, and knowledge alone does not enable him to perform it well. Further, there is no necessary connection between knowledge of the intelligible notions temperance and wealth and the activity of bringing these notions into actual existence. The activity depends on a further condition, the desire and the decision to perform it. The conjunction "if" *(idhā)*, which Alfarabi employs in both instances, implies a condition that is not necessarily present in the possessor of theoretical science. Beyond this, Alfarabi ceases to speak of *us* in divine science and human or political science in part 1, and thus we begin to suspect that the absence of the desire and decision that he specifies here affects the theoretical study of divine and human things, as distinguished from logic and physics, where the common ground hinted at by the frequent reference to *us* was most apparent. Absence of the will in the addressee to actualize voluntary intelligible notions in cities and nations somehow affects his theoretical understanding of them, or it produces a lack of enthusiasm for divine and human things as distinguished from logic and physics.

Be this as it may, the addressee is excluded from part 3. The theme of this part is no longer the argument that the possessor of theoretical virtue must also possess the highest deliberative and moral virtues and the highest practical art—that is, that he must become a true prince. Rather, it describes what a prince who has achieved these virtues must learn and do. Since he ought to be able to actualize the specialized virtues and arts in cities and nations, Alfarabi proceeds to explain how he ought to teach and form the character of his subjects, persuade and conquer, legislate, order the classes of his subordinates, and lead cities and nations and every group and every individual to the ultimate happiness for which they are equipped by nature. The implication of this material with reference to the addressee seems to be clear. It is up to him to decide whether he wishes to become a prince. If he decides to become one, and succeeds, this will be his reward. If not, he will be excluded from this great power and glory, and Alfarabi excludes him from it now in a symbolic way by not addressing him and not including him among the "supreme rulers" who, among other things, will have the power to control the teaching and investigation of the theoretical sciences.

Prince, Philosopher, Legislator, and *Imām*

With the termination of part 3, the treatment of the subject matter of the *Attainment of Happiness,* strictly speaking, is completed. The four human things whose possession leads to happiness have been dealt with, both in themselves and in respect to the ways whereby they are realized in nations and cities. A cursory glance at the opening and concluding remarks of each one of the first three parts suffices to show that Alfarabi supplies a rigid framework to remind the reader of the steps of his argument and that within this framework the concluding remarks of part 3 announce that the subject matter upon which the author had embarked is now definitely terminated. Part 4 seems to be a kind of epilogue that is extraneous to the theme formulated in the opening sentence of the *Attainment of Happiness.* Were the latter indeed the true theme of the work, it would be difficult to justify the presence of this last part.

Moreover, part 4 introduces a number of new topics, all of which are treated with relative haste. It begins with a praise of theoretical science and traces its origins. It explains the meaning of "philosophy" and "religion" and the relation between them "according to the Greeks." It explains the ideas as well as the *names* of "prince," "philosopher," "legislator," and *imām* (aristocrat). It explains how the same human being can be a philosopher and a religious lawgiver. It distinguishes between the false and true philosopher and asserts the latter's claim to rule. Finally, it traces *this* kind of philosophy to the Greeks in general and to Plato and Aristotle in particular, and this serves as a transition to the remaining two parts of the trilogy. The swiftness with which these topics are treated is compensated for, however, by relatively frequent direct references to authorities, a practice Alfarabi had avoided up to this point with a single exception: the reference to Plato with respect to the education of the prince in part 3 (sec. 40, 30.7).

Once we consider these references, we begin to discern the general theme of this part and the relationship between it and the theme of part 1. We remember that part 1 concluded with the assertion that *theoretical* science encompasses knowledge of the four human things whereby cities and nations attain ultimate happiness and that Alfarabi took it for granted that the addressee understood what this assertion meant. But consideration of the problem whether theoretical science is sufficient for realizing these four things led to the conclusion that, not one, but *four* kinds of science are required: (1) theoretical sciences that make intelligible the things that are by certain demonstrations; (2) rhetorical sciences that present these same intelligibles by way of persuasion; (3) poetic sciences that supply representations of these intelligibles by way of persuasion; and (4) sciences extracted from the first three for each nation (sec. 46, 35.2–8). Alfarabi does not tire of repeating in this part that the first kind is the highest. But his intention is to convince the addressee that he should accept the other three sciences as necessary and useful and that these sciences should be employed to fulfill the purpose of theoretical science, which is man's ultimate happiness (sec. 52, 38.9–13; cf. sec. 44, 34.1). The addressee does not need to be convinced of the superiority of theoretical science. Alfarabi tried to prove in part 2 that, by themselves, the theoretical sciences are not sufficient for the realization of ultimate happiness, and he proceeded in part 3 (apparently without noticing whether the addressee was able or willing to follow this discussion) to elaborate the activities of the prince who teaches the citizens and forms their character by their consent and by compulsion. Originally, the addressee was asked to admit that other things are needed in addition to theoretical science. Now he is being asked to admit that the other kinds of science are needed besides the theoretical.

Alfarabi does not call these three kinds "rhetorical," "poetic," and "national"; but these names are appropriate if we consider their definitions. If we place ourselves in the position of the addressee, the first question that comes to mind is whether Alfarabi is justified in calling the nontheoretical disciplines "sciences" or whether the usage is arbitrary. Through frequent repetition of the name "science," by itself and in conjunction with the demonstrative pronoun, "*this* science," "*these* sciences," and "*those* sciences," Alfarabi forces the addressee to wonder about this question, distracts him from other objections he might have had, and almost reduces the whole issue to one of *names*. Then he proceeds to show his own competence as an authority on names and their meaning, that his manner of using names is based on solid authority and understanding, and that the addressee should learn this from him.

The problematic character of names emerges in this part as follows. Alfarabi justifies the existence of the other sciences on the ground that they are necessary for the instruction of the vulgar. He sets forth the distinction between the vulgar and the elect on the basis of the distinction between common opinion and knowledge. But the names "vulgar" and "elect" are not applied in general usage to those who accept com-

mon opinions and those who seek to know, respectively; they are not
employed strictly on the basis of knowledge but on the basis of belief:
people who are skilled in a certain art say that they themselves belong to
the elect and that others are vulgar, because they believe that they themselves possess knowledge and that others follow generally accepted opinions (sec. 50, 37.3–14). Alfarabi introduces this common and imprecise
usage, not to cast doubt on the true distinction between the vulgar and
the elect, but to support it. The common usage, based on what people
think or believe, reflects the true meanings of these names. The distinction between the vulgar and the elect is known best, not by the practitioners of the arts who are confined to their own belief about what they
know, but by the practitioners of the sciences, especially those of them
who possess the highest science, which is not based on generally accepted opinion.

Alfarabi turns from the practitioners of the arts to the practitioners of
this science, attempts to determine which was the first or earliest group
to possess it, and tries to find out what the name "science" meant according to "them." But here he meets with the following problem. Tradition relates ("it is said") that the first to possess this science were the
Chaldeans and that it passed from them to the Egyptians, the Greeks,
the Syrians, and finally the Arabs. Alfarabi did not have the literature of
the Chaldeans or the Egyptians on the subject, or he did not trust what
went under that name in his time. (He did not know, for instance,
whether what was reported to be the wisdom of the Chaldeans and of
the Egyptians meant "this [theoretical] science" or "the other sciences.")
The only literatures he knew embodying the expression of this science
were in the Greek, the Syriac, and the Arabic tongues. In order to find
out the earliest uses of the name "science," he had to go back to the
Greeks ("among whom it remained for some time"). They are Alfarabi's
best authority, both because they possessed this science and because we
have the names they applied to it and know what they meant by these
names.

In part 3, Alfarabi broadened the meaning of science to include the
other three kinds of science besides the theoretical, and he broadened
the function of science to include a political, besides a cognitive, role.
Now he defends all this as the original meaning and function of science
"among the Greeks who possessed *this* science." The first name they had
for it was "absolute wisdom" and the "highest wisdom"; they gave the
name "science" to the acquisition of that wisdom. They had a specifically
Greek name, "philosophy," for the scientific state of mind; but what they

meant by philosophy was the *love* of that highest wisdom. The one who acquires this wisdom is not named "scientist" by them, but "philosopher," by which name they meant the *lover* of the highest wisdom. Alfarabi's account of these names thus shifts away from "science" to "wisdom" and "love of wisdom"—to philosophy and the philosopher. Finally, he reports the view or opinion of the Greek philosophers about the object of their love, the highest wisdom (that potentially it encompasses *all* the virtues), reports the names they gave to it ("the science of sciences" and so forth), and explains what they meant by such names.

The conclusion is this. Alfarabi is not an innovator. The innovators are those who restrict the meaning of science to theoretical science only. Whatever the advantages of this restriction, it departs from the original meaning of "wisdom" and "philosophy." Seen in that original and wider perspective, the investigations of theoretical science alone do not constitute the search for the highest wisdom, and the philosophy that obtains theoretical science without the power to instruct and form the character of the multitude is incomplete philosophy. Alfarabi's notion of science, wisdom, and philosophy is the original notion, which is also the perfect and most complete notion.

In comparison, the concept of science as merely theoretical is an innovation and a partial or incomplete concept. Seen in this partial perspective, the philosopher need not be the supreme ruler; but were one to recover the original, unrestricted concept of the philosopher (the notion of the absolute philosopher), then "philosopher" and "supreme ruler" would mean the same thing. Moreover, by returning to the original use of names, we recover, concomitantly with the older, more authoritative, and unrestricted meaning of "philosophy," the meaning of "religion" according to the ancients and the relationship between philosophy and religion, which finds its highest expression in the activity of the philosopher-lawgiver. Finally, the recovery of the original Greek names "wisdom," "science," and "philosophy" teaches us, not only the original meanings of these names and the relationship among them, but also how different names can indicate different aspects of the same thing. It enables us to see how these names indicate separate things when we think only of the restricted signification of the names and that to find out their true meaning is to recover their unconditional or unrestricted signification. For instance, "lawgiver" signifies the discovery of the particular conditions under which happiness can be sought by a particular political community.

But this presupposes that the lawgiver knows what happiness is, or that he has acquired philosophy. The name "philosophy" has acquired the restricted significance of theoretical virtue. But the existence of the theoretical virtue in its last perfection requires the presence of the other, nontheoretical virtues as well. The name "prince" signifies complete power. But to possess complete power without restriction means to possess also the inner power of thought, virtue, and art. The name "*imām*" (cf. sec. 40, 29.18, passim) in Arabic means being followed and accepted as a guide. But in order to be followed and accepted without condition or restriction, a guide should have the highest purpose, science, virtue, and art. Alfarabi returns to the original meaning of "science," not merely to justify his own manner of using this name or to recover the original meaning of "wisdom" and "philosophy," but to recover the way Greek philosophers (the ancients) would have thought about names (such as *imām*) that were not known to the Greeks but whose meaning has to be sought out "according to the Arabic language."

This, then, seems to be the immediate object of part 4: to train the addressee in the method of transcending the restricted signification of names. In the third of the four instances in which Alfarabi speaks directly to the addressee, and in the second of the three instances in which he employs the formula "make it evident to yourself," he commands him to learn that the logical, abstract, or unrestricted meaning *(maʿnā)* of the utterances *(alfāz)* "philosopher," "supreme ruler," "prince," "lawgiver," and *imām* is one and the same (sec. 58, 43.18–19). He also alludes to the way he, the addressee, can learn the unity underlying this diversity of expressions:

> Whichever one of these utterances you take, proceeding then to consider what each one of them signifies according to the majority of those who speak *our language,* you will find that in the end they all agree by signifying one and the same meaning. (Sec. 58, 43.19–44.2; emphasis added)

Thus the addressee cannot learn what Alfarabi asks him to learn merely by taking the utterances themselves, but only by going further and finding out what they signify among those who speak *our* language.

Had we not become aware of the problem of language and the central place it occupies in the present part, and also of the fact that (apart from the colophon) this is the sole instance in it in which Alfarabi refers to us, we might have been satisfied with the apparent linguistic meaning of *our* language—Arabic, the language spoken by Alfarabi and his addressee. But immediately prior to this command Alfarabi explained the *meaning* of *imām* "in the language of the Arabs" and said that "it signifies merely the one whose example is followed and who is well received." Then he proceeded to explain how one must understand this definition: when the implied restriction of the signification of the name is lifted, then *imām* will come to mean the same as "philosopher." The latter signification is surely not "according to the language of the Arabs."

Further, the name "philosopher" is Greek and not Arabic. Alfarabi had labored so hard to point out the importance of recovering the original Greek meaning of names such as "science" and "wisdom" that he could not be asking the addressee to accept, as his final authority on what the name "philosopher" signifies, its signification among the majority of those who do not speak Greek. They could not, for instance, surmise by looking at the word *faylasūf* that it means "the one who loves and is in quest of the highest wisdom," which, according to Alfarabi's report, is the authoritative meaning given to the Greek name by those among the Greeks who possessed the highest science. By the same token, *our* language could not mean Greek, for *imām* is not a Greek word. And although Alfarabi mentions the fact that the highest science was expressed "in the Greek tongue," he never explains the meaning of any name according to the Greek tongue, but only according to "those among the Greeks who possessed this science." These two are not necessarily identical. For instance, in the Greek tongue, "philosopher" means the one who loves or is in quest of wisdom; while those among the Greeks who possessed this science "meant by 'philosopher' the one who loves and is in quest of the *highest* wisdom."

In his explanation of the meaning of *imām*, which goes beyond the meaning of the name "in the language of the Arabs," Alfarabi does not follow the signification of the name according to the Greek tongue but follows the practice of "those among the Greeks who possessed this science" and who gave Greek names meanings that go beyond the common meaning of the expressions in question. *Our* language is, therefore, neither Greek nor Arabic; it is the language of "those who possess this science," whether Greeks or Arabs. It is also not the language common to Alfarabi and his addressee. The addressee, we found out, is a neophyte in *this* language: he is commanded to learn it. The estrangement between Alfarabi and his addressee, which reached its climax in part 3, is not resolved here through a common denominator (the Arabic language). Alfarabi only holds forth the promise that the addressee can join a new community to which he does not yet belong, provided he learns its language. Only by learning this new language can he know what "philosophy," "legislation," and "religion" truly mean and that mere knowledge of theoretical science is the sign of the counterfeit, vain, and false philosopher.

Although Alfarabi does not specify further who the Greeks or the ancients who spoke this language were, there is a figure who plays a significant role in this part and, as it were, embodies the authority on which Alfarabi bases his reinterpretation of the meaning of "science." Plato enjoys the distinction of being the only philosopher whose name is mentioned in the text of the *Attainment of Happiness*. He is mentioned for the first time in part 3 where, in connection with the education of *imāms* and princes and their political role, Alfarabi refers the reader to Plato's account (in the *Republic*) of the steps that they should follow in learning the sciences and acquiring the habits of character from their childhood until they become the supreme rulers of the city (sec. 40, 30.7). Although it is evident that he is the primary authority for the entire part, it is only in part 4, after Alfarabi's reference to the ancients and their view of the relation between philosophy and religion, that Plato emerges as the key figure in the *Attainment of Happiness*. Alfarabi refers to what Plato does in the *Timaeus* as the model for the production of sensible images of intelligible things (sec. 55, 41.5). This image-making activity is said to be characteristic of religion in contrast to philosophy, which presents a demonstrative account of the things themselves.[6] Then, in the concluding discussion concerning the distinction between the true and the false philosopher, Alfarabi refers again to Plato's account in the *Republic* of the necessary equipment that the student of theoretical science should possess in order not to end up as a counterfeit, vain, or false philosopher (sec. 61, 45.17–18). In the same connection, he refers again to the "fire [sun] of Heraclitus" mentioned by Plato (in the *Republic*) to illustrate how the light of theoretical science learned by the false philosopher who lacks natural equipment, and by the vain philosopher who lacks proper habits, is quenched as they grow old (sec. 61, 46.2).

If we now consider these four references to Plato, we see that they are concerned exclusively with the proper education of future philosophers and the relationship between philosophy and religion. They refer to two of Plato's works, the *Republic* and the *Timaeus*, which are also the only writings mentioned in the *Attainment of Happiness*. What Plato

---

6. There is a mysterious figure (41.6) who is said to have represented matter by abyss or darkness or water, and nothingness by darkness. Alfarabi does not mention the name of this anonymous prophet, but the suggestion that he imitated Plato is strengthened by the hint that "philosophy precedes religion in time" (41.12).

does in the *Timaeus* is presented as a model for the imitative activity that resulted in what the ancients called "religion." What he mentions in the *Republic* is presented as the normative account of the upbringing and education of the true philosopher.

According to Alfarabi, Plato specifies in the *Republic* that, in order to avoid becoming a false philosopher, the student of theoretical science "should have sound convictions about the opinions of the religion in which he is reared, hold fast to the virtuous acts in his religion, and not forsake all or most of them" (sec. 60, 45.6–7). This statement is patently ambiguous. Nevertheless, on the basis of it, no student of theoretical science can be considered a true philosopher if he turns his back on the opinions and actions of his religion or pursues theoretical science in utter disregard of the religious community in which he lives. If we remember that Alfarabi's references to Plato appeared after Alfarabi abandoned the common ground on the basis of which he could refer to himself and the addressee of the *Attainment of Happiness* as *we,* and that Plato is the only one among those who speak our language who is mentioned by name and whose works are cited by Alfarabi, we begin to perceive the apparent implication of this change of attitude toward the addressee. Plato is the authority to whom Alfarabi refers the addressee to support his reevaluation of the status of theoretical science. If the addressee is to become a true philosopher and not a mere student of theoretical science or a false philosopher, he should learn the language of Plato—that is, what Plato does and says in the *Timaeus* and the *Republic.*

The argument of part 4, especially the emphasis on the education of the future philosopher-prince and the relation between philosophy and religion, prepares us for the dominant theme of the concluding remarks, which is the distinction between philosophy itself, the ways leading to philosophy, and the ways through which philosophy is to be reconstructed or reestablished when it has become defective or extinct (sec. 63, 47.4–5). But it does not prepare us for the assertion that the philosophy described by Alfarabi in part 4 (the only part in which the name "philosophy" appears) "has come down to us through the Greeks from Plato *and* Aristotle" (sec. 63, 47.3–4). Aristotle is not mentioned anywhere else in the *Attainment of Happiness.* He is undoubtedly the main authority for the logical methods and the natural science described in part 1; yet even there Alfarabi avoids mentioning him by name. Subsequently, Alfarabi leads the addressee to a view of science that seems to be characteristically Platonic and postpones the mention of philosophy until after he mentions Plato and until he can equate philosophy with the new view of science emerging from the wider meaning of philosophy. The argument of the work as a whole deliberately culminates in the education of the future philosopher-prince according to the program offered in Plato's *Republic,* on the one hand, and in indicating the philosophic importance of the question of religion that finds its solution in Plato's *Timaeus,* on the other. Yet after having led us to this conclusion, Alfarabi now affirms unequivocally that we can learn *this* philosophy from *Aristotle* as well. Still, Plato and Aristotle gave us two separate accounts of philosophy and of the ways to it and to reestablishing it. Alfarabi calls them "Plato's philosophy" and "Aristotle's philosophy," respectively, and announces his intention to present a separate account of each. (Alfarabi's trilogy, the *Philosophy of Plato and Aristotle,* was also known under the title the *Two Philosophies.*)

Without indicating the manner in which these two philosophies have become *the* philosophy described by him in the *Attainment of Happiness,* Alfarabi turns to his addressee with a final request (sec. 63, 47.9). He asks him to learn "from this" (from the preceding account, from the following two separate accounts, or from both) that Plato and Aristotle had a single purpose and that they aimed at giving an account of a single philosophy. The addressee is asked next to go beyond what Alfarabi is offering him in this trilogy, to seek for the evidence regarding the unity of the purpose and aim of Plato and Aristotle. Alfarabi leads the addressee to the two philosophies and ends by pointing toward their purpose and aim, but he does not show them to him. This is something the addressee has to find for himself. The only aid the addressee receives from Alfarabi in this respect is a number. The *Attainment of Happiness* begins with the number 4, leads the addressee by the hand to the number 2, and requests him to look by himself for the number 1. The trilogy begins with the *Attainment of Happiness* as part I, followed by the "two" philosophies in parts II and III. But there is an unwritten "fourth" part in which the addressee is asked to look for the common purpose and aim of the two philosophies. This "fourth" part is hinted at again at the beginning of part III, where a new set of four things is introduced and recalled in the remarks that conclude the trilogy.

All this seems rather enigmatic. It certainly does not offer a direct answer to the difficulties encountered in Alfarabi's concluding remarks, when they are considered, not as a transition to the two parts of the trilogy yet to come, but as a conclusion of the *Attainment of Happiness.* Yet if we are concerned with Alfarabi's purpose and aim, we must proceed to study parts II and III, in which Alfarabi hides behind Plato and Aris-

totle, to see if they shed further light on part I, where he is presenting
his own account of the way to their philosophy. Although the concluding
remarks raise more questions than they answer, they are helpful in one
decisive respect. They vitiate the conclusion to which every step in the
Attainment of Happiness seemed to be leading, and for which the surface
movement of the argument seemed to offer massive support, that is, that
Alfarabi is leading his addressee away from the philosophy of Aristotle
and to the philosophy of Plato. We now know that the work is designed
to lead the addressee to the philosophy of Aristotle as well as of Plato;
that he needs an account of the philosophy of Aristotle just as much as
that of Plato; and that the work aims at training the addressee to understand, not only Alfarabi's account of Plato's philosophy, but his account
of Aristotle's philosophy as well. Why, then, did Alfarabi preserve complete silence about Aristotle until the last moment? The Aristotle who
was not mentioned earlier in the *Attainment of Happiness* is an Aristotle
who leads up to Plato. But there is another Aristotle, who will be engendered by Plato and who "sees the perfection of man as Plato sees it and
more."

On Aristotle's Starting Point

Alfarabi's *Philosophy of Aristotle* is the last part of a trilogy entitled the *Philosophy of Plato and Aristotle*. The trilogy begins with the *Attainment of Happiness,* proceeds to the *Philosophy of Plato,* and concludes with the *Philosophy of Aristotle*. The complete title of this last part is *The Philosophy of Aristotle, the Parts of His Philosophy, the Ranks of Order of Its Parts, the Position from Which He Started and the One He Reached.*

In the *Attainment of Happiness* Alfarabi begins with the enumeration of the human things in virtue of which nations and citizens of cities attain happiness and ends with an account of religion and philosophy. He concludes with the statement that the philosophy about which he has been speaking in the *Attainment of Happiness* "came down to us" from Plato and Aristotle and invites his addressee to make clear to himself the unity of the aim or purpose of their philosophy. Yet nowhere in the *Philosophy of Plato* or the *Philosophy of Aristotle* does either Plato or Aristotle, or Alfarabi, disclose that aim or purpose. There are many indications, both in the titles and in the internal arrangement of the *Philosophy of Plato* and the *Philosophy of Aristotle,* that the unity of their aim or purpose is to be sought in the order of their investigations, as well as in the relation between the three parts of the trilogy. The *Attainment of Happiness* is the first part of the trilogy. Yet the account of philosophy presented in the *Attainment of Happiness* is not the first account of true philosophy as Alfarabi understood it but the last of three accounts of that very same philosophy. This is true, of course, in a temporal sense. But it is true also inasmuch as large portions of the *Attainment of Happiness* are not intelligible without the *Philosophy of Plato* and the *Philosophy of Aristotle*.

The relation between the *Philosophy of Aristotle* and the *Philosophy of Plato,* similarly, is ambiguous. The *Philosophy of Aristotle* comes after the *Philosophy of Plato* and assumes Plato's view of human perfection. Yet

Alfarabi's Aristotle decides to start from a position anterior to the position from which Plato started. Therefore we need to pay some attention to the significance of, and the relation between, the three starting points in the trilogy.

The only one of the three accounts of philosophy not presented by Alfarabi as in any way dependent on the other two is the account presented in the *Philosophy of Plato*. It can therefore be said that the first account, or the account of the beginning, of true philosophy as Alfarabi understood it is his account of the philosophy supplied by Plato. But it is not an account of the historical beginning of philosophy: an independent account of pre-Platonic philosophy in the broader sense is not considered necessary for understanding the philosophy of Plato.

Quite a bit is said in the *Philosophy of Plato* about Socrates. But Alfarabi does not begin with Socrates or the pre-Socratics (e.g., Parmenides); these are included in Plato's philosophy in the sense that their positions are investigated by Plato and presented within its parts and the ranks of order of its parts. He asserts that Plato's philosophy, or investigations, covered all the sciences and arts and ways of life generally known among nations and cities. Although Plato's philosophy is not the beginning of philosophy simply, and certainly not the beginning of all theoretical or practical arts, in a way it encompasses all of philosophy and all the theoretical and practical arts generally known among nations and cities; it is the most comprehensive beginning of philosophy that had come down to Alfarabi. Also, it is a philosophy that forms a whole, with recognizable parts, a recognizable rank of order among these parts, and a beginning and an end. It is the center around which both the *Attainment of Happiness* and the *Philosophy of Aristotle* revolve and from which they take their bearing.

Whereas Alfarabi began the *Attainment of Happiness* by enumerating the human things by which nations and citizens of cities attain happiness in this life and ultimate happiness in the life beyond, Alfarabi's Plato begins by subordinating the investigation of happiness to the investigation of the perfection of man as man and subordinating man's social or political happiness to the happiness associated with or proceeding from man's last perfection. The questions of practical life (the virtues) and politics emerge as questions within this framework. For Alfarabi's Plato, human perfection consists of a desired science and a desired way of life (*Philosophy of Plato*, secs. 1–4). This means that the desired science alone is not sufficient for achieving human perfection. The distinction between the theoretical virtues, on the one hand, and the deliberative virtues, moral virtues, and practical arts, on the other, in the *Attainment of Happiness* (secs. 22ff.) originates here. The theoretical virtues (the theoretical sciences and theoretical perfection) are not sufficient. But not sufficient for what? The *Attainment of Happiness* (sec. 21) suggests the following answer: for the attainment of ultimate happiness by the citizens of cities and nations. The *Philosophy of Aristotle* does not pursue this question.

It is true that Alfarabi's Plato says a great deal about the desired way of life—that of the philosopher or the initiate and that of the multitude, and the relation between the two—but tells us very little about the content of the desired science. Still, it is Alfarabi's Plato who defines the desired science as the science of the substance of each one of all the beings or of natural and divine beings (*Philosophy of Plato*, secs. 3 and 33); faces and solves the question whether such a science is possible (*Philosophy of Plato*, sec. 5), a question on which the philosophic enterprise as a whole depends according to Alfarabi (see the distinction between certainty, conviction, and belief early in *Attainment of Happiness*, secs. 2–3); and faces and solves the question whether this science is obtained by chance, by nature alone, or by investigation, study, and instruction that make use of an art and a power based on an art (*Philosophy of Plato*, sec. 6, and *Attainment of Happiness*, secs. 4ff.). Plato, then, is the one who stands at the beginning of this philosophy, sets up its framework, raises the question of the possibility of philosophy and the possible way to it, and investigates philosophy as a problem, defending it against the significant doubts raised against it and explaining what it is to be a philosopher and to be set apart from the nonphilosophic multitude. Finally, there are the Platonic investigations of the theoretical and practical arts and the ways of life (*Philosophy of Plato*, secs. 7–18) that take place before Plato himself supplies the true theoretical art and the true practical art. That is, it is Plato who first investigates what in the *Philosophy of Aristotle* (sec. 14, 84.3–4) are called "the things that stand in the way" of the certain science.

For these reasons, Plato's investigations are presented by Alfarabi "as entirely independent of the investigations of any predecessors" (Strauss 1945, 4 n. 7). Plato's relation to his predecessors—his rejection, or total or partial adoption, of their views—is presented in the course of Alfarabi's exposition of Plato's writings themselves; he considered these writings sufficient for understanding the philosophy supplied by Plato. Further, Alfarabi "presents Plato as a man who had to discover the very meaning of philosophy entirely by himself, thus implying that he had no philosophic predecessors whatsoever" (Strauss 1945, 20, and n. 46 [the reference in this note is to secs. 19 and 37]).

In this respect, the case of Aristotle's philosophy as offered in the *Philosophy of Aristotle* is somewhat different. Aristotle's writings and the philosophy present in these writings presuppose Plato's philosophy as given in the *Philosophy of Plato*. This is shown by the actual sequence of presentation—first Plato, then Aristotle—and also by the first sentence in the *Philosophy of Aristotle,* where Aristotle is said to agree with Plato on the guiding theme of the latter's philosophy: what constitutes human perfection. Thus one cannot begin with Aristotle. Aristotle, unlike Plato, does not make a philosophic beginning. Moreover, as presented by Alfarabi, Aristotle's writings do not contain the philosophy of all of his predecessors, which in the most important respect means that they do not contain Plato's philosophy, at least not sufficiently. Otherwise, Alfarabi could have ignored Plato and said that the whole of the philosophy he describes in the *Attainment of Happiness,* while perhaps originating with Plato, is adequately or sufficiently contained in the writings of Aristotle and that the writings of Plato can therefore be dispensed with. In this respect, he would have thought as a true Aristotelian is supposed to think, that is, that the whole of philosophy, or the whole substance of philosophy, is contained in the writings of Aristotle and that the thought of his predecessors—and this includes Plato—as far as they had something that is interesting or significant to say, or as far as they made an important contribution to philosophic knowledge, is contained in the philosophy and writings of Aristotle.

Alfarabi was not an Aristotelian in this sense. On the contrary, in the body of the *Attainment of Happiness,* where he speaks in his own name, he "hides" Aristotle and mentions only Plato. At the end of that work he asserts that the philosophy he has been describing came to us from Plato and Aristotle, not from Aristotle alone. The *Attainment of Happiness* is structured in a way that makes the presentation of Plato, which follows immediately, seem natural and intelligible, requiring no explanation or justification. The way Plato begins his investigations is easily accounted for in individual Platonic works. In the case of Aristotle (who is not mentioned in the *Philosophy of Plato* either), on the other hand, his very beginning has to do with his relation to Plato, with his being in full agreement with Plato on the most important and overarching question of philosophy—what constitutes human perfection.

Thus, the question that arises is not "Why Plato?" but "Why Aris-

totle?" The introduction of Aristotle needs justification. The justification
is Aristotle's departure from Plato based on a Platonic requirement,
which Aristotle understands to be the need for certainty and demonstration. And Alfarabi does not find Aristotle's departure from Plato accounted for or sufficiently explained in any one of Aristotle's writings.
Alfarabi's Aristotle (unlike the Aristotle whose writings on the subject
Alfarabi knew) seems to be reticent on his departure from Plato and on
the starting point of his own philosophy. Instead, Alfarabi has to canvass
all of Aristotle's writings in order to disengage, explain, and justify Aristotle's departure from Plato.

The result is a lengthy Introduction in which Alfarabi accounts for
Aristotle's departure from Plato and justifies his inclusion of Aristotle
altogether.[1] This stands in sharp contrast to the *Philosophy of Plato*, where
Plato himself introduces his philosophy and justifies it (*Philosophy of
Plato*, secs. 1–19). In Alfarabi's Introduction, Aristotle, unlike Plato,
does not engage in argument with alternative views regarding the possibility of the desired science or how it is attained, nor does he engage in
argument with the competing theoretical arts; and, again unlike Plato,
he is not concerned directly with the fate of Socrates, who is not mentioned in the *Philosophy of Aristotle*. Instead, his first concern is with what
everyone thinks and desires.

To engage this starting point, Alfarabi finds it necessary to reconstruct what Aristotle thought before writing his works, and he does this
before giving an account of these works one by one, starting with the *Categories*. (Unlike Porphyry, whose *Introduction* to the *Categories* deals with
language and the predicables, Alfarabi introduces the entire logical and
physical corpus of Aristotle in his Introduction.) For Alfarabi, then, the
philosophy of Aristotle is not coextensive with his writings. Aristotle's
writings need an introduction and a conclusion. Therefore, the account
of his philosophy begins before the account of his writings.

And it does not end with the account of his writings, which account
ends with the *Metaphysics*. Alfarabi does not say at the end of the *Philosophy of Aristotle*, "this is where Aristotle's philosophy terminated," although he does make such a remark at the end of the *Philosophy of Plato*.
And if we now look at the title again, we will notice that "the position
from which he started" and the position he "reached" are ambiguous,
which is not the case with the title of the *Philosophy of Plato*. The tradi-

1. By "Introduction," I mean the part that precedes the account of Aristotle's writings
that begins with an account of the *Categories*, that is, *Philosophy of Aristotle*, 59.5–72.16, or
secs. 1–3 and part of sec. 4.

tional starting point of Aristotle's writings is the *Categories*. This starting point is not self-explanatory, and Alrarabi proposes to explain it. This is true also of the position Aristotle reached; for there, too, Alfarabi proposes to explain what Aristotle achieved in his writings.

The Question of Human Perfection

Alfarabi begins the *Philosophy of Aristotle* (sec. 1, 59.5–7) with a statement on Aristotle's agreement as well as disagreement with Plato: Aristotle's opinion regarding human perfection is the same as Plato's opinion, very much and emphatically the same; and Aristotle is even more emphatic in holding the Platonic opinion regarding human perfection than Plato himself. Alfarabi continues: but this (Platonic-Aristotelian opinion regarding human perfection) is neither self-evident nor easy to explain by a demonstration that leads to certainty; therefore Aristotle was of the opinion that he should start at a point before the position from which Plato started.

Alfarabi repeats the expression "opinion," or rather the verb "to see" or "to opine,"[2] in connection with both the agreement on human perfection and the disagreement regarding the proper position from which to start. An opinion can very well be true, but, as opinion, it is not necessarily true. It is to be contrasted to what is evident by itself, what cannot and need not be demonstrated but can be ascertained through (dialectical) examination, and to what is explained or made evident by means of a demonstration—starting, ultimately, from self-evident things—with which one attains certainty.

That Alfarabi's Plato did not consider his view of human perfection self-evident is clear from the fact that he engaged in successive investigations until "it became evident to *him*" that human perfection is a particular science and a particular way of life (*Philosophy of Plato*, secs. 1–2) and until "he attained" what these two things are (*Philosophy of Plato*, secs. 3–4, and sec. 5, beginning). Nor do we have reason to believe that Alfarabi's Plato thought it easy to make human perfection as he saw it evident to oneself or to others through a demonstration that would give one certain knowledge of it. Alfarabi states that Plato's view of human perfection became evident to him (Plato), that he (Plato) attained or realized what its two component parts are, and that it was he (Plato) who supplied the arts that provide these two parts (*Philosophy of Plato*, sec. 19). And he suggests that the only method sufficient for supplying the desired

2. The expression occurs five times in *Philosophy of Aristotle*, sec. 1. *Yarā (doxein)* is the verb from which *ra'y (doxa)*, "opinion," is derived; like *doxein*, it means "to resolve."

science, which is the greater of the two human perfections, is a method that is other than dialectic—that is, according to Alfarabi, the demonstration leading to certainty (*Philosophy of Plato*, sec. 12; Alfarabi, *Rhetoric*, 55). But nowhere in the *Philosophy of Plato* does he state or suggest with respect to Plato's view of human perfection that his Plato either himself attained it through a demonstration or tried to explain it in his writings through a demonstration leading to certainty. (The expressions "certainty" and "demonstration" do not occur in *Philosophy of Plato*.) In fact, Alfarabi does not even say that his Plato explained his view of human perfection, but only that it became evident or plain to Plato.

Now, it seems unlikely that Aristotle would be so emphatic in adopting Plato's view of human perfection just because it had become evident to Plato or merely on Plato's authority—that is, if it had not become evident to Aristotle also and if he, too, had not attained it and realized in his own soul that it is the true view of human perfection. It seems, however, that being "evident to him" (himself), which was sufficient for Plato, is not sufficient for Aristotle. Is that because Aristotle is the inventor of "demonstration" as a full-fledged art through which what is not self-evident in itself, yet is true necessarily and always, can be demonstrated to be such both to one's own satisfaction and to the satisfaction of others? Or is Aristotle's invention of the art of demonstration due rather to his dissatisfaction with the situation that Plato's view of human perfection should remain "undemonstrated"? Plato is said elsewhere by Alfarabi to have "perceived the methods of demonstration" through exceptional natural endowment, that is, "without having established the general rules" of the methods of demonstration as an art that were developed by Aristotle (Alfarabi, *Rhetoric*, 55). But even at this early stage (i.e., before we learn anything about demonstration as an art) Aristotle seems to be concerned with the difficulty of demonstrating Plato's view of human perfection and with the question whether the guiding theme of Plato's philosophy (and, for him, of philosophy simply) should not also be communicated to others as true necessarily and always. Of course, we do not know as yet whether and how in fact Aristotle will demonstrate this view; so far, we are still dealing with Aristotle's "opinions" or with what he "sees." But, initially at least, the question of demonstrating and communicating the certain truth to others—what is eventually to be Aristotle's view of true science, or "wisdom" (secs. 7–19)—seems to be stimulated by the desire to communicate Plato's (and his own) view of human perfection in such a manner that others do not think that it is merely Plato's or Aristotle's opinion.

Alfarabi then proceeds (sec. 1, 59.8–17) to give Aristotle's ground for deciding to start at a point before the position from which Plato started. Throughout this account, Aristotle does not investigate but looks around in order to see how things stand. Aristotle's agreement with Plato regarding his view of human perfection recedes now to the background. Unlike Plato, Aristotle does not begin by asking and investigating the question "What is the perfection of man as man?" or any other question in particular. The things he sees and describes are for the most part not even specifically human but things that humans share with other animals; and it has yet to be seen how this starting point can lead to the question of human perfection. Generally, however, one may say that unlike Alfarabi's Plato, who immediately recognizes the insufficiency of the things most men seek, and then himself recognizes what is needed instead of or in addition to them, his Aristotle begins by *describing* the things he sees without at first judging them, as though he has no purpose in mind but to find out how it is that, from these brutish beginnings, by stages—and without philosophy (or Socrates) around to goad them or "corrupt" them or show them the way—men are ultimately driven to ask the question about human perfection, showing how this question becomes necessary and how it is answered or must be answered. What is not yet clear is whether such a starting point and this way of necessitating the question affect the question itself by determining its direction and character, and finally whether it remains the same question and elicits the same answer as the question investigated by Alfarabi's Plato.

To begin with, Alfarabi's Aristotle looks for things that have four characteristics: that *(a)* are the "first" things sought by "all," *(b)* are seen (opined) by "all" as desirable goods, *(c)* are, "as it were," desired and sought "by nature" immediately (or, from the beginning), and *(d)* are not preceded in time by "other" pursuits. He sees that such things are four in number: (1) sound bodies, (2) sound senses, (3) sound capacity for knowing *(ma'rifa)* how to discern the things that lead to the soundness of these two (items 1 and 2), and (4) sound power to labor at what leads to the soundness of these two (items 1 and 2). Of the four things, items 3 and 4 seem to be instrumental for the soundness of items 1 and 2, the body and the senses. Knowledge and speech are not first but derivative.

There follow various characterizations and elaborations of items 3 and 4. Item 3 is the "useful-necessary" knowledge. Item 4 is the "useful-necessary" labor, as well as what is "preferred before everything." Of items 3 and 4, item 4 is more than "useful-necessary"; it is also "preferred

before everything" else, that is, even before knowledge. At the beginning
men prefer to labor and to labor in deed rather than to labor in speech.
This means that initially a human being's unquestioned preference is to
do things, to labor in deed, rather than to think about what ought to be
preferred or avoided. The useful-necessary labor does not require reflection or consideration. Further, this labor (item 4) has the two characteristics just mentioned in all of the following cases, that is, when a human being

>   (A) labors alone for himself; labors for himself and others labor for
>   him; or labors for himself and labors for others;

and

>   (B) either labors by deed, this being the useful-necessary and prior
>   deed; or labors by speech, this being the useful-necessary
>   speech.

Finally, we meet with the following assertion: that these four things being in the most "excellent" *(afḍal)* state of their soundness "may also be
preferred" (sec. 1, 59.17–18).

It is to be noted that a "human" (rather than "all") occurs in item 4
only, in connection with (A) laboring "alone" or "alone" and together
with others, that is, when others also labor for him or when he labors for
others also; as well as in connection with (B) "speech," the only specifically human activity mentioned here. "Speech" is subordinated to "deed,"
or unlike "deed" it is not said to be preferred before everything. However, like the knowledge in item 3, both the labor by deed and the labor
by speech are only of the useful-necessary kind.

Furthermore, the "useful-necessary" (in none of the four cases is the
expression "useful *and* necessary") means that subdivision of the useful
which is the necessary.[3] The useful-virtuous (according to Plato) is mentioned in the *Philosophy of Aristotle* (sec. 1, 59.18) with respect to the
four things, and it is said that this "may be preferred" rather than "is
preferred" or "preferred before everything" (59.13–14). This means that
it is preferred by some rather than all or not before everything, that is,
sometimes or after other needs are satisfied. Thus not even the virtuous
or excellent state of bodies and the virtuous or excellent state of senses
are seen by all as goods (*khayrat,* 59.8); they are preferred only by some
and only after they have satisfied what is "preferred before everything."

---

3. The other subdivision of the useful is the "virtuous" or "gainful"; see *Philosophy of
Plato,* secs. 13–16 and 20. The last section says that philosophy is the useful-necessary. See,
however, the later development of the notion "useful" in *Philosophy of Aristotle.*

(This additional preference is the horizon of practical science in sec. 3, 60.20–61.21.) What is pursued at this stage is the useful-necessary for all, not the pleasure of the body, of society, of possessions (wealth), or of honor and glory, which are pursued by men in cities that rise above the association meant to serve the useful-necessary things. Associating with others is not specifically human, and speech does not seem to be used here for a specifically human end. The city is not mentioned here.[4]

Finally, the division under (B) applies to all three divisions under (A). In (B), deed has priority; speech does not.

Brutish Beginnings and Human Excellence

Alfarabi's Aristotle sets aside the question of the perfection of man as man. Instead, he looks for the first things pursued by all, as well as seen by all, as desired goods. He accommodates the beginning of his investigation or of his philosophy to the human beginning simply, the beginning that antedates by far the beginning of philosophy and the questions raised by philosophy. To make sure that this is in fact the beginning, he looks for the first things that all men, not only pursue, but also see (at the level of opinion) as the desired goods; he looks for the first pursuits on which men agree in deed and in speech, in action and in opinion. For if all men pursued certain things and yet thought that they ought to desire other things, that would mean that we have not reached back to the true beginning or else that the first beginning is problematical and therefore has no distinct contribution to make to the inquiry into human perfection. The only characteristic that does not seem to be quite definite is whether these four things are desired and pursued from the beginning by nature. But Alfarabi's Aristotle sets this question—related to the question of what is human perfection—aside also; at this stage, the question is left open: they are desired and pursued, "as it were," by nature. He does not settle the question whether they are in fact desired and pursued by nature and, if so, what is meant here by the expression "by nature." It will turn out not to be specifically human nature but that nature a human shares with other animals (sec. 3, 67.17–18).

Still, they are the things pursued first in time—that is definite. The search for the beginning leads Alfarabi's Aristotle to reconstruct the human beginnings in time: what one might call the original state of man or of the first humans, who are pursuing, desiring, and thinking about the first things and who are acting according to their first or original

4. It is not mentioned until sec. 3, 68.7ff., where it occurs in connection with specifically human deeds.

nature, as it were. He finds these first things to be the soundness of their bodies and senses, and the sound knowledge and labor needed to maintain their bodies and senses. He searches, not so much for a clear beginning, but for a clean beginning that is as yet unencumbered by the things about which all men do not agree in their deeds and opinions and that lead them to pursue or desire different things, have different preferences, and think different thoughts. This is the human beginning with which Alfarabi's Aristotle decides to start, and here is the position that is before the position where Plato started.

Alfarabi characterizes the way his Aristotle sees or views the beginning as Aristotle's opinion, not as something that Aristotle found—Aristotle does not begin to "find" things until section 2. This so-called state of nature is not something one can find by looking around; it is a construct. In contrast, the four things Alfarabi's Plato investigates first are things that his Plato found by looking about among the citizens of the nations and cities of his own time (*Philosophy of Plato,* sec. 1). Yet this is an opinion that is meant to reflect the opinion of all men as to the first things and as to the character of their own desires and pursuits. The question whether these four things are desired and pursued by nature is left open because it involves knowledge of what nature is and what human nature is, which is not available to all at the beginning.

The question as to why men desire and pursue these four things at the beginning is not raised at the beginning. Men do not ask: Why do we need to protect ourselves (our bodies and senses) from wild animals, or to eat, clothe ourselves, sleep, procreate, and so forth? Self-preservation and the satisfaction of bodily needs are desired and pursued at the beginning, and knowledge and labor (in deed and speech) are at first in the service of the soundness of the body and the senses.

Also, the question whether the most excellent state of the soundness of these four things is preferred is, like "by nature," left open at this stage because, to begin with, it is not clear what that is. The soundness of the four things is thought to be clear and definite. But once we consider the various states of their soundness (this includes knowledge and labor, i.e., deed and speech) and then the most excellent state of their soundness, we are no longer considering definite things that all men desire and pursue; and the beginning for Aristotle, it seems, must be a definite beginning. Men will need to come to know or have an opinion about what excellence is. So far they agree only concerning the useful-necessary. Nevertheless, the most excellent state is characterized as something that may be preferred, and the investigation of the ground of this preference

leads Alfarabi's Aristotle to find out the things that drive human beings
to transcend brutish beginnings.

Assuming that the question of human perfection lurks in the background of Aristotle's search, a comparison with Plato's starting point will
be instructive as to the difference between their procedures. According
to Alfarabi, Plato's initial investigation of the perfection of man as man
led him to investigate four things, too. But he was not concerned with
the beginning of man as Alfarabi's Aristotle articulates this beginning.
The four things Plato investigates are not that subdivision of the useful
which is the necessary, but the higher subdivision which is the virtuous
(excellent) or gainful—that is, everything up to and including honor and
glory, the highest thing desired and pursued in the city just below that
other thing which, it became evident to him, is the perfection of man as
man. Although Plato knew of that subdivision of the useful which is the
necessary, he is not concerned with it or with man's brutish beginnings;
his concern is with the highest or most excellent or desirable things
achieved by men and cities and nations up to and including his own
time. He asks the question whether some or all of these constitute the
perfection of man as man and finds them wanting.

To begin here, Aristotle seems to think, is to begin at too advanced a
stage in the inquiry into the perfection of man; it does not help make
Plato's view of human perfection (which, according to Alfarabi, Aristotle
shares) clear or evident, or easy to demonstrate to others and enable them
to attain certainty about it. Because he disregards what all men seek and
desire by nature (or, as it were, by nature), and because of his radical criticism of generally accepted opinions (including the highest and noblest)
regarding human perfection, Plato cannot—in any case he does not—
explain how his view of human perfection and the need to search for,
find, pursue, and achieve it emerge among human beings. For human
beings constitute a species of beings that to begin with—and, according
to Aristotle, up to a very advanced stage of its existence—does not seem
to differ from the rest of the beings that constitute the natural world but
seems to be given its perfection and the means to achieve it rather than
having to discover it. Plato seems to think that all humanity culminated
and ought to culminate in his own search for what human perfection
must be, which is radically different from everything that was hitherto
believed to be man's perfection. But he does not explain the stages that
led to and necessitated his question, or what drove humanity in a direction that, in the end, made this question possible and necessary.

On Philosophy and Religion

*T*he second and central part of Alfa-
rabi's *Book of Letters* is devoted to what looks like a history of the emergence of philosophy and religion and the relation between them. Philosophy and religion are relative latecomers in the history of the human arts.
Their emergence presupposes the full development of the practical arts
and of all the popular arts (sec. 140) and all the vulgar arts mentioned
so far (from sec. 114 to sec. 139; cf. sec. 139, 149.1–3)—that is, the five
arts listed in section 138 and the practical and political arts that precede
them (but not the "theoretical affairs" and the "ruling art simply"). For
only after these have been developed (sec. 140, 150.2–3) do human
souls desire to understand the causes of sensible things that appear on
earth and in the heavens and to know many of the things (figures, numbers, colors, etc.) discovered by the practical arts. This desire, in turn,
prompts some human beings to investigate the reasons for these phenomena (sec. 140, 150.6, cf. 150.3). The investigation engendered by
the desire to know the causes or reasons characterizes a new epoch in
the development of the human arts that unfolds in stages as follows.

The Syllogistic Arts: Five Stages of Their Development

1. First (sec. 140, 150.7 and 9), the investigation is conducted by means
of rhetorical methods because rhetoric is the first syllogistic method to
be perceived by human beings (cf. sec. 140, 150.9, with sec. 108, 131.5;
sec. 111, 132.14; and sec. 129, 142.6ff.). Rhetoric has already been practiced in connection with language and politics (secs. 127, 129, and 138),
but not in the investigation of the causes of things. Now it is used out
of the desire for knowledge, investigation, verifying opinions for oneself,
instructing others, and verifying things when one is challenged by others
(cf. sec. 164). Human beings begin to use rhetoric to investigate mathe-

matical things and nature. These two subject matters were initially mentioned in this order: physics, mathematics. Now the order is reversed (cf. sec. 140, 150.9–10, with 3–6). The earlier ones among the ancients used rhetoric, the early physicists used dialectic, and the "divine" thinkers used demonstration. The "divine" thinkers *(ilāhiyyūn)* are Plato and Aristotle.[1]

2. The second stage (sec. 141) is reached when inquirers come to learn about dialectical methods. A long time passes during which they continue to use rhetorical methods, resulting in differences of opinions and a multiplicity of doctrines, frequent discussions about the opinions that each verifies for himself, and frequent occasions in which they challenge each other's positions. As they contend against one another, each will need to firm up the methods he uses and try to make them irrefutable or difficult to refute. They continue this effort and keep testing the firmer methods until they learn to use dialectical methods. Initially, or when dialectical methods are being learned, rhetoric, sophistry, and dialectic are mixed together. Then rhetorical methods are rejected in favor of dialectic. But because there is a similarity between dialectic and sophistry, both are at first used in the investigation and verification of opinions. The distinction between sophistry and dialectic is the last step in this stage, whereupon sophistry is rejected and used only for the purpose of examination or testing.

The steps taken in this second stage seem to be as follows.[2] The use of rhetoric leads to the emergence of a variety of views and positions, and inquirers confront each other. Each will try to defend his position by refining his method and to contend against the methods and opinions of the others. In the process there emerges a mixture of rhetoric, sophistry (contentiousness), and dialectic. Since sophistry has been used in criticizing rhetorical methods, the rejection of rhetorical methods leaves sophistry and dialectic. And since sophistry "resembles" dialectic, what is left may be largely dialectical or largely sophistic; some inquirers will use largely the one, others the other. Alfarabi first mentions the emergence of dialectic, then the distinction between dialectic and sophistry. But he also notices that the "similarity" between the two leads "many

---

1. Secs. 142–43; cf. further secs. 215ff. on the various methods; also secs. 96–98 on the views on nonbeing held by the multitude, the earlier ones among the ancients, the early physicists, and the "divine" thinkers.

2. We are dealing with the investigation of theoretical matters: physics and mathematics (sec. 140, 150.9–10, and sec. 141, 150.11 and 151.5).

people" to use sophistry (not dialectic) in the investigation and verification of opinions. It is only later that the inquiry into theoretical affairs and their investigation and verification settles upon dialectical methods alone, and sophistry is set aside for use in testing and examination only.

Thus sophistry is not presented as a separate "historical" stage. It is present at the end of the rhetorical stage and at the beginning of, or alongside, the dialectical stage; then it is kept for use under special circumstances. It is one of the two lines of development after the rhetorical stage: a false line of development that is rejected as the inquiry into theoretical things settles on dialectical methods (cf., however, sec. 142; *Rhetoric*, 55.12–14). The reason rhetoric leads to a variety of opinions has something to do with the fact that it uses primary, figurative, and metaphorical meanings indifferently (cf. secs. 127 and 163–65). Accidentally, dialectic and sophistry also make use of figurative and metaphorical meanings (sec. 164); hence, perhaps, the confusion with respect to these methods.

3. The third stage begins (sec. 142) with the discovery of the insufficiency of dialectic and ends with the completion of philosophy (sec. 143, 152.6). Two steps are taken in this third stage. First, dialectic is employed until dialectical forms of address are perfected. It then becomes evident by the use of these very dialectical methods that they are not sufficient for attaining certainty. This leads to the investigation of the methods of instruction and certain science. Second, while this is happening, two new directions emerge. *(a)* Men "fall upon" or discover the "methods of mathematics" or the proper methods for the investigation of "mathematical affairs" (cf. sec. 140, 150.9); these methods become perfect or almost perfect. And it appears that as a result of all this the difference between the methods of dialectic and the methods of certainty begins to appear to the inquirers and they begin to distinguish between the two to some extent. *(b)* Men become inclined to the "science" of "political affairs" (as distinguished from theoretical affairs, physics and mathematics), and these are investigated with a mixture of dialectic and the certain methods, at a time when dialectical methods have become so firm as to be almost scientific. This situation continues until "philosophy" reaches the state it reached at the "time of Plato."

It is important to notice that Plato's philosophy or the philosophy of "Plato's time" is not contemporaneous with the discovery of dialectic. The discovery of dialectic, the dialectical inquiry into theoretical affairs, and even the separation of dialectic from rhetoric and sophistry and the rejection of the latter two had occurred earlier. Rather, it is contemporaneous with the very end of the dialectical period when philosophy is about to be completed. It is preceded by the discovery of the insufficiency of dialectic for attaining certainty. This discovery, attributed to dialectic itself, appears to lead also to the discovery of certain correlations between the methods of instruction, on the one hand, and of the certain science, on the other.

The discovery and the subsequent perfection of the methods of mathematics seem to be a *parallel* development. But the coming of age of the methods of mathematics precedes the coming of age of the methods of certainty (in physics and politics), and both seem to contribute to the development of the inquiry into the methods of instruction and the certain science. The advance in the methods of mathematics and the inquiry into the methods of instruction and the certain science, in turn, enable men to see the "difference" *(farq)* and distinguish "to a certain extent" between dialectical methods and the methods of certainty (cf. secs. 162–65).

In *On Philosophy* (frag. 8 Ross), Aristoteles/Aristocles does not emphasize the place of mathematics. He moves from natural science to the highest wisdom. Alfarabi assumes that physics and mathematics were being investigated from the beginning of the "theoretical" epoch (sec. 140, 150.9–10). Although physics seems to be the theoretical science proper (sec. 141, 151.5) that is being investigated rhetorically, sophistically, and dialectically, we learn (sec. 142, 151.10) that the methods of mathematics are distinct and that their rapid advance contributes to the clarification of the distinction between dialectic and certainty and to the development of the scientific method in general. Again, in *On Philosophy*, Aristoteles/Aristocles distinguishes between the inquiry into nature and the highest wisdom; in Alfarabi, the latter inquiry seems to correspond to the beginning of the search for the methods of the certain science initiated by the development of mathematics and politics.

Alfarabi's and Aristoteles/Aristocles' accounts converge when they speak about the emergence of the "knowledge of political affairs" (sec. 142, 151.12). Aristoteles/Aristocles connects this event with Socrates. Alfarabi says that "men become inclined to" this knowledge but does not explain why; neither does Aristoteles/Aristocles. The implication is that the perfection of the methods of mathematics, the distinction between dialectic and certainty, and in general the investigation of the methods of instruction and of the certain science lead inquirers to set apart matters not subject to the methods of certainty—not mathematical and, generally, not "theoretical" in this sense. Their principle is will and choice. As men begin to see that these matters cannot be investigated by the method they have come to regard as the highest science and that they have a different kind of principle, they incline to know them. This seems to form part of their effort to understand the distinctions among various subject matters and their desire for a comprehensive science of all things. Although they had known a great deal about political matters (in a practical way, on the basis of generally accepted opinions, etc.), now that they have come to learn about the methods of instruction and the certain science and to distinguish among the methods—that is, now that they know the limits of rhetoric and dialectic—they are inclined to know political affairs scientifically or with certainty.

The way of Socrates, according to Alfarabi, consisted in the attempt to make his people understand their ignorance of "scientific investigation" (*Philosophy of Plato*, sec. 36, 22.1–2); and Socrates possessed the ability to conduct "*scientific* investigation of justice and the virtues" (*Philosophy of Plato*, sec. 36, 22.5; emphasis added). Hence the event described here (sec. 142, 151.12–15) does refer to Socrates. Socrates emerges out of a physical and mathematical tradition, which he supplements with the scientific investigation of political affairs. His primary achievement is not the refutation of sophistry. This had happened earlier (sec. 141). What characterizes Socrates' (and Plato's) "stage" is the search for the certain science or for certainty. He investigates political affairs with a mixture of dialectical and certain methods in which the dialectical component has become so firm as to be almost scientific. Alfarabi is silent here about the contribution of Thrasymachus (*Philosophy of Plato*, sec. 36, 22.1–8), which is postponed for a later stage (sec. 143, 152.2ff.; cf. the parallel account in *Rhetoric*, 55.13–16).

4. The fourth stage is reached (sec. 143) when the matter rests in the way it rested in the "days of Aristotle." At this stage, scientific inquiry reaches "the highest level" (*yatanāhā*); all the methods are distinguished from each other; and theoretical and "universal" practical philosophy becomes complete with no place in it for further investigation. Philosophy becomes an art that is only learned and taught. It is taught in a twofold manner: privately to the few and publicly to the many. Private instruction is conducted by means of demonstrative methods only. Common, or public, instruction is conducted by means of dialectical, rhetorical, and poetic methods (not sophistical, see sec. 142, 151.6; *Rhetoric*, 57.4). Of these three, rhetorical and poetic methods are more likely to be employed in instructing the multitude in theoretical and practical things that have been established as correct by demonstration.

The position of poetic methods in the development described so far is rather curious. While poetry as images and as the activity of imaging forth was present from the beginning of the discussion (sec. 108, 131.9ff.), there was no such thing as "poetic philosophy" (as there was a "sophistic philosophy," for instance; sec. 108, 131.5, and sec. 110, 132.7, passim), and "poets" did not figure in the enumeration or ranking of those who belong to the few (sec. 113, 134.12–15). Then, in the account of the emergence of the popular arts, poetry developed "alongside the development or after the development" of the (syllogistic) art of rhetoric (sec. 129, 142.12), but the account (142.12–17) and explanation of its development as a syllogistic art dealt with the practice of poetry rather than with the general rules of the art as distinguished from the general rules of the other syllogistic arts, all of which presumably had to wait for Aristotle. Next, the poets are included among the wise men of the nation and the authoritative source of its language (sec. 130, 143.4–6). Finally, the art of poetry is enumerated among the five popular arts and its function is described (sec. 138, 148.14–19), and it is said emphatically that all these arts and those who occupy themselves with them are vulgar (sec. 139).

In the epoch whose stages we are describing here, in contrast, the sequence is rhetoric, followed by dialectic and sophistry, followed by science and certainty. Poetry reemerges only in the postdemonstrative period as one of the three methods of common, or popular, instruction (the other two are dialectic and rhetoric) especially appropriate in instructing the multitude in theoretical and practical things established by demonstration. What is missing is the role of poetry in the inquiry into the causes of things.[3] With reference to what follows, one must keep in mind Socrates' disclaimer of knowledge about "divine" things. Hence, only "human" religion is at issue here (see the comments on sec. 148 below).

5. The fifth stage (secs. 144–45) comprises what will be needed "after *all* these things" mentioned in the four preceding stages—that is, to give the *nomoi*. This need is felt by the men of demonstration (otherwise, Alfarabi could not have said that this need arises only "after *all* these things"), and the *nomoi* needed here are the *nomoi* to be given by de-

---

3. Cf. Alfarabi's *Summary of the Organon* (Bratislava University, MS 231, TE 41, fol. 180b) on philosophic poetry: Empedocles and the Pythagoreans. On the logical methods, especially with reference to sec. 143, 152.2–6, cf. ibid., fols. 180b, 217b, 218a, 219a, 219b, and *Philosophy of Aristotle*. On the postdemonstrative use of rhetoric, see *Rhetoric*, 57.4–9. On a curious aspect of postdemonstrative rhetoric and poetry, see sec. 165.

monstrative men, the philosophers who know all the arts listed above (sec. 143). These are obviously "human" *nomoi*. Sections 144–47 recapitulate and, in part, repeat sections 108–13. The first question is why (assuming that the order of this part of the book is correct) Alfarabi began his discussion with sections 108–13 before proceeding to the account of the beginning in sections 114ff. Then there is the question of the differences between the two blocks.

The beginning of what might be called part 2 recalls the beginning (frag. 8 Ross) of *On Philosophy*, with Socrates going to Delphi, perhaps to be interpreted as the beginning of "human religion" or the religion legislated on the basis of philosophy. There follows the account of the true beginning, which (in the cyclical view) is arbitrary in any case (152.5–8 repeats 131.8–10). This is to be compared with Maimonides' *Logic* (chap. 14, end), where Maimonides says: "In these times, all this— I mean the regimes and the *nomoi*—has been dispensed with, and men are being governed by divine commands." This is one interpretation of the sequence: philosophy, human religion *(nomoi)*, divine religion (commands). So "religion, if it is assumed to be human" (sec. 108, 131.6), comes after philosophy; if it is "divine," it may come at any time. One could perhaps say that, since Alfarabi is commenting on Aristotle's *Metaphysics*, he deals exclusively with predivine religion or *nomoi*. It is curious, however, that the phrase ("if it is assumed to be human," sec. 108, 131.6; cf. sec. 146, 153.10–11, and sec. 147, 153.14, "we required") is about all that is said about "other" kinds of *nomoi* or religion.

"Giving the *nomoi*" is an art. Its aim or the only thing that one seeks from practicing it (cf. sec. 108, 131.7) is instructing the multitude in those theoretical and practical things or affairs that have already been discovered in philosophy (cf. 131.8). The theoretical things are the ones discovered, finished with, and verified by demonstration, whereas the practical things are the ones discovered by the faculty of prudence. Hence philosophy comprises demonstration and prudence.

The "art of giving the *nomoi*" comprises the ability to do three things. *(a)* The first is excellent imaging forth of the theoretical intelligibles that the multitude find hard to conceive (the ones they can conceive with ease can be given as they are; see Averroes, *Decisive Treatise*). *(b)* The second is excellent discovery of every political activity that is useful for reaching happiness (see *Attainment of Happiness*). This is done by the exercise of the faculty of prudence, whose activity is not confined to these practical things but covers the art of giving the *nomoi* in general.

(c) The third is excellent persuasion about both of the former two things (the theoretical and the practical) by means of *all* the methods of persuasion (see *Rhetoric* and *Philosophy of Aristotle*). These include arguments and external methods: threats and promises.

Religion comprises the *nomoi* concerning both of these "genera" (the theoretical and the practical) and, in addition, the methods by which the multitude are persuaded and instructed, by which their characters are formed, and by which they are made to follow everything by which they achieve happiness (cf. *Attainment of Happiness*). The *nomoi* are indispensable but not sufficient (as *Attainment of Happiness* explains). In addition, the lawgiver must practice and provide for the ways of instructing the multitude and forming their characters.[4]

Unlike the things that emerge in the first four stages, the emergence of everything needed in the fifth stage (religion, jurisprudence, and theology) is expressed through conditional sentences ("if . . . then," and so forth; cf. the context of the conditional expression in sec. 109, 131.15). This is perhaps meant to hint that the legislation of this philosophic religion is not a normal or necessary development but something that is desirable or an object of wish, and to hint at the superior arrangement in which philosopher-legislators or givers of a philosophic religion succeed each other (and thus ensure the rule of living wisdom or continuous, original legislation; cf. *Attainment of Happiness, Virtuous City,* and *Political Regime*).

The art of jurisprudence accepts the *"particular* practical things" (cf. sec. 112, 133.9; emphasis added) declared by the giver of the religion and discovers what he had not declared, following his intention. Nothing is said here about the content of the things discovered. Theology, on the other hand, discovers the "theoretical *and universal,* practical affairs" not declared, or other than the ones declared, by the giver of the religion, following his intention. It is stated emphatically that this is "another art" (sec. 145, 153.4). Theology also defends the religion. This latter function is contingent on the presence of a group who try to refute the religion. It comes in the second place. "The art of these two faculties" (jurisprudence and theology) is "only possible through the common methods, that is, the rhetorical." This means that in the religion legislated by philosophers, jurisprudence and theology dispense with dialectical and poetic methods, which are also "common" (cf. sec. 143, 152.4, and sec.

4. So far, sec. 144 elaborates and explains the earlier version in sec. 108. Further elaborations can be found in *Attainment of Happiness, Philosophy of Aristotle,* and *Plato's "Laws."*

111, 132.21–22). In sections 109–12 Alfarabi spoke more elaborately of the subordinate character and the "posteriority" of jurisprudence and theology in relation to religion and indirectly to philosophy. The context was wider than that of "demonstrative" philosophy and the religion based on it, which is "repeated" in sections 147ff. The character of jurisprudence and theology depends on the religion, which in turn depends on the character of the philosophy on which the religion is based.

In any case, given what religion does (sec. 111, 132.12), theology perceives only persuasive things and verifies them through persuasive methods and arguments. The premises and opinions used by theologians in verifying opinions are rhetorical and, at best, dialectical. "Theoretical things" are mentioned specifically (sec. 111, 132.12 and 18). Theology verifies and defends (sec. 111, 133.3); nothing is said about "deduction" or "discovery" *(istinbāt)* in section 111.

In section 112 (on the relation between the jurist and the prudent man), the jurist (like the prudent man) discovers the "correct opinion in particular practical" matters. But the difference is in the character of the premises: the jurist uses premises received from the giver of religion (these are *particular* practical matters), while the prudent man uses premises that are generally known to all and other premises that he obtains by experience.

The difference between jurisprudence and theology is not based on the distinction between discovery and defense as in the *Enumeration of the Sciences,* chapter 5, but on the distinction between the discovery of *"particular practical* things" and the discovery of *"universal practical and theoretical* things." Defense is an additional function. Thus theology occupies a more exalted position in the *Book of Letters* (cf. *Attainment of Happiness*) than in the *Enumeration of the Sciences,* chapter 5.

The account of the prehistory and history of the rise, development, and succession of *all* the syllogistic arts in *all* nations is now concluded (sec. 146). This is the "order" according to which the syllogistic arts arise or should arise in the nations out of their own innate dispositions and natural makeup—that is, it is not necessarily the order according to which they may be imported from other nations (cf. sec. 147, 154.12–15). The next chapter (chap. 24, sccs. 147–53) proceeds to discuss, first, the modifications of this order within the nation itself and, second, the question of transnational movement of these arts. Also, this order is said to be "the order which we required [or narrated]" (sec. 147, 153.14), indicating that it is perhaps the natural or correct model, which may, however, be modified by accident or luck or art.

Philosophy and Religion: Internal Development

The correct religion is the religion based on a philosophy that is fully developed after all the syllogistic arts have been distinguished from each other, according to the order detailed above (sec. 147). The following are the possible departures from that order.

1. When a philosophy is not yet "demonstrative, based on certainty," but verifies its opinions by rhetoric, dialectic, or sophistry, it may contain untrue opinions. It may happen that these untrue opinions are wholly untrue, yet it is not perceived that they are untrue. And all the philosophy, or most of it or much of it, may consist of such untrue opinions. The fact that philosophy is not yet making use of scientific demonstrations does not mean that the opinions it contains are necessarily untrue: they may be untrue. It is the truth or validity of the opinions that is relevant for the religion based on philosophy, not how these opinions were arrived at. In the present case, the philosophy is based on mere opinion or falsification. If a religion is subsequently based on such a philosophy, it, too, will contain many untrue opinions.

2. If, in addition, the religion dispenses with many of these untrue opinions and substitutes their similitudes, which a religion normally does with difficult things that are hard for the multitude to conceive, this religion will be still further from the truth: it will be a corrupt religion, and its corruption will not be perceived. (Cf. sec. 109, 131.10ff.)

That for many things it is necessary for religion to dispense with the things themselves and substitute for them their similitudes and images is accepted throughout. It is also sensible to say that a religion that substitutes similitudes for the things themselves is further removed from the truth than a religion that presents the things themselves (were such things easy to understand by the multitude). Why should it be especially corrupt? It seems that "many of those untrue opinions" (154.2) include the untrue versions of opinions that, were they to have been true, it would not have been necessary to dispense with and choose their images instead. We may thus be considering the worst case (mentioned in 153.17) where the entire philosophy may consist of entirely false opinions. When the religion, in turn, consists of a vast number of untrue opinions and, in addition, a large number of these are set aside in favor of their similitudes (154.3–4; the religion does this, not just because it is necessary, but also because it is in the habit of doing it), then the religion is corrupt in addition to being false; that is, it is not based on correct opinions and lacks good similitudes for those correct things that are correctly judged to be hard to understand in themselves. It is also corrupt in the sense that it hides its untrue opinions. In the first case listed above, the falsehood may eventually be perceived; in this case, the "corruption cannot be perceived," apparently because demonstrative philosophy has not yet emerged.

3. It is assumed that under normal conditions the philosophy described above (153.15–18) will continue to develop until it becomes demonstrative in the manner explained earlier. Under these conditions the giver of the *nomoi* must take the opinions he needs for his religion from "the philosophy that happens to exist in his own time" (154.5–6). If this philosophy is not yet fully developed (which is true of the first case listed above), the religion will not be correct; but this is unavoidable. The extremely bad or corrupt case, even more corrupt than the second case listed above, is the case of the giver of the *nomoi* who neglects the philosophy of his time (contemporary philosophy) and adopts instead the opinions given in an earlier or the very first religion (i.e., that of 153.18ff.) as though they were true and then (following the practice of the giver of the *nomoi* in the second case listed above) proceeds to use their similitudes to instruct the multitude.

Cases 1 and 2 are assumed to be contemporaneous or alternative ways of basing religion on predemonstrative philosophy at a time when demonstrative philosophy (or an improved version of the earlier forms of predemonstrative philosophy) has not yet emerged. A giver of the *nomoi* who "comes afterward" will come at a time when demonstrative philosophy is emerging or has been completed. The philosophy of his time will be demonstrative philosophy. Thus the degree of corruption is determined by the distance of the similitudes from the truth as well as the availability of the truth. In the present case (3), the giver of the *nomoi* presents distant similitudes of untrue opinions at a time when he has the opportunity to adopt true opinions as the basis of his religion.

4. If a giver of the *nomoi* should come after the one just mentioned (3) and choose to follow him instead of turning to an even more complete demonstrative philosophy, his religion will be still more corrupt.

Assuming that the development of philosophy is in the direction of demonstration and certainty and perfection, Alfarabi requires that the *nomoi* and religion be based on the most developed and up-to-date philosophy. The need for a new lawgiver and religion arises when philosophy or science has progressed to a point where it becomes necessary to reform the earlier *nomoi* or religion. Once theoretical and practical philosophy is completed (in the sense of sec. 143), the religion based on it will be the last and final religion (as in sec. 144; this lawgiver may be called the "seal" of lawgivers), which will need jurisprudence and theology for practical purposes only. This will be the correct (154.8) religion in the true sense; all others are corrupt to various degrees (hence the twofold division of 154.8–10).

The statement that in both cases religion comes to exist *after* philosophy (after the philosophy based on certainty, which is true philosophy, in the one case, and the philosophy based on opinion in the other) does not mean that any religion that comes after true philosophy must be "correct." On the contrary, religions existing in the time of or even after true philosophy may be extremely corrupt (cases 3 and 4 listed above). Still, correct religion *can* exist only after true philosophy. Corrupt religions exist after predemonstrative philosophy, and this "after" may continue during and even after the emergence of true philosophy. After true philosophy, there is "need" for a religion based on it (sec. 144, 152.7), but this need may not be satisfied. It is contingent on the philosopher-king, the philosopher who possesses the art of the lawgiver (sec. 144).

Again, all the above refers only to the development of philosophy and religion within the nation itself and out of its innate disposition and natural makeup, not when they are imported from "outside" (divine source or other nations). Thus the departures from the model enumerated above (sec. 147) take place also within this context. The departures that follow (secs. 148–51) are, in contrast, due to the transfer of religion and philosophy from one nation to another.

Philosophy and Religion: Cross-national Movements

First, Alfarabi states the general principle. If a religion belonging to one nation is transferred (either as it is or after altering it by addition, subtraction, etc.) to another nation and it is used to form the character of, to instruct, and to govern this second nation, then it is possible that in the second nation a religion—that is, a religion based on philosophy—may develop before *(a)* philosophy and (even) before *(b)* the arts of dialectic and sophistry. Similarly, if philosophy does not develop naturally in a nation but is transferred to it from some other group (belonging to another nation) among whom it had existed earlier, it is possible for philosophy to develop in this nation after its acceptance of the religion based on philosophy that had been transferred to it earlier.

The question of the correctness or corruption of religion is not at issue. The religion that is transferred to a nation may very well be correct, and the changes made in it to adjust it to the new circumstances may be correct also. The founder of the new religion may be a stranger and may even be a true philosopher-lawgiver. But it is more likely that he belongs to the nation to which the religion is being transferred. In this case, he may have traveled abroad, studied the philosophy and religion of a foreign nation, and come back with a religion for his own nation. Or he may be ignorant of philosophy altogether, someone who borrows a religion about which he may have heard from foreigners. In any case, his own nation lacks an indigenous philosophy and may even lack indigenous dialectic and sophistry. It is assumed to possess indigenous rhetoric and poetry, which are needed for the instruction of the many in the imported religion.

In the case of the philosophy transferred to a nation from another group (philosophy belongs to a group, not to a nation as a whole), it can develop in this nation after the religion that was transferred to it earlier. It can, of course, also be transferred to it before the religion is transferred. The question is whether philosophy can be transferred "out of season" and what this means. The answer will depend in part on whether the study of a foreign philosophy by one or a few travelers can be considered adequate transference or whether one needs a school or a tradition that must take root in the new nation. If the latter is the case, can this happen without the development of the stages that must precede demonstrative philosophy when it develops as an indigenous tradition? Does Alfarabi mean that the course of development will be rhetoric, then religion (jurisprudence/theology), then dialectic/sophistry, then demonstrative science? Or does he mean that the stage of dialectic/sophistry can be dispensed with? One thing is clear: religion can be transferred from the rhetorical stage on; it does not need to wait until after the demonstrative stage. This parallels the development of an indigenous religion. The difference, presumably, is that the transferred religion can be a higher religion because it can be imported from a nation in which religion is based on a later stage or development in philosophy.

What does Alfarabi have in mind? Did he live in a nation in which this possibility was realized? Surely his religion came *before* philosophy (and dialectic and sophistry) and, correspondingly, his philosophy came after religion. Yet he is not concerned with the historical origins of that religion or where it came from. His account of the origin and development of language and of the arts preceding the philosophic arts indicates that the Arabs in the years 90–200 after the founding of their religion were still occupied with the science of language (sec. 135) or that the indigenous development of the arts among the Arabs was still at the stage (presented in chap. 22, secs. 129–39) of the practical arts and the other popular arts (150.2). Further, "the philosophy that exists today among the Arabs was transferred to them from the Greeks" (sec. 156, 159.1; cf. sec. 142, 151.15–16, sec. 143, 151.18, and *Attainment of Happiness,* where true philosophy came from the Greeks—from Plato and Aristotle).

Why is Alfarabi silent about the origin of the religion existing today among the Arabs? Is it because it is divine and therefore something about which Alfarabi, like Socrates, feigns ignorance? See Alfarabi's *Summary of the Organon:*

> What some people believe is by some *divine* act. . . . Let us leave this to whoever practices external philosophy. . . . Rather, we say that we are now talking about that instruction which is *human* and is included in the philosophy which comprehends *human* intelligibles. . . . (fol. 177a; emphasis added)

But does it make any difference where that religion came from, whether it is divine or human? Alfarabi discusses this issue in the *Book of Religion,* the *Virtuous City,* and the *Political Regime.* He concludes that it makes no difference, at least not after the perfection of philosophy in the Socratic school and after a "philosophic religion" has become possible. It is curious, to say the least, that he insists on giving the impression (an impression based on what one may deduce from what he says about the language of the Arabs and the philosophy existing among them in his time) that the religion of the Arabs (like Christianity before it) came from the Greeks at a time when the Arabs lacked philosophy and dialectic and sophistry and were at the state of the prephilosophic arts.

We must understand his intention through his aim. What he plans to teach the philosophers of his time and his coreligionists is that their religion consists of similitudes of true philosophy. And what he plans to *do* for his coreligionists is to reform the religion in this direction (acting as a theologian who discovers "theoretical and universal practical affairs which the founder of the religion has not declared," cf. sec. 145, 153.2–3). He may also have in mind such things as the history of the influence of Platonic "religious" ideas on Christianity and Islam and on the dialectic and rhetoric of the Muslim theologians, which he, in turn, brings to completion or perfection by recovering the most perfect philosophy, the true origin of that "religion." There is, finally, the question of the authority of philosophy, the philosophic defense of religion, and the dangerous situation in which philosophy may find itself, to which he turns in what follows.

1. The first case discussed by Alfarabi in this connection is this (sec. 149). A religion based on a perfect philosophy, but in which all or most of the *theoretical* matters are given through similitudes, is transferred to a nation that is ignorant of the fact that this religion is based on philosophy or that its contents are similitudes of theoretical matters verified in philosophy by means of certain demonstrations. Someone (presumably the founder) remained silent about this fact. As a result, this nation believes that these similitudes are the truth and the theoretical affairs themselves. Afterward, the (perfect) philosophy on which the religion depends for its excellence is transferred to that nation.

In this case, there is no assurance against or it may very well happen that *(a)* this religion will oppose philosophy and its followers will contend against philosophy and reject it; and philosophers will contend against this religion so long as they do not know that this religion consists of similitudes of the contents of philosophy. However, *(b)* when philosophers learn that this religion consists of similitudes of the contents of philosophy, they will not contend against this religion; yet the followers of this religion will continue to contend against them. This will lead to the following results. (i) Philosophy and the philosophers will have no authority (rule) over, and both will be rejected by, that religion or its followers. (ii) Religion will not be defended to any appreciable degree by philosophy. (iii) Philosophy and the philosophers are in danger of being greatly harmed by that religion and its followers. (iv) The philosophers may be *forced* at this point to contend against the followers of religion "in search of the *safety* of those who are engaged in philosophy." They choose or try not to contend against the religion itself but only against the belief of the followers of the religion that religion contradicts philosophy. They exert themselves to remove this belief by trying to make the followers of the religion understand that the contents of their religion are similitudes.

The explanation of the reason for the silence about the truth of the dependence of this religion on perfect philosophy may have been given earlier (in sec. 148). Religion was transferred before the transference of philosophy and therefore the new founder (whether he knew about the fact of the matter or not is not now at issue) could not disclose the dependence of his religion on philosophy. Even if he knew the fact of the matter, he may have been wise to remain silent: his followers could not have understood what he was talking about. Whether, to what extent, and to whom this fact is disclosed in the model nation is not discussed but can be learned from the *Virtuous City* and the *Political Regime,* where those who show signs that they will be able to contend against philosophy are trained not to do so. This is assumed to be what the philosophers will do later on in the nation whose case is under discussion. Hence the conflict between religion and philosophy in this particular context results from the reversal of the historical sequence of the appearance of philosophy and religion.

This reversal seems to be responsible also for the predicament that the philosophers themselves do not as yet know that religion consists of similitudes of the theoretical contents of philosophy. In the model situation, the appearance of demonstrative philosophy goes hand in hand with the criticism of rhetoric, dialectic, and sophistry, the development of mathematics, and the inclination to the science of political affairs. It is only after philosophy (both theoretical and practical) is completed that philosophers begin to understand the public use of rhetoric and poetry and the need for lawgiving and religion. In the present case, religion (and jurisprudence and theology) are already there, and it is assumed that philosophers have not yet reached the point of realizing the need for founding a religion or appreciating the need for the religion that is already there. Religion and theology appear to be part of the rhetoric, dialectic, and sophistry that the philosophers are trying to reject. Yet the time has arrived when the fact of the matter can be revealed both to the followers of the religion and to the philosophers, for the benefit of both.

The benefit to religion is that it will not be opposed and in fact will be "greatly defended" by the philosophers, while the benefit to philosophy is that it will avoid the "great harm" that religion can inflict on it. These two benefits go hand in hand in the sense that the safety and development of philosophy will redound to the strength of religion, and a more enlightened religion will in turn tend to support and protect philosophy.

Indirectly, Alfarabi depicts a happy and peaceful picture of what may happen when the followers of religion and the philosophers are enlightened about the true relationship between religion and philosophy. Religion will not oppose philosophy. Its followers will not contend against philosophy but welcome it. Philosophers will not contend against religion. Philosophy and the philosophers will occupy a *ruling* position in that religion and will be accepted and honored. Philosophy will "greatly defend" the religion.

Otherwise, and out of concern for their own safety, philosophers may have to contend against religion. They choose not to contend against religion itself (they are not in a position to oppose it directly and openly, but consider the case of al-Rāzī). They will be satisfied with removing the belief that religion contradicts philosophy and making the followers of the religion understand that their religion consists of similitudes. And they will exert themselves to do just this, because this is the crux of the matter. For, once they succeed in this, the rest follows. They will have established that philosophy is the source and the truth itself, and that religion is the stepchild of philosophy. They will be honored and elevated to the rank of prophets.

Alfarabi does not blame religion or its followers for their attitude to philosophy and philosophers. He understands the dangers and their source; and he does not expect relief from that front. The key to the solution is in the hands of the philosophers. First, they must be educated to understand the true relation between philosophy and religion. Then they must be taught what they need to do to improve their position: theirs is an educative role. The myth of the origin of religion is part of the new lawgiving activity of the new philosophers. (The larger narrative describes the situation as Alfarabi found it and his proposed solution.) The myth is absolutely essential for the proposed solution; any other myth is intolerable to demonstrative philosophy.

2. The second case is this (sec. 150). The imported religion was origi-nally based on a "corrupt ancient" philosophy (rhetorical, dialectical, and/or sophistic). This religion is assumed to have been imported first; and it is left open whether or not the fact that this religion was originally based on such a philosophy is known to the followers of the religion. Next, "correct and demonstrative philosophy" is imported to this na-tion. In this situation, philosophy and religion will be totally opposed to each other. Alfarabi begins with philosophy. Philosophy (demonstrative philosophy) will oppose both the religion and its philosophic basis. And because of this, religion will oppose this philosophy. The situation is pre-sented as a state of total war in which each of the contestants seeks com-plete victory and the destruction (refutation) of the other. Each tries to subdue the nation and remove the other from the field. What could be the existential reference of this case and why this inordinate boldness? Could Alfarabi be referring to non-Muslim religions that are completely inhospitable to philosophy? Or to certain forms of Zandaqa, Epicurean-ism, and so forth, which are mentioned at the end of the *Virtuous City*? There philosophy joins hands with the religion based on perfect philoso-

phy to fight the religions based on predemonstrative philosophy. He could also be referring to certain unacceptable interpretations of Islam by certain radical practitioners of *kalām* and to al-Rāzī.

3. The third case discussed by Alfarabi (sec. 151) is the case of the nation already in possession of a well-established religion when dialectic and sophistry are imported. They will be harmful to religion and will make those who believe in it think that it is of little or no importance. The power of dialectic and sophistry consists of proving and disproving the same thing. Therefore their use shakes the hold of religious beliefs, generates doubts about them, and reduces them to things that have not as yet been verified, or else makes one perplexed about them to the point that he begins to think that nothing can be affirmed, neither these beliefs nor their opposites. This is why lawgivers, as well as the princes set up to protect religion, emphatically forbid the practice of dialectic and sophistry. This is true of all religions.

Alfarabi does not say what kind of religion he is talking about and implies that this makes little difference. Dialectic and sophistry (useful as they are for the development of philosophy) are harmful and destructive so far as religion is concerned. He seems to approve of the position taken by lawgivers and princes against these two arts. (He reminds us of the position of Averroes in the *Decisive Treatise,* where dialectic and sophistry are rejected in favor of rhetoric and demonstration.) It is assumed that the religion in question is established by means of rhetoric and poetry.

In the context of the development of the philosophic arts, sophistry and dialectic form a later and higher stage. They are inherently superior to rhetoric and poetry as methods of investigation. A religion based on rhetorical persuasion has little chance of winning in a situation where dialectic and sophistry have a free hand. The only way it can prevent their victory is by the use of nonargumentative means: legal exclusion from the community.

The case will be different when religion allies itself with demonstrative philosophy and gains its support. Philosophy knows the uses of rhetoric and poetry as public (postdemonstrative) arts. It knows the philosophic counterparts of the things imaged or expressed through similitudes in religion. Above all, it knows what dialectic and sophistry are all about; it knows their shortcomings and how to silence those who practice them.

Alliance between Religion and Demonstrative Philosophy

Alfarabi (like Averroes after him) is therefore proposing an alliance between religion and demonstrative philosophy against dialectic and sophistry. Theology must be cleansed of dialectic and sophistry and become more rhetorical, following the example of the lawgiver. This alliance is profitable to both religion and philosophy: religion will be well supported by demonstrative philosophy in its conflict with dialectic and sophistry; and philosophy will be supported by religion in its conflict with dialectic and sophistry. Section 152 begins by enumerating four groups who have shown four different attitudes to philosophy: (1) sympathized with or encouraged it, (2) permitted its pursuit, (3) remained silent about it, and (4) forbade it. Alfarabi is silent about the first three groups. The third was mentioned in section 149. The fourth was also the attitude of the lawgivers and princes toward dialectic and sophistry. The rest of the section deals with the reasons for the fourth attitude, just as section 151 explained the reason for forbidding dialectic and sophistry. This indicates that the groups in question are lawgivers (see 156.19) and princes set up to protect religion (perhaps theologians and jurists as well). To "forbid" means to forbid every follower of the religion (the entire nation) in contrast to the first three attitudes, which imply that some may pursue philosophy.

The main obstacle to this alliance is that a minority of lawgivers have forbidden the followers of their religions to engage in philosophy. The explanation of the interdiction against philosophy is sought by Alfarabi in the character of the nation and in the characters of the religion and the lawgiver.

A lawgiver may forbid the nation to engage in philosophy because its character is such that it cannot be taught the truth or theoretical affairs as they are. The natural makeup of the people who compose the nation is such, or the lawgiver's "purpose in it or from it" (see 156.15) is such, that it should not be acquainted with the truth itself but have its character formed by similitudes of the truth only. Or else it may be a nation whose character is such that it must be formed by "actions, deeds, and practical things only, not by theoretical affairs or only by very few of these" (156.16–17).

It is assumed that the lawgiver had made a correct assessment of the character of the nation, determined what and how much it can know, and forbade philosophy because it is incompatible with the character of the nation and its natural makeup. The nation may also have been meant to play a subordinate role in the universal scheme envisaged by the law-giver for a large number of nations (cf. *Attainment of Happiness*), which is perhaps what is meant by the "purpose in it or from it." But what if philosophy develops in such a nation despite the lawgiver's declared interdiction? The lawgiver (who legislated for his own time; see *Political Regime* and *Book of Religion*) was correct when he forbade philosophy; but things have now changed, and the law must be interpreted and sup-plemented to take account of the new conditions, even though the phi-losopher will not be able to disclose the true reason for the earlier legis-lation.

The philosopher must justify philosophy in terms of the new condi-tions. He may argue that the religion was in fact based on true philoso-phy; the interdiction was appropriate earlier but must now be lifted; and philosophy must now be permitted, among other things, for its use in the defense of religion against dialectic and sophistry. In any case, the appearance of philosophy in the nation despite the lawgiver's interdiction indicates a change in conditions and points to the need to discover new opinions and practices (which is the function of theology and jurispru-dence). It is possible that the original lawgiver was not a philosopher and yet knew something about philosophy or something like philosophy and its impact.

This does not make much difference. The interpretation of the inten-tion of the lawgiver in this respect depends on whether the rise of philos-ophy is an accident and a passing phenomenon or an event indicating a fundamental change in the character of the nation (as described in 156.13–17). If it is an accidental and a passing phenomenon, then per-haps the philosopher will do well to migrate or remain silent and leave the nation at peace with its religion. If, on the other hand, a fundamental change has taken place in the character of the nation, then the religion must be interpreted and supplemented to enable philosophy as much freedom of action as necessary, something that the original lawgiver would have done had he lived under the new conditions.

The new interpretation is necessary for the sake of the philosopher as well as the believers who are now in a position to question the religious beliefs in their original form. The latter will need room to ascend to the degree of understanding corresponding to their respective capacities. Otherwise, they will reject the beliefs and find no higher interpretation in which they can believe—that is, they will reject the beliefs simply. This will harm the religion. It will lose its more intelligent followers, and their public questioning and rejection of beliefs will threaten the faith of the community at large. It may be necessary to present the new supplement to the religion as an interpretation of the old religion rather than as an innovation. But this is something the philosopher must decide on in his capacity as theologian and jurist.

But a lawgiver or founder of a religion may also forbid philosophy because it does not serve his private interest. He brings forth a "corrupt and ignorant" religion (156.18; see *Political Regime, Virtuous City,* and *Book of Religion*) through which he seeks, not the nation's happiness, but his own; he uses the nation to make himself, not the nation, happy. He is afraid that, should he permit inquiry into philosophy, the nation will come to understand the corrupt character of the religion and of what he sought to establish in the souls of the people. This case, or something very close to it, was spoken of earlier (in sec. 150), where the rise of philosophy led to total war with religion. It is to be assumed that the same consequences apply here also.

It is apparent, Alfarabi concludes (sec. 153), that, if a religion contends against philosophy, so will the art of theology in that religion; and theologians will contend against philosophers to the same degree that the religion contends against philosophy.

This proposition is obvious to the extent that the theologian does not discover things not declared by the lawgiver and remains attached to the lawgiver's original purpose. But the theologian's function is also to deduce propositions appropriate to new conditions. What is meant, apparently, is religion as it exists at any particular time. Since the theologian is a servant of religion, he will oppose what the religion opposes. This does not take into account the possibility that theologians may be divided into groups with different attitudes to philosophy, or the activity of the philosopher in reforming religion and enlightening the believers about the true relation between religion and philosophy (as explained in sec. 149). It simply warns the philosopher that he must be prepared to contend with opposition, not only from the religion itself or the lawgiver's declared statements and intention, but also from the theologians, who tend to defend the lawgiver's intention, elaborate his statements, and then defend them by all the means available to them.

Religion and the Cyclical View of History

It is fitting that the text for the fol-
lowing remarks on religion and the cyclical view of history be taken from
the last philosopher to reflect seriously on the topic. In sections 61 and
62 of part 3 of *Beyond Good and Evil,* entitled "Das religiöse Wesen,"
we read:

> The philosopher as *we* understand him, we free spirits—as the man
> of the most comprehensive responsibility who has the conscience for
> the overall development of man—this philosopher will make use of reli-
> gions for his project of cultivation and education, just as he will make
> use of whatever political and economic states [circumstances] are at
> hand . . . religion is one more means for overcoming resistances, for the
> ability to rule—as a bond that unites rulers and subjects and betrays
> and delivers the consciences of the latter, that which is most concealed
> and intimate and would like to elude obedience, to the former. And if
> a few individuals of such noble descent are inclined through lofty spiri-
> tuality to prefer a more withdrawn and contemplative life and reserve
> for themselves only the most subtle type of rule (over selected disciples
> or brothers in some order), then religion can even be used as a means
> for obtaining peace from the noise and exertion of *cruder* forms of gov-
> ernment, and purity from the *necessary* dirt of all politics. That is how
> the Brahmins, for example, understood things: by means of a religious
> organization they gave themselves the power of nominating the kings
> of the people while they themselves kept and felt apart and outside, as
> men of higher and supra-loyal tasks. . . .
>
> In the end, to be sure—to present the other side of the account of
> these religions, too, and to expose their uncanny dangerousness—one
> always pays dearly and terribly when religions do *not* want to be a means
> of education and cultivation in the philosopher's hand but insist on
> having their own *sovereign* way, when they themselves want to be ulti-
> mate ends and not means among other means. (Translated by Walter
> Kaufmann)

If these statements on the relation between philosophy and religion seem somewhat bold, they are not, I suggest, revolutionary. Nor do they represent an innovation, but only a renovation, restoration, or revival of a strain in the philosophic tradition that had always been closely connected with, and in most cases actually derived from, a cyclical view of history that assumed "eternal return" of one form or another. To conduct a proper investigation so as to recover this strain and show the importance of its place in the philosophic venture throughout its long history will require nothing less than the kind of penetration into, and restatement of, the core of that tradition for which Nietzsche was eminently qualified. I shall be satisfied if, through what archeologists call a rapid surface sounding, I can persuade the reader that there is something worth digging for here.

By "history," we have come to mean at least two things. "History" may mean an account of individual periods, institutions, ideas, or achievements. History in this sense existed, of course, in classical and medieval times, and its practical use and modest theoretical value were recognized by all. The term can also be used to indicate an account or a view of the overall course of human events, such as historical progress, the rise and decline of civilizations, the view that every teaching is essentially relative to the historical situation, or the view that these historical situations are repeatable or not repeatable.

The following observations are intended to show that a view of history in this second sense was very much part of classical and medieval philosophy in general and political philosophy in particular. I shall sketch this view in outline and explain how it helps us understand certain features of premodern political philosophy and provide us with a clearer idea of the change in perspective that took place with the abandonment of that view in modern times. It is to be hoped that these observations will show also that, to understand this change in perspective, one needs an account of the premodern view as articulated, not only in classical philosophy, but in medieval philosophy as well; and that this is particularly important for clarifying the changing relationship between philosophy and religion.

History is said to consist of movement in time. Time has been thought of as the greatest of gods, encompassing all things, or as one of two or more gods or principles of equally eternal power. But this is not the time of man and his history. Historical time is time as experienced by man and by which man measures the movement of human things. In its simplest form, it is like a series of points arranged regularly in a straight line or a curved line forming a circle.

The movement of history on a straight line can be infinite (having no beginning or end) or finite (having both a beginning and an end, preferably a beginning and an end that are not so distant from each other that they lose their relevance for the present) or semifinite (having a beginning but no end). Finite and semifinite straight lines required an account of the beginning—that is, whether it was brutish and insecure or a golden age due to the presence of gods among men or the rule of reason, philosophy, or science in human affairs. An infinite straight line must have a direction (up or down) or else contain variations (seasonal or contraction and expansion). Movement in a circle can have a beginning and an end (a single great cycle ending in a universal conflagration or an eschatological cataclysm) or, like a pure circle, have no beginning or end. There will then be eternal return. It is as if the demiurge had taken the line and bent it into a circle (Plato, *Timaeus,* 36b) so that every point and phase precedes and follows every other point or phase in time; and yet, wherever one chooses to start from or happens to be, there is a before and an after, and there is a measured distance between that point and the preceding or following points. The arrangement of the series is such

> that it returns back in a circle to the point from which it began and thus secures continuity and identity of composition. . . . If then human life is a circle, and a circle has neither beginning nor end, we should not be "prior" to those who lived in the time of Troy nor they "prior" to us by being nearer to the beginning. (Aristotle, *Problemata,* 17.3.916a17 ff.)

The view that human history moves in an eternally recurring circle is said to be Babylonian in origin and is known to be at the root of Chaldean astrology. Those who prefer a cosmos of a limited duration characterize this view as antihistorical, as a static view of the future that annuls the irreversibility of time. But if the duration of the cosmos is not limited, or not limited for all practical purposes relevant for human history, then the view of history and the future based on a cosmos of a limited duration must be set aside. Accordingly, cyclical, "eternal" return appears as the more sensible way of viewing the overall course of human history.

Aristotle's and Aristoteles/Aristocles' Accounts

The classic account of this view is found in Aristotle and in the fragments from the work of Aristoteles/Aristocles. Aristotle's low estimate of the theoretical status of history is well known. Whether this estimate applies only to the historical accounts of others (the historians) or applies to his own historical research as well need not concern us here. We merely notice that Aristotle did not leave a specialized account of history as he did of many other subjects, such as logic, natural science, politics, and poetry. His account must be pieced together from a few short passages.

Exploration, Perfection, and Loss
(*Metaphysics*, Lambda 8.1074b1 ff.)

Our quest for the beginning, for "our ancestors in the remotest ages" and the traditions handed down from them, is complicated by the following fact. We have no assurance that the loss or forgetfulness was complete, or that the traditions handed down to us in mythical form were of our ancestors' own invention or divination. In this particular case, Aristotle distinguishes between two layers: first, mythical forms that divinely express the truth about what encompasses the whole of nature; and second, other forms (added to the former) "for the persuasion of the multitude and for their legal and social uses" (e.g., the view "that these gods are in the form of men or are like some of the other animals"). Now if "arts and philosophies" have been often explored and perfected, but lost, then the first layer could be understood as an ancient relic of a once-perfected philosophy. The second layer, too, can be understood as an ancient relic of a once-perfected legal and political art, even though its crudeness may suggest crude legal and political conditions that do not go hand in hand with the perfection of legal and political art.

The Five Phases of the Cycle
(Aristoteles/Aristocles, *On Philosophy,* frag. 8 Ross)

On Philosophy seems to have begun with an account of the beginning of the last phase: Socrates going to Delphi. There are also references to "ancient philosophy," first among the Chaldeans (the Magi and Zoroaster, who was connected by Eudoxus with Plato, calculating the distance between them as 6,000 years, or one great year) and next among the Egyptians. And proverbs are said to be "relics, saved by their conciseness and cleverness when ancient philosophy perished in the widespread destruction of mankind."

Aristoteles/Aristocles is defining a term that is broader and more ambiguous than "philosophy"—that is, "wisdom" *(sophia)*: "it brings hidden things to light" *(phōs)*. The movement from the darkness of ignorance to the light of knowledge is presented in a historical account. Men perish in diverse ways: *(a)* plagues, famines, earthquakes, various diseases, and so forth; *(b)* above all, by more violent cataclysms, such as the one in the time of Deucalion, but not the greatest of all, for herdsmen and those on the mountains and foothills were saved. Not having the means of sustenance, they were: (1) "Forced by *necessity* to think of useful devices—the grinding of corn, sowing, and the like—and they gave the name of wisdom to such thought, thought which was useful to the necessities of life." (2) They devised the arts, going on to the production of *beauty and elegance,* and called it wisdom. (3) They turned their attention to *politics* and invented laws and all such things that hold a city together. They called such thought wisdom. (The Seven Wise Men were men who attained *political* virtues.) (4) Then they went further. They proceeded to "bodies themselves and the nature that fashions them." They called it *natural science,* and "we" describe its possessors as wise in the affairs of nature. (5) "Fifthly, men applied the name in connection with *things divine,* super-mundane, and completely unchangeable, and called the knowledge of these things the *highest wisdom.*"

If human life is a circle, the circle appears to begin after a cataclysm and to have five phases characterized clockwise by (1) necessities, (2) beautiful things (mythical forms i), (3) politics (mythical forms i and ii), (4) natural science, and (5) divine science (highest wisdom).

As a mathematical model, the circle is perfect but has no beginning or end and no source of movement in one direction or another. What is it, then, that makes human life move in this fashion? Natural phenomena, such as earthquakes and other cataclysms of a certain intensity, can arrest or terminate any one of the phases of the cycle and force a return to the beginning. Plagues, famines, and certain diseases, on the other hand, are human phenomena and can be the by-product of a certain lifestyle—crowded cities, international commerce, extensive wars, and so forth—and tend to influence the later phases of the cycle. The end and the necessity of a fresh start can, then, be explained on grounds both external and internal to human life. As to the movement within the cycle, Aristotle distinguishes between two broad aspects. The first consists of man's concern for himself, for the satisfaction of his needs and desires. The principles that govern here are necessity and (human) nature: "We must believe, then, that these and many other (political) things were discovered several times over in the course of the ages—indeed, times without number. For *necessity* itself may be supposed to have been the mother of indispensable inventions: on this basis, and with these once provided, it was *natural* that discoveries that made for the adornment and graces of life should have steadily developed; and the same rule must be held to be true in the things of the *politeia*" (*Politics,* 7.10.1329b25– 31, translated by Ernest Barker). The second aspect consists of man's thought of god and divine things, and fragment 12 of *On Philosophy* states that "men's thought of god sprang from two sources—the experi- ence of the soul and the phenomena of the heavens" (Ross).

The recurrence or return does not necessarily require an external con- tinuity between the cycles, or that some of phase 5 be actually remem- bered, even vaguely, and be expressed in myth in phase 2 of the next cycle. Phase 5 may be completely forgotten or lost. But it will be redis- covered. What is necessary is the continuous existence of the two sources of men's thought about the gods: the experiences of the soul and the phenomena of the heavens. The rediscovery will take place through "the inspiration and prophetic power of the soul in dreams." Men will observe what takes place in their souls and the heavenly bodies, begin "to suspect the existence of something divine" (frag. 12 Ross), and move on. Neces- sity, human nature, the experience of the soul, and the phenomena of the heavens give every cycle a definite beginning, direction, and end— which is philosophy. Aristotle had reports about ancient Chaldean and Egyptian philosophy and suspected the existence of a pre-Homeric Greek philosophy; and he had reports about cataclysms. Hence the Socratic phase of the cycle, which culminated in Aristotle himself, was not the first or the last philosophic phase. Yet his own accomplishment in per- fecting this philosophy means that he will be followed by an age of dark- ness, but an age of darkness that will be the beginning of new cycles and new movements that will end again (at least in some cases) in a philo- sophic phase. Assuming that the heavens and the human species are eter- nal, there will be an infinite number of such cycles in the future just as there must have been an infinite number of them in the past.

Alfarabi's *On the Rise of Philosophy* and *Book of Letters*

Alfarabi concludes part I of his *Philosophy of Plato and Aristotle* as fol- lows: "The philosophy that answers to this description [i.e., 'highest wis- dom,' etc.; cf. secs. 53ff.] was handed down to us by the Greeks from Plato and Aristotle only. Both have given us an account of philosophy, but not without giving us also an account of the ways to it and the ways to reestablish it when it becomes confused and extinct." Thirteen centuries after Aristotle, Alfarabi was naturally curious about what had actually happened since Aristotle's time.

Alfarabi wrote a work on the name and rise or the cause of the appearance (or reappearance) of philosophy of which only fragments are extant. The "name" recalls the various meanings of "wisdom" in Aristoteles/ Aristocles' *On Philosophy*. The "cause of its rise or appearance" *(zuhūr)* refers both to its earlier appearance or appearances, its decline and disappearance, and its reappearance after a period of "concealment" *(sitr)*. The few surviving fragments deal with the survival of Aristotle's writings and the tradition of teaching them in Greece, then Alexandria, and then Rome; with the coming of Christianity, the abandonment or suppression of philosophic learning in Rome, and the new policy (initiated by the ruler and the council of bishops) to abandon or suppress the most important part of the Aristotelian philosophic tradition and limit public instruction to the part thought to be useful for the defense of their religion, that is, for theology (the suppressed art continued to exist, but in concealment—*mastūr*, i.e., taught only in private); next, with the coming of Islam, the movement of the school and the books from Alexandria to Antioch, and then to Marv and Ḥarrān.

At one point (in Antioch), the transmission depended on the survival of a single man who had two students, each of whom had two students; but one individual from each of these two pairs devoted himself to religious affairs, so that again there were only two left who taught philosophy. Then, Muslim students and teachers, like Alfarabi himself, were able to read Aristotle's logical works and go as far as they could. The concealment is thus connected with religion (Christianity). What had happened earlier as a result of natural cataclysms and been done unconsciously through myth now happened through religion by design and consciously. Philosophy survived but had to go underground because of a human or divine cataclysm.

In his *Book of Letters* (which is a commentary on parts of Aristotle's *Metaphysics* with a somewhat exaggerated interest in Lambda 8.1074b1 ff.), Alfarabi introduces the notion of the human religion that should come after philosophy *in time* and teach the multitude the theoretical and practical matters that had been discovered in philosophy by means of persuasion and/or image-making. The notion that one can and should set up a human religion that accords with philosophy or science is not strange to Aristotle's *Metaphysics* and is urged in Plato's *Republic* and *Laws*.

The *Book of Letters* consists of three parts. The first and third deal with the question of being, or in how many ways a thing is said to be. The central part deals with the question of the relation between philosophy and religion, analytically and genetically through what appears to be a historical account. The aim is to return—or to push forward, which in this context means the same thing—to a philosophic religion with which to arrest the cycle at its highest point (secs. 108–13). The phases of Alfarabi's cycle are not substantially different from those of Aristoteles/Aristocles: they are (1) necessary or indispensable affairs (secs. 114–20), (2) elegant and beautiful things (secs. 121–38), (3) political arts and virtues (sec. 139 and passim), (4) mathematics and natural science, and (5) the highest wisdom (secs. 140–43). But there are two differences. First, Alfarabi describes the ascent toward the highest wisdom in terms of the progressive refinement of the methods of investigation—from the poetic to rhetoric, sophistry, dialectic, and demonstration. Second, and this is a clear departure from Aristotle, he sees the need for something after phase 5, for a kind of addition to phase 5 that would prevent or delay the end of the cycle as far as it is in the power of man to do so. The instrument is the philosopher-lawgiver who establishes the human religion, so that the theoretical and practical things discovered by demonstration and prudence are taught to the multitude through rhetorical and poetic methods, and everyone is persuaded to accept correct opinions and perform salutary practices.

All this is characterized as the natural, internal development. Throughout, religion is dependent on philosophy or science and comes after it in time. Philosophy is the original model; but, most important, it is the ultimate authority and the ruling power. Science cannot just engage in the initial act of establishing a religion and retire. It must stay in power and look after religion, make sure the images and arguments are not changed, constantly rejuvenate the religion and make it keep abreast of the developments and changes in the character of the public, and meet external dangers and challenges. It needs to stay in power also for self-preservation, for the public may turn against philosophy and persecute it as being different from and even opposed to religion. The most that Alfarabi envisages as a concession in the *Virtuous City* is that wisdom may retain a share of the highest authority—that there be a ruling group one of whom is the wise man. Otherwise, decline is inevitable; the cycle will move on again. To arrest the cycle, wisdom (or philosophy) and political authority must be combined and stay combined. The cycle is arrested at the very end of phase 5 with the establishment of the human religion based on the perfected highest wisdom.

Alfarabi's Successors

The notion of a "philosophic" religion as propounded by Alfarabi is elaborated and applied by the major figures in medieval Islamic and Jewish philosophy as well as by the so-called Averroists in the Latin West to interpret the history of the revealed religions, in the exegesis of revealed texts, and to define the task of philosophy in relation to theology and jurisprudence.

Maimonides expounds an account of the cycle within the Jewish community or nation when he speaks of the Sabians and Abraham's revolt against Sabianism and of Moses as the supreme philosopher-legislator— that is, a Plato or Aristotle who legislates a philosophic religion that accords to, or had to take into account, the pagan or Sabian temper of the time. Because of this, the Bible and the Midrashim contain "strange but correct notions attained by the speculation of the most sublime of those who have philosophized" (*Guide*, I.70), presented enigmatically, too strange to be understood by the vulgar. (To understand their correct meaning, therefore, one must become a "most sublime philosopher.") The context is the explanation of the expression "to ride" *(rakhob)* in the dictum "the rider of the heavens" (Deut. 33:26) and the relation between the heavens and God (cf. Aristotle, *Metaphysics,* Lambda 8, above).

This account is followed immediately (in the chapter devoted to a critique of *theology* in *Guide,* I.71) by an account of the causes of the disappearance of "the many sciences devoted to establishing the truth regarding these matters that have existed in our religious community." These causes are the length of the *time* that has passed; our being dominated by the ignorant nations —nations, that is, that lack correct "divine science" and the corresponding practices; and the fact that it is not permitted to divulge these matters to all the people (they were transmitted by a few men belonging to the elite to a few other men of the same kind). Such were the causes that led to "the disappearance of these great roots of knowledge from the nation," leaving only slight indications and pointers: "These are, as it were, a few grains belonging to the core, which were overlaid by many layers of rind, so that people were occupied with these layers of rind and thought that beneath them there was no core whatever." Maimonides' account runs parallel to Alfarabi's account of what happened with the coming of Christianity. And, like Alfarabi, Maimonides evidently thought the time had come to revive that "core" of which he speaks and reestablish it as the foundation and life-giving source of the divine law, as well as to recover the position of authority that philosophy held before its concealment and disappearance.

The so-called Latin Averroists had to face greater difficulties in their relations with the theologians. In Islam and Judaism, one could simply deny theology the authority to limit or proscribe the study of philosophy or philosophic investigations by having recourse to the authority of the divine law and the authority of the prince. In Latin Christianity, one could achieve this freedom only by denying the authority of theology *and* the authority of the councils and the pope. One's only recourse in so doing was to the protection of a secular prince.

The first step had to be the emphasis on the self-sufficiency of human reason, the supremacy of human science, the this-worldliness of man's supreme end or happiness—all of which was done by the "Averroistic" commentators on Aristotle's *Nicomachean Ethics* (investigated by commentators such as Grabmann and Gauthier). The essence of the struggle against theology was the defense of demonstrative science against what was seen as rhetoric, sophistry, and dialectic. (The Thomistic synthesis may have satisfied the church; it did not satisfy the philosophers.) The thinker who gave the clearest political expression to this philosophic anti-clericalism was Marsilius of Padua, who argued against the coercive power of the church, its this-worldly authority, its title to rule in this world, and so forth. The church could teach about and have the "other" world—that is, rewards and punishments in the other world—all to itself.

This must be understood in terms of the *Defender of Peace,* 1.5.11, on philosophic religions or acts laid down or invented by the wise philosophers. Their use, he says, can be *demonstrated* (it is rational). They contribute to peace and welfare in this world. The correct views concerning God and the true priesthood, on the other hand, cannot be known by reason. The church should not rule in this world and contribute to war and misery. Marsilius tries to isolate the church, and in this he may be looked at as one of the fathers of the doctrine of the separation of church and state.

The New Perspective: Machiavelli and Nietzsche

In the new perspective initiated by Machiavelli, both the cyclical view of history and the political-theological notion of a philosophic religion as the means of conquering the cycle are preserved. But these are radically modified through a novel view of philosophy or science. Man's thought of nature (including human nature) and man's thought of God and divine things are no longer legitimate prephilosophic opinions, and the philosophers' natural and divine sciences are no longer legitimate areas of inquiry and do not constitute the highest wisdom. Both philosophy (metaphysics) and religion (Christianity) as hitherto understood must be eliminated. According to Polybius, cyclical change occurs "according to nature" just as it did for Aristotle. According to Machiavelli, cyclical change occurs "by chance" or unforeseen accidents.

The heaven-gods, too, are replaced by *fortuna*. Nature and the gods are not our friends but our enemies. We should not aspire to know them, let alone love or be loved by them. Above all, we must not allow ourselves to be terrorized by them and thereby become weak and lose our manhood and virtue. We must recognize them as nothing more than *fortuna* and be men enough to "regulate" her, "to beat her and to pound on her" (*Discourses*, 3.30; *Prince*, chap. 25). Accepting the cyclical view of history as propounded by Polybius, Machiavelli blames the ancients for acquiescing to it, for their lack of resolve, courage, and the will to fight and control the cycle by political means—that is, by continuously renewing the political regime. The ancients' view of science, their contemplative ideal, was a cowardly surrender to the forces of nature, both external and human. They condemned themselves to being chained down in the cave; they could not manage to come out and stay on top. A religion based on such a philosophy is another form of that surrender. Man can control his own destiny and conquer nature by means of science, which is now seen as a servant to be used rather than a master to which one submits. With the political order well under control, the new science offers limitless vistas for progress in the future. The cycle should be arrested at phase 3, and the circle unbent, *in deed*, by eliminating the phases that follow the high point of political virtue.

The old activities in phases 4–5 sponged on phase 3 and contributed to its decline. The new science—religion—and rhetoric will be based solidly on the practical political art that will preserve the high point of political virtue (*Florentine Histories* 5.1; *Discourses*, 1, preface, and 3.1).

Nietzsche's innovation was not the cyclical view of history that he called the "eternal return teaching" or even the much quoted view that "Christianity is Platonism for the people." His innovation was, to begin with, bringing to the foreground a view that lurked in the background of the philosophic tradition and formulating it as an explicit and principal teaching; and then presenting eternal return as a ground for the "radical rejection of even the concept of being" and as a substitute for "metaphysics" and religion.[1]

1. See *Die fröhliche Wissenschaft* (The Gay Science), aphorism 104, end, in Nietzsche 1960, vol. 2, 111. See also vol. 3, 560 *(Nachlass)*.

REFERENCES

Primary Sources

Alfarabi

Attainment of Happiness. Arabic text: *Taḥṣīl al-Saʿāda* (Hyderabad, A.H. 1345). English translation in *Alfarabi: The Political Writings, "Philosophy of Plato and Aristotle,"* translated and with an introduction by Muhsin Mahdi, rev. ed. (Ithaca, N.Y., 2001), pt. 1. References in the present volume are to the sections of the English translation and to the pages and lines of the Hyderabad edition. See notes to the Arabic text of the *Attainment of Happiness* in *Alfarabi: The Political Writings, "Philosophy of Plato and Aristotle,"* 149–56. The *Attainment of Happiness,* the *Philosophy of Plato,* and the *Philosophy of Aristotle* make up a trilogy.

Book of Letters. Arabic text edited by Muhsin Mahdi, *Alfarabi's "Book of Letters" (Kitāb al-Ḥurūf): A Commentary on Aristotle's "Metaphysics"* (Beirut, 1969). Revised Arabic text by Muhsin Mahdi (Beirut, forthcoming). English translation by Muhsin Mahdi, *Alfarabi: The Political Writings, "Political Regime" and Other Texts,* edited and with an introduction by Charles E. Butterworth (Ithaca, N.Y., forthcoming). References in the present volume are to the sections as well as the pages and lines of the Beirut edition.

Book of Religion. Arabic text edited by Muhsin Mahdi, *Alfarabi's "Book of Religion" and Related Texts (Kitāb al-Milla wa Nuṣūṣ Ukhrā)* (Beirut, 1968). English translation in *Alfarabi: The Political Writings, "Selected Aphorisms" and Other Texts,* edited and translated, with an introduction, by Charles E. Butterworth (Ithaca, N.Y., 2001). References in the present volume are to the sections as well as the pages and lines of the Beirut edition.

Enumeration of the Sciences. Arabic text edited by ʿUthmān Amīn, *Iḥṣāʾ al-ʿUlūm,* 2d ed. (Cairo, 1949). English translation of part of chapter 5 by Fauzi M. Najjar, "The Enumeration of the Sciences," in *Medieval Political Philosophy: A Sourcebook,* edited by Ralph Lerner and Muhsin Mahdi with the collaboration of Ernest L. Fortin (New York, 1963; reprint, Ithaca, N.Y.: Cornell Paperbacks,

1984), sec. 1. English translation of chapter 5 by Charles E. Butterworth, *Alfarabi: The Political Writings, "Selected Aphorisms" and Other Texts*. Two Latin versions of the work, one a translation, the other an adaptation, together with the Arabic text and a Spanish translation, can be consulted in Ángel Gonzalez Palencia, *Al-Fārābī: Catálogo de las ciencias*, 2d ed. (Madrid, 1953). The Latin translation (pp. 117–76), literal and generally accurate, is by Gerard of Cremona. The adaptation (pp. 83–115), first published by Camerarius, is ascribed on reasonable grounds to Gundissalinus (who made use of Alfarabi's classification of the sciences in his own work, "De divisione scientiarum") and was edited under his name by Manuel Alonso Alonso, S.J., *Domingo Gundisalvo: De scientiis* (Madrid, 1954). References in the present volume are to the pages and lines of the Cairo edition.

Epistle on the Intellect. Arabic text edited by Maurice Bouyges, S. J., *Al-Fārābī, Risāla fī-al-ʿAql* (Beirut, 1938). English translation by Arthur Hyman, "Letter concerning the Intellect," in *Philosophy in the Middle Ages: The Christian, Islamic, and Jewish Traditions*, edited by Arthur Hyman and James J. Walsh (New York, 1967). References in the present volume are to the sections of the Beirut edition.

Harmonization. The Harmonization of the Two Opinions of the Two Sages, Plato the Divine and Aristotle (Al-Jamʿ Bayna Raʾyay al-Ḥakīmayn, Aflāṭūn al-Ilāhī wa Arisṭūṭālīs). Arabic text edited by Friedrich Dieterici, *Al-Thamarāt al-Marḍiyya* (Leiden, 1890). New Arabic text edited by Fauzi M. Najjar and translated into French by Dominique Mallet, *L'harmonie entre les opinions de Platon et d'Aristote* (Damascus, 1999). English translation by Charles E. Butterworth and Fauzi M. Najjar, *Alfarabi: The Political Writings, "Selected Aphorisms" and Other Texts*. References in the present volume are to the pages and lines of the Leiden edition.

Introductory "Risāla" on Logic. Arabic text *(Risāla ṣuddira bihā al-Kitāb)* edited by D. M. Dunlop, "Al-Fārābī's Introductory *Risālah* on Logic," *Islamic Quarterly* 3 (1957): 224–35.

On the Purposes of Aristotle's "Metaphysics." Arabic text *(Fī Aghrāḍ al-Ḥakīm)* edited by Friedrich Dieterici, *Al-Thamarāt al-Marḍiyya* (Leiden, 1890).

On the Rise [or Reappearance] of Philosophy. Fragments. In Ibn Abī Uṣaybiʿa, *ʿUyūn al-Anbāʾ fī Ṭabaqāt al-Aṭibbāʾ*. Arabic text edited by August Müller (Cairo and Königsberg, 1882–84), 2:134ff.; Nachtragsband, pp. 49, 78. German translation in Franz Rosenthal, *Das Fortleben des Antike im Islam* (Zurich and Stuttgart, 1965), 74–76. (Translated into English by Emile Marmorstein and Jenny Marmorstein, *The Classical Heritage of Islam* [Berkeley, Calif., 1975].) Partial German translation in Max Meyerhof, *Von Alexandrien nach Baghdad: Ein Beitrag zur Geschichte der philosophischen und medizinischen Unterrichts bei den Arabern*, SPAW phil-hist. Kl. 23 (Berlin, 1930), 387–429. Partial German translation by Gotthard Strohmaier, "'Von Alexandrien nach Bachdad'—Eine fictive Schultradition," in *Aristoteles: Werk und Wirkung—Paul Moraux gewidmet,* edited by Jürgen Wiesner (Berlin, 1987), 2:380–89. English translation of a supplementary fragment by Muhsin Mahdi, "Al-Fārābī," in *Dictionary of Scientific Biography,* 4:523–26. French translation of fragments from al-Masʿūdī in Michel Tardieu, "Ṣābiens coraniques et 'Ṣābiens' des Ḥarrān," *Journal asiatique* 274 (1986): 1–44.

Philosophy of Aristotle. Arabic text edited by Muhsin Mahdi, *Al-Fārābī's "Philosophy of Aristotle" (Falsafat Arisṭūṭālīs)* (Beirut, 1961). English translation by Muhsin Mahdi, *Alfarabi: The Political Writings, "Philosophy of Plato and Aristotle,"* pt. 3. References in the present volume are to the sections as well as the pages and lines of the Beirut edition, all of which are indicated in the English translation.

Philosophy of Plato. Arabic text edited and translated into Latin by Franz Rosenthal and Richard Walzer, *Alfarabius De Platonis Philosophia (Falsafat Aflāṭun)* (London, 1943). English translation by Muhsin Mahdi, *Alfarabi: The Political Writings, "Philosophy of Plato and Aristotle,"* pt. 2. References in the present volume are to the sections of the English translation and to the pages and lines of the London edition, all of which are indicated in the English translation.

Plato's "Laws." Arabic text and Latin translation by Francesco Gabrieli, *Alfarabius Compendium Legum Platonis* (London, 1952). New edition and French translation by Thérèse-Anne Druart, "Le sommaire du livre des 'Lois' de Platon *(Djawāmiʿ Kitāb al-Nawāmīs li-Aflāṭūn)* par Abū Naṣr al-Fārābī," *Bulletin d'études orientales* 50 (1998): 109–55. English translation by Muhsin Mahdi, *Alfarabi: The Political Writings, "Political Regime" and Other Texts.* References in the present volume are to the pages and lines of Druart's edition.

Political Regime. Arabic text edited by Friedrich Dieterici, *Alfārābī's Abhandlung der Musterstaat* (Leiden, 1895). Reprinted as *Kitāb al-Siyāsāt al-Madaniyya* (Hyderabad, 1927). Fauzi M. Najjar, *Al-Fārābī's "The Political Regime" (al-Siyāsa al-Madaniyya: Also Known as the "Treatise on the Principles of Beings")* (Beirut, 1964). Partial English translation by Fauzi M. Najjar in *Medieval Political Philosophy: A Sourcebook,* sec. 2. English translation by Charles E. Butterworth, *Alfarabi: The Political Writings, "Political Regime" and Other Texts.* References in the present volume are to the pages and lines of the Beirut edition.

Rhetoric. Edited, with French translation, by J. Langhade and M. Grignaschi, *Al-Farabi: Deux ouvrages inédits sur la Rhétorique (Kitāb al-Khaṭāba)* (Beirut, 1971).

Selected Aphorisms. Edited by Fauzi M. Najjar, *Al-Fārābī's "Fuṣūl Muntazaʿa" (Selected Aphorisms)* (Beirut, 1971). Partial edition and English translation by D. M. Dunlop, *Al-Fārābī: The Fuṣūl al-Madanī (Aphorisms of the Statesman)* (Cambridge, 1961). English translation by Charles E. Butterworth, *Alfarabi:*

The Political Writings, "Selected Aphorisms" and Other Texts. References in the present volume are to the aphorisms as well as the pages and lines of the Beirut edition.

Utterances. Arabic text, edited with introduction and notes by Muhsin Mahdi, *The Utterances Employed in Logic (al-Alfāẓ al-Mustaʿmala fī al-Manṭiq)* (Beirut, 1968).

Virtuous City. Principles of the Opinions of the Inhabitants of the Virtuous City. Arabic text edited by Friedrich Dieterici, *Ārāʾ Ahl al-Madīna al-Fāḍila* (Leiden, 1895). Arabic text and English translation by Richard Walzer, *Al-Farabi on the Perfect State: Abū Naṣr al-Fārābī's "Mabādiʾ Ārāʾ Ahl al-Madīna al-Fāḍila,"* revised text with introduction, translation, and commentary (Oxford, 1985). References in the present volume are to the pages and lines of Dieterici's edition unless followed by "Walzer."

Aristotle
The Politics of Aristotle. Translated, with an introduction, notes, and appendixes, by Ernest Barker (London, 1972).

Averroes
Decisive Treatise (Faṣl al-Maqāl). Arabic text edited by George F. Hourani (London, 1959). Translated by George F. Hourani, *On the Harmony of Religion and Philosophy* (London, 1961).

Parva naturalia. Arabic text edited by Harry Blumberg, *Averrois Cordubensis compendia librorum Aristotelis qui "Parva naturalia" vocantur* (Cambridge, Mass., 1972). English translation by Harry Blumberg, *Averroes Epitome of "Parva naturalia"* (Cambridge, Mass., 1961).

Avicenna
On the Divisions of the Rational Sciences (Fī Aqsām al-ʿUlūm al-ʿAqliyya). Arabic text in: *Tisʿ Rasāʾil* (Cairo, 1908). Partial English translation by Muhsin Mahdi in *Medieval Political Philosophy: A Sourcebook,* sec. 5.

"Condemnation of 219 Propositions." Translated by Ernest L. Fortin and Peter D. O'Neill in *Medieval Political Philosophy: A Sourcebook,* sec. 18.

Falaquera
Reschith Chokhmah. Edited by M. David (Berlin, 1902).

Ghazālī, al-
The Deliverer from Error (Al-Munqidh min al-Ḍalāl). Arabic text edited by Jamīl Ṣalība and Kāmil ʿAyyad, 3d ed. (Damascus, 1939). Translated by Richard Joseph McCarthy, S.J., *Freedom and Fulfillment* (Boston, 1980).

Incoherence of the Philosophers (Tahāfut al-Falāsifa). Arabic text edited by Maurice Bouyges, S.J. (Beirut, 1927). Translated into English by Sabih Ahmad Kamali (Lahore, 1958).

Ibn Ṭufayl

Ḥayy ibn Yaqẓān. Arabic text and French translation in Léon Gauthier, *Hayy ben Yaqdhân: Roman philosophique d'Ibn Thofaïl,* 2d ed. (Beirut, 1936). Partial English translation by George N. Atiyeh, "Ibn Tufayl, Hayy the Son of Yaqzan," in *Medieval Political Philosophy: A Sourcebook,* sec. 9.

Maimonides

Logic. Arabic text edited by Mübahat Türker, "Mûsâ İbn-i Meymûn'in *Al-Makāla fī Ṣinā'at al-Manṭik:* Inin Arabça Asli," *Ankara Üniversitesi Dil ve Tarih Coğrafiya Fakültesi Dergisi* 18, 1–2 (1961): 40–64. English translation of chapter 14 by Muhsin Mahdi in *Medieval Political Philosophy: A Sourcebook,* sec. 11.

Guide. Arabic text *(Dalālat al-Ḥā'irīn)* edited by S. Munk, *Le guide des égarés,* 3 vols. (Paris, 1856–66). English translation by Shlomo Pines, *The Guide of the Perplexed,* translated and with an introduction and notes by Leo Strauss (Chicago, 1963). Partial translation by Ralph Lerner and Muhsin Mahdi in *Medieval Political Philosophy: A Sourcebook,* sec. 12.

Ṣā'id al-Andalusī

Classes of Nations (Ṭabaqāt al-Umam). Arabic text edited by Louis Cheikho (Beirut, 1912).

Secondary Sources

Burke, Edmund. *Orations and Essays.* New York, 1900.

Gilson, Étienne. *History of Christian Philosophy in the Middle Ages.* New York, 1955.

Heidegger, Martin. *An Introduction to Metaphysics.* Translated by Ralph Mannheim. New York, 1961.

Klein, Jacob. *A Commentary on Plato's "Meno."* Chapel Hill, N. C., 1965.

Lane, Edward William. *Arabic-English Lexicon.* London, 1863–93.

Madkour, Ibrahim. *La place d'al-Fārābī dans l'école philosophique musulmane.* Paris, 1934.

Mahdi, Muhsin. "Al-Ta'ālīm wa al-Tajriba fī al-Tanjīm wa al-Mūsīqā." In *Nuṣūṣ Falsafiyya Muhdāt ilā al-Duktūr Ibrāhīm Madkūr,* edited by 'Uthmān Amīn. Cairo, 1976.

Nietzsche, Friedrich. *Werke.* Edited by Karl Schlechta. 3 vols. Munich, 1960.

———. *Beyond Good and Evil, Prelude to a Philosophy of the Future.* Translated, with commentary, by Walter Kaufmann. New York, 1966.

Shehadi, Fadlou A. *Ghazali's Unique Unknowable God.* Leiden, 1964.

Sherif, Mohamed A. *Ghazali's Theory of Virtue.* Albany, N.Y., 1975.

Strauss, Leo. "Eine vermisste Schrift Fârâbîs." *Monatsschrift für Geschichte und Wissenschaft des Judentums* 80 (1936): 96–106.

———. "Farabi's Plato." In *Louis Ginzberg Jubilee Volume.* New York, 1945.

ACKNOWLEDGMENTS

Earlier versions of the chapters included in this volume were published or submitted for publication as follows.

1. "The Political Orientation of Islamic Philosophy," Center for Contemporary Arab Studies, Occasional Papers Series (Washington, D.C., 1982).

2. "Philosophy and Political Thought," *Arabic Sciences and Philosophy* 1 (1990): 9–29.

3. "Al-Fārābī and the Foundation of Islamic Philosophy," in *Islamic Philosophy and Mysticism,* edited by Parviz Morewedge (Delmar, N.Y.: Caravan Books, 1981), pp. 3–21.

4. "Science, Philosophy and Religion in Alfarabi's *Enumeration of the Sciences*," in *The Cultural Context of Medieval Learning,* edited by J. E. Murdoch and E. E. Sylla (Dordrecht, Holland, and Boston, Mass.: D. Reidel Publishing Co. 1975), pp. 113–47.

5. "Alfarabi on Political Philosophy and Religion," paper read at public lecture, Institut du Monde Arabe, Paris, 6 June 1995.

6. "Alfarabi," in *History of Political Philosophy,* edited by Leo Strauss and Joseph Cropsey (Chicago: Rand McNally, 1963), pp. 160–80.

7. "Prophecy and Revelation in Alfarabi's Political Philosophy," in *Les doctrines de la science de l'Antiquité à l'Âge classique,* edited by R. Rashed and J. Biard (Louvain: Peeters, 1999), pp. 165–88.

8. "Remarks on Alfarabi's *Attainment of Happiness*," in *Essays on Islamic Philosophy and Science,* edited by George F. Hourani (Albany, N.Y.: State University of New York Press, 1975), pp. 47–66.

9. "Alfarabi on Aristotle's Starting Point," in *Philosophies of Being and Mind: Ancient and Medieval,* edited by James T. H. Martin (Delmar, N.Y.: Caravan Books, 1992), pp. 221–33.

10. "Alfarabi on Philosophy and Religion," *Philosophical Forum* 4.1 (1972): 5–25.

11. "Religion and the Cyclical View of History," in *Langages et philosophie, hommages à Jean Jolivet,* edited by A. De Libera, A. Elamrani-Jamal, and A. Galonnier (Paris: Vrin, 1997), pp. 3–11.

INDEX

Abed, Shukri, xiv
Abraham, 237
acquired intellect, 154–56, 161–62
actions, 83, 89–91, 93–99, 102–5, 122, 126, 137, 206, 236; noble, 128–29; noble and base distinguished, 128; and reason, 126; and revelation, 103–5. *See also* religious actions, activities, and practices
active intellect. *See* divine mind, active intellect of
agriculture, 80
Albert the Great, 30; and reformation of Christian theology, 37
Alcinous, *Didaskalikos,* xi
Alexander the Great, 154
Alexandria, school of, 1–2, 52–56; tradition of philosophic learning in, 52–54; —, Alfarabi's continuation of, 53. *See also* Alfarabi, works: *On the Rise [or Reappearance] of Philosophy*
Alfarabi (Abū Naṣr al-Fārābī, ca. 870–950)
  account of religion of, 149–51, 182; as human wisdom, 151; Platonic-Aristotelian basis, 2 (*see also* Alfarabi, works: *Book of Religion;* Alfarabi, works: *Enumeration of the Sciences*)
  achievement of, 169–70
  on Aristotle's achievement, 200–201
  as believer, 165
  and classical political philosophy, 3, 30, 52–53, 56, 83–85, 122, 125–28
  cosmology of, xii, 4, 82; relationship to political and religious teachings, 4, 9–10, 59
  as founder: of Islamic political philosophy, xi, xvii, 29, 56, 60–61; of

main tradition of Islamic philosophy, 47
  harmonization of Plato and Aristotle, 148, 194–95
  importance of, 3, 65, 125
  intention of, 221
  interpretation of Aristotle, 56, 196–202
  interpretation of Plato, 36, 56, 137, 196–202
  and Islamic philosophy, 3, 52
  justice of, 169–70
  life of, 1–2, 95
  lost writings of, 51–56, 154, 156; modern recovery of, xi–xii, xiv, xvi–xvii, 4–5. *See also* writings *below in this entry*
  manner of writing, 175
  and medieval philosophy, 3
  and Middle Platonism, xi–xii, 2
  and Neoplatonism, 3, 48, 56
  originality of, 168n, 169
  as "the philosopher of the Muslims," 174
  piety of, 169–70
  Platonism of, 158–59, 168, 199
  political science of, 83–96, 121–23; and ancient political science, 83, 122–23; central theme, 84
  political teaching of, xi, xvi, 2, 60, 65
  political theology of, 82
  on prophecy, 149–50
  rejection of Neoplatonism, xii–xiii, 2–3
  on revelation, 149–54
  and school of Alexandria, 52–56
  secondary literature on, xii–xv, 5–6, 9, 149, 157
  as "second teacher" (after Aristotle), xiv, xvii, 3, 125

249